PRAISE FOR THE THIRD EDITION

"Dominic Bright's excellent book A Practical Guide to the Small Claims Track has already established itself as essential reading for litigants in person, practitioners and many judges alike. With its characteristically clear and easily accessible style and practical approach, the Third Edition will be a welcome and indispensable addition to the bookshelf of all those who find themselves navigating this significant area of the work in the County Court."

– District Judge Redpath-Stevens

South Eastern Circuit

"A valuable and much welcomed third edition of this excellent guide to the Small Claims Track. The book is an essential tool for both litigants in person and lawyers, in what can be complex litigation in the County Court. User friendly, relevant and insightful, the book arms the reader with everything they need know and what to expect on their day in court. An indispensable read, and one that I am delighted to recommend".

– District Judge Asjad

Midland Circuit

"I am delighted to be able to endorse the third edition of this invaluable guide. This book is a great resource for both lawyers and litigants in person, providing clear, comprehensive, and practical guidance on navigating the complexities of the small claims court. The updated edition continues to excel in demystifying the legal processes, offering step-by-step instructions and insightful tips that are crucial for achieving fair and efficient outcomes. Whether you are a seasoned legal professional or a self-represented litigant, this book equips you with the knowledge and confidence needed to effectively present your case. I highly recommend this book as an indispensable tool for anyone involved in small claims litigation."

– District Judge Nathan Banks

Northern Circuit

"In the last week I have dealt with nine small claims trials out of a total of twenty cases. That demonstrates the proliferation of such matters before the county court. The availability and/or quality of representation in these hearings can be variable. This book provides a structured and comprehensive walk through of the entire process from start to finish. Any representative, lay or legal, appearing before a District Judge would be well advised to read and familiarise themselves with its contents. It is invaluable."

– District Judge Justin P. Evans
Wales Circuit

PRAISE FOR THE SECOND EDITION

"A comprehensive and practical guide to the Small Claims Track. Dominic Bright has set out a clear and extensive guide which will be invaluable to all practitioners who deal with Small Claims; as well as those in the voluntary sector, who assist Litigants in Person."

– District Judge & Recorder Pollard
South Eastern Circuit

"The second edition of A Practical Guide to the Small Claims Track continues to be essential reading for all those involved in conducting small claims. Written in a clear, accessible style, Dominic Bright's detailed yet concise guide sheds light on all aspects of the small claims procedure. With up-to-date information on changes in practice precipitated by the Covid-19 pandemic, this book is an invaluable resource particularly for litigants in person and those who are unfamiliar with the court process."

– District Judge Dias
South Eastern Circuit

"In this book, Dominic Bright has managed to produce a detailed and comprehensive guide to dealing with all aspects of a case in the small claims track which is both easy to understand and to navigate. Although small claims cases are normally for less than £10,000, the amounts claimed and in dispute can still be life changing for parties. The book will assist practitioners and litigants in person in preparing and presenting cases in the best and most effective way."

– District Judge James Britton
Western Circuit

"Mr Bright has written a thorough, detailed yet easy to follow guide to all using the small claims procedure in the County Court. It will be an invaluable aide to litigants in person, practitioners and the newly appointed District Judge, and I cannot commend it highly enough."

– District Judge Bishop
South Eastern Circuit

PRAISE FOR THE SECOND EDITION

"A comprehensive and practical guide to the Small Claims Track. Dominic Bright has set out a clear and extensive guide which will be invaluable to all practitioners who deal with Small Claims; as well as those in the voluntary sector, who assist Litigants in Person."

– **District Judge & Recorder Pollard**
South Eastern Circuit

"The second edition of A Practical Guide to the Small Claims Track continues to be essential reading for all those involved in conducting small claims. Written in a clear, accessible style, Dominic Bright's detailed yet concise guide sheds light on all aspects of the small claims procedure. With up-to-date information on changes in practice precipitated by the Covid-19 pandemic, this book is an invaluable resource particularly for litigants in person and those who are unfamiliar with the court process."

– **District Judge Dias**
South Eastern Circuit

"In this book, Dominic Bright has managed to produce a detailed and comprehensive guide to dealing with all aspects of a case in the small claims track which is both easy to understand and to navigate. Although small claims cases are normally for less than £10,000, the amounts claimed and in dispute can still be life changing for parties. The book will assist practitioners and litigants in person in preparing and presenting cases in the best and most effective way."

– **District Judge James Britton**
Western Circuit

"Mr Bright has written a thorough, detailed yet easy to follow guide to all using the small claims procedure in the County Court. It will be an invaluable aide to litigants in person, practitioners and the newly appointed District Judge, and I cannot commend it highly enough."

– District Judge Bishop
South Eastern Circuit

PRAISE FOR THE FIRST EDITION

"Dominic Bright has balanced a thorough, careful review of the Small Claims Track procedure with a helpful analysis of the most common areas of law the County Court sees. The wealth of sensible, practical advice for those coming to court helps further set this book apart."

– District Judge Cridge
South Eastern Circuit

"… it has the potential to be a genuine game-changer in the pro bono sector … Despite its small size, [it] takes in everything from the pre-action stage right the way through to costs and appeals. … It seems inevitable that [it] will quickly become the go-to small claims book for practitioner volunteers (and junior practitioners generally), especially those unfamiliar with handling claims allocated to the small claims track, as well as an indispensable self-help guide to LiPs."

– Richard Pitkethly
In-house counsel and head of learning & practice at LawWorks
'A pro bono game-changer' in the *Law Society Gazette*
Five Stars

"Barrister Dominic Bright comes from Lamb Chambers and he has written a masterful account of what to do when you are faced with dealing with a small claim."

– Phillip Taylor MBE
Reviews Editor of *The Barrister*
Five Stars

Dominic is a barrister at Lamb Chambers.

He practises commercial, construction and property law.

Dominic is a member of the British Institute of International and Comparative Law, Chatham House, Civil Mediation Council, Commercial Bar Association, Property Bar Association, and Technology and Construction Bar Association.

A Practical Guide to the Small Claims Track

Third Edition

A Practical Guide to the Small Claims Track

Third Edition

A Practical Guide to the Small Claims Track

Third Edition

Dominic Bright

Barrister, Lamb Chambers

Law Brief Publishing

Published 2024 by Law Brief Publishing, an imprint of Law Brief Publishing Ltd
30 The Parks
Minehead
Somerset
TA24 8BT

www.lawbriefpublishing.com

Paperback: 978-1-916698-57-4

For my mother.

FOREWORD TO THE THIRD EDITION

I am delighted to have been asked to write a foreword to the 3rd edition of Dominic Bright's book "a practical guide to the small claims track". I have read the book to write this foreword, and it does exactly what it says, namely provide a practical guide to those involved in claims in this track. For example, bringing extra copies of documents and what to do if you are late. Claims on the small track make up a substantial volume of the work of the County Court and anything that can be done to help those cases run smoothly will not just help the litigants involved in the case, but also the judiciary, court staff and the litigants involved in other cases by reducing delay and increasing efficiency.

I agree with and reiterate what the 2 authors of the forewords to the 1st and 2nd editions have said, in particular with regard to the rule of law. It is also important to consider that "small" claim does not necessarily mean to the people involved that it is "small" or insignificant. This book will help unrepresented parties and those who represent them to get the best out of the system and contribute to achieving a fair result.

His Honour Judge Marquand
Senior Circuit Judge
Designated Civil Judge for West London

PREFACE TO THE THIRD EDITION

Fully revised, updated, and relevant to over 70% of civil claims.

Even clearer. Even more comprehensive. Even more concise.

New guidance on cross-examination, closing submissions, and skeleton arguments; new authority on mandatory mediation, putting your case, and setting aside judgment; and a step-by-step guide to carriage, drafting, and agreement, of minutes of order.

The law in England and Wales is stated as at 1 October 2024.

Dominic Bright
Lamb Chambers, Temple, London
October 2024

FOREWORD TO THE SECOND EDITION

A litigant in England and Wales is most likely to come into contact with the civil courts, principally the county court, in connection with a claim proceeding on the Small Claims Track which, despite the name, is the track to which nearly all the cases worth up to £10,000 are allocated, a very significant number of cases every year. Such litigants are often faced, for the first time, with a set of rules of practice and procedure and legal principles which they will never have seen before and which some might find somewhat bewildering. They need not fear. In the Second Edition of his book Dominic Bright has provided a comprehensive, step-by-step, guide to the Small Claims track which will take the litigant by the hand and lead them through the process from beginning to end. In the course of that journey the author addresses everything which the reader might want to know about the court, the system, the processes and the participants, including what technology the litigant might need to be familiar with and how to "break the ice" with the other side. The book is learned, practical, readable and useable.

I think that no one will doubt that 2020 has been a challenging year for everyone, including the courts, HMCTS, the judges and all the court users, professional and lay. Each has had to adapt to ensure that cases can continue to be heard and, as Her Hon Judge Walden-Smith commented in the Foreword to the First Edition of this book, to ensure that there is the proper system for the judicial resolution of disputes between citizens and that the rule of law can continue to be upheld. The proper functioning of the Small Claims Track is crucial to the maintenance of the rule of law. The author has addressed the challenges which 2020 has brought to those courts with specific sections dedicated to remote hearings and C-19. It is to be hoped that C-19 will not need to appear in what I am sure will be a Third Edition of this splendid book in due course.

The book is, in my view, essential reading not only for litigants in person, but for all practitioners who handle small claims (whether as advocates or in the earlier stages of the case). I also have no doubt that the judges of the county court (whether salaried or fee-paid) would benefit considerably by reading this book and keeping it by their side when giving directions or trying cases on the small claims track or hearing the occasional appeal from a decision made on the track. The Practical Guide to the Small Claims Track is an excellent book.

His Honour Judge Marc Dight CBE
Senior Chancery Circuit Judge
Designated Civil Judge Central London and
Mayor's & City of London Courts
Lead Diversity and Community Relations Judge
Royal Courts of Justice
London

PREFACE TO THE SECOND EDITION

Fully revised and updated.

Clearer. More comprehensive. More concise.

Guidance on remote preparation, conferences and final hearings; new authority on bias, unfairness and litigants in person; and step-by-step advice for efficiently working from home.

The law in England and Wales is stated as at 1 November 2020.

Dominic Bright
Working from home
November 2020

FOREWORD TO THE FIRST EDITION

Over recent years, a succession of Lord Chancellors and Ministers of Justice have been keen to emphasise their commitment to protecting judges and upholding the rule of law. Such commitments are not without meaning and while the rule of law is a phrase often said, it is rarely examined. It is not an arid legal doctrine but is the foundation stone of much that creates a fair and just society.

It may be thought that the rule of law is of no relevance to a foreword about a book giving practical guidance to claims within the small claims track in the County Court. On the contrary, the rule of law is front and centre. It is because people with a dispute, however low in value and lacking complexity, can bring a claim before an impartial judge, that we can function as a civilised society where business can be done and wrongs remedied. The small claims procedure is a very real example of the rule of law in operation.

The District Bench across England and Wales is under pressure as it has never been before, with both the volume and variety of work that judges are obliged to hear. Added to that, judges generally, and the District Bench in particular, has to be able to reach both legal and factual decisions often without the benefit of the parties having legal representation. In order to fulfil their role properly and in order to continue with their duties to uphold the rule of law, without fear or favour, both full-time and deputy District Judges need to be able to manage heavy lists of both civil and family cases. A sizeable part of the daily diet of the District Bench will be civil claims which are allocated to the small claims track.

As Dominic Bright sets out, small claims account for approximately 60% of all allocations of civil work in the County Court and three-quarters of all civil claims disposed of by way of final hearing. The financial value of a small claim is now £10,000 or less and the track is designed to provide a proportionate procedure by which the most straightforward of these relatively low value claims can be decided without substantial pre-hearing preparation and without the formalities of a traditional trial. Of course, most people with a claim worth £10,000 or less are unlikely to consider the sums involved to be "small" and the title given to this track must not be seen to belittle the importance of the dispute to the parties involved. What is important is that the track provides a proportionate means of resolving a dispute between parties which can be of considerable practical importance and, despite the categorisation of small, considerable financial worth to the individuals involved.

In this comprehensive guide to the small claims track, Dominic Bright has set out all that a practitioner could possibly need to know about how to deal with a small claim, from allocation to judgment and through to any potential appeal. He covers the court's duty to manage cases actively and the overriding objective and, in doing so, points out the duty of the court to take into account the fact that a litigant is without representation when exercising powers of case management albeit that all rules, practice directions and orders apply equally to represented and unrepresented litigants. It is, of course, incumbent upon a practitioner, as well as the court, to act in furtherance of the overriding objective. An unrepresented litigant is not only entitled to a fair hearing, he is entitled to understand that he is obtaining that fair hearing.

Further to the specifics of how the court will deal with a small claim, including the pleadings, the allocation and the hearing itself, Dominic Bright has included guidance on a wide range of matters, such as ethics and ways to behave when in court, which will be of assistance to any junior practitioner appearing in a civil case at an early stage of their career. The inclusion of the civil procedure rules and practice directions relating to the small claims track, and also to pre-action conduct and protocols and to the overriding objective and the court's duty to manage cases, means that this guide provides a useful toolkit of relevant rules and practice directions.

This Practical Guide to the Small Claims Track will be of benefit to practitioners, particularly those new to practice. It will therefore be of benefit to the District Judges and their deputies who hear small claims. Undoubtedly, the better informed and prepared the representatives are, the better it is for the judges who hear such claims to enable them to concentrate on reaching the correct legal and factual conclusions in furtherance of upholding the rule of law.

HHJ Karen Walden-Smith
Senior Circuit Judge
Designated Civil Judge for
the County Court in East Anglia
November 2019

PREFACE TO THE FIRST EDITION

My aim is to shine light upon the 'what', 'when', and 'how' of the small claims track. This practical guide is written with junior *barristers* and *solicitors* in mind, however, *litigants in person* may also find it of some assistance. This is because the *special* procedure for dealing with these claims is designed so that *litigants* may conduct their *own* case.

It purports to be *clear*, *comprehensive*, and *concise*.

'Clear' because *short*, *descriptive* sub-headings are used to marshal content, often comprising just a few sentences; and sometimes, only one, *importance* sentence, containing a *single*, but *key* point.

'Comprehensive' because the full timeline of a claim is covered: from *pre-action*, through *final hearing*, to *appeal*. There are many, more comprehensive, authoritative texts on civil procedure in general, advocacy, and on the small claims track within the Intellectual Property Enterprise Court.

'Concise' because every effort has been made to remove jargon unencumbered with merit, unwarranted primary authority, and unnecessary secondary sources.

It aspires to be well-thumbed, throwing a beacon of light onto issues, *before*, and *when* they arise, so that they can be dealt with *confidently*, to the benefit of *lay* and *professional* clients, and enabling *the court* to achieve the overriding objective to deal with cases justly, and at proportionate cost.

The law in England and Wales is stated as at 1 November 2019.

Dominic Bright
Lamb Chambers, Temple, London
November 2019

PREFACE TO THE FIRST EDITION

My aim is to shine light upon the 'what', 'when', and 'how' of the small claims track. This practical guide is written with junior *barristers* and *solicitors* in mind, however, *litigants in person* may also find it of some assistance. This is because the *special* procedure for dealing with these claims is designed so that *litigants* may conduct their *own* case.

It purports to be *clear*, *comprehensive*, and *concise*.

'Clear' because *short*, *descriptive* sub-headings are used to marshal content, often comprising just a few sentences; and sometimes, only one, *importance* sentence, containing a *single*, but *key* point.

'Comprehensive' because the full timeline of a claim is covered: from *pre-action*, through *final hearing*, to *appeal*. There are many, more comprehensive, authoritative texts on civil procedure in general, advocacy, and on the small claims track within the Intellectual Property Enterprise Court.

'Concise' because every effort has been made to remove jargon unencumbered with merit, unwarranted primary authority, and unnecessary secondary sources.

It aspires to be well-thumbed, throwing a beacon of light onto issues, *before*, and *when* they arise, so that they can be dealt with *confidently*, to the benefit of *lay* and *professional* clients, and enabling *the court* to achieve the overriding objective to deal with cases justly, and at proportionate cost.

The law in England and Wales is stated as at 1 November 2019.

Dominic Bright
Lamb Chambers, Temple, London
November 2019

"It is not the critic who counts; not the man who points out how the strong man stumbles or where the doer of deeds could have done them better. The credit belongs to the man who is actually in the arena, whose face is marred by dust and sweat and blood; who strives valiantly; who errs, who comes short again and again, because there is no effort without error and shortcoming; but who does actually strive to do the deeds; who knows great enthusiasms, the great devotions; who spends himself in a worthy cause; who at the best knows in the end the triumph of high achievement, and who at the worst, if he fails, at least fails while daring greatly, so that his place shall never be with those cold and timid souls who neither know victory nor defeat."

Theodore Roosevelt
Sorbonne, Paris
April 1910

CONTENTS

1. Overview

This chapter summarises the special procedure for dealing with claims that have been allocated to the small claims track.

The remaining chapters provide guidance as to when to rely upon specific rules, and when to deploy authority interpreting them.

a. Small claim

The rules of civil litigation in England and Wales are prescribed in the Civil Procedure Rules ("CPR").

Part 27 of the CPR is entitled: 'The small claims track'.

A "small claim" is a claim that: falls under this Part which sets out the procedure for dealing with small claims; and limits the amount of costs that can be recovered (CPR 27.1(1) and (2)).

The special procedure for dealing with claims that have been allocated to the small claims track 'is intended to provide a proportionate procedure by which most straightforward claims with a financial value of not more than £10,000 can be decided, without the need for substantial pre-hearing preparation and the formalities of a traditional trial, and without incurring large legal costs' (Practice Direction ("PD") 26 at [15]).

It is regrettable that these are referred to as "small claims".

First, they make up about three-quarters of all civil claims disposed of by way of final hearing. Secondly, many would not accept that £10,000 is a "small" sum. Thirdly, the claimant bringing the claim, and the defendant defending against it, are not likely to agree that the importance of their dispute is "small".

b. Context

In January to March 2023, 25,000 cases were allocated to the small claims track. This is more than 70 percent of all allocations.

Of the claims that went to a final hearing, three-quarters were allocated to the small claims track: 8,600. This is a decrease of about one-third when compared to the same quarter in 2023.

A claim takes about 52 weeks to go to a final hearing (Ministry of Justice, *Civil Justice Statistics Quarterly, England and Wales, January to March 2024,* 6 June 2024).

c. Allocation

Generally, the small claims track is the "normal track" for three types of claim (CPRs 26.9 and 27.1(2)).

First, any claim with a value of not more than £10,000. In practice, this forms the overwhelming majority.

Secondly, a "claim for personal injuries" where: the value of the claim is not more than £10,000; and the value of any claim for 'damages for personal injuries' arising from a road traffic accident is not more £5,000, or £1,000 in the circumstances prescribed in CPR 26.10, and £1,500 in any other claim.

A "claim for personal injuries" is one in which 'there is a claim for damages in respect of personal injuries to the claimant or any other person'.

"Damages for personal injuries" means 'damages claimed as compensation for pain, suffering and loss of amenity and does not include any other damages which are claimed'.

"Road traffic accident" means 'an accident resulting in bodily injury to any person caused by, or arising out of, the use of a motor vehicle on a road or other public place in England and Wales unless the injury was caused wholly or in part by a breach by the defendant of one or more of the relevant statutory provisions.

Thirdly, any claim which includes a claim by a tenant of residential premises against a landlord where: the tenant is seeking an order requiring the landlord to carry out repairs, or other work to the premises; the cost is estimated to be not more than £1,000; and the value of any other claim for damages is not more than £1,000.

If a tenant is claiming a remedy in respect of harassment, or unlawful eviction, it will not be allocated to the small claims track.

d. Civil Procedure Rules

CPRs and PDs apply, unless a CPR or PD under CPR 27 prescribes otherwise (CPR 27.2(2)).

CPRs relating to the following do not apply (CPR 27.2):

1 interim remedies (except as they relate to interim injunctions);
2 disclosure and inspection;
3 evidence (except the power of the court to control evidence);
4 miscellaneous rules about evidence;
5 experts and assessors (except the duty to restrict expert evidence; experts' overriding duty to the court; the court's power to direct that evidence is to be given by a single joint expert; and instructions to a single joint expert);
6 further information (although the court may, on the court's own motion, order a party to provide further information if the court considers that it is appropriate);
7 Part 36 offers to settle; and
8 hearings (except the general rule that hearings are to be in public; communications with the court; and recording and transcription of proceedings).

e. Final remedy

The court may grant any final remedy that may be granted if the proceedings were allocated to another track (CPR 27.3).

f. Preparation

After allocation, the court will do one of the following (CPR 27.4).

Give *standard* directions, and fix a date for the final hearing.

Give *special* directions, and fix a date for the final hearing, or direct that the court consider what further directions are to be given, no later than 28 days after the date that special directions were given.

Fix a date for a *preliminary* hearing.

Give notice that the court proposes to deal with the claim *without* a hearing, and invite the parties to notify the court by a specified date if they agree.

"Standard directions" means: 'a direction that each party shall, at least 14 days before the date fixed for the final hearing, file and serve on every other party copies of all documents (including any expert's report) on which he intends to rely at the hearing'; and any other standard directions prescribed in PD 27A.

"Special directions" means 'directions given in addition to or instead of the standard directions.'

The general rule is that the court will give the parties at least 21 days' notice of the date fixed for the final hearing. The exception is where the parties agree to accept less notice.

In any event, the court must inform the parties of the amount of time allowed for the final hearing.

g. Experts

No expert evidence may be given at a hearing without the court's permission (CPR 27.5).

h. Preliminary hearing

A preliminary hearing may only be held in three circumstances (CPR 27.6).

First, *special directions are needed* to ensure a fair hearing, and it appears that it is necessary for a party to attend at court, so as to ensure that that party understands what she must do to comply with the special directions.

Secondly, *to dispose of the claim*, on the basis that one of the parties has no real prospect of success.

Thirdly, *to strike out (part of) a statement of case*, on the basis that it discloses no reasonable grounds for bringing, or defending, the claim.

When deciding whether or not to hold a preliminary hearing, the court must have regard to the desirability of limiting the expense of the parties that will be incurred by attending court. The parties must be given at least 14 days' notice of the date of such a hearing.

If the parties agree, the court may treat a preliminary hearing as a final hearing.

At, or after, a preliminary hearing, the court will do three things. First, fix the date of the final hearing (if it has not already been fixed), and give the parties at least 21 days' notice of the same, unless the parties agree to accept less notice. Secondly, inform the parties of the amount of time allowed for the final hearing. Thirdly, give any appropriate directions.

i. Additional or amended directions

The court may add to, vary, or revoke, directions (CPR 27.7).

j. Final hearing

There are six rules for the final hearing (CPR 27.8).

First, the court may adopt any method of proceeding that is fair. Secondly, hearings will be informal. Thirdly, the strict rules of evidence do not apply. Fourthly, evidence need not be on oath. Fifthly, the court may limit cross-examination. Sixthly, the court must give reasons for its decision.

k. Non-attendance

If a party does not attend the final hearing, but satisfies the following conditions, the court will take into account that party's statement of case, and any other documents that she has filed when the claim is decided (CPR 27.9).

First, at least seven days before the hearing, written notice ("notice") that she will not attend has been filed with the court, and served on the other party.

Secondly, at least seven days before the hearing, she has served any other documents on the other party that she has filed with the court.

Thirdly, in the notice, she has requested that the court decide the claim in her absence, and she has confirmed her compliance with the first and second condition.

Otherwise, the court may strike out the claim (CPR 27.9(2)).

The court may decide the claim solely on the evidence of the claimant if two conditions are satisfied (CPR 27.9(3)).

First, a defendant does not attend the hearing, or give notice. Secondly, the claimant does not attend the hearing, or give notice that she will not attend.

The court may strike out a claim, defence, and counterclaim, if neither party attends, nor gives notice (CPR 27.9(4)).

l. Disposal without a hearing

The court can dispose of a claim without a hearing in two circumstances. First, if both parties agree (CPR 27.10). Secondly, until 1 December 2024 (unless it is extended), without the agreement of the parties in certain circumstances (PD 51ZC at [1]).

m. Set aside & re-hearing

Where the following are met, a party may apply for an order that judgment is set aside, and that the claim is re-heard (CPR 27.11).

First, she was neither present, nor represented, at the hearing of the claim. Secondly, she has not given notice, in accordance with the rule for non-attendance at the final hearing. Thirdly, the application must be made not more than 14 days after the day on which notice of the judgment was served on her.

Where these conditions are satisfied, a court may grant the application, but only if the applicant satisfies a further two conditions.

First, she had a good reason for not attending, or being represented at, the hearing, or giving notice in accordance with the rule for non-attendance at the final hearing. Secondly, she has a reasonable prospect of success.

If judgment is set aside, the court must fix a new date to hear the claim. This may take place immediately after the application. It may also be heard by the judge who granted the application.

An application to set aside cannot succeed, where a claim was disposed of without a hearing and with the agreement of the parties.

n. Costs

There are three overarching rules.

Pre-allocation. After allocation. Re-allocation.

i. Pre-allocation

CPRs 46.11 and 46.13 apply before allocation (CPR 27.14(1)).

Generally, once a claim is allocated to the small claims track, the rules that apply to costs on this track apply to the periods *before and after* the claim was so allocated (CPR 27.14(1) and (5)).

Any cost orders made before a claim is allocated to the small claims track will not be affected by allocation (CPR 46.13(1)).

Where costs are assessed on the standard basis following the conclusion of a claim that had not been allocated, costs may be restricted to those that would have been allowed on the track to which the claim would likely have been allocated (CPR 46.13(3)).

ii. After allocation

Generally, a party can only be ordered to pay the following in respect of another party's costs, fees, and expenses, including those relating to an appeal (CPR 27.14; and PD 27A at [7]):

1. fixed costs of issuing the claim in Table 2 of PD 45;
2. not more than £260 in respect of legal advice and assistance in proceedings that include a claim for an injunction, or an order for specific performance;
3. any court (hearing and application) fees;
4. expenses which a party, or a witness, has reasonably incurred in travelling to, and from, a hearing, or staying away from home so as to attend a hearing;
5. not more than £95 for any loss of earnings / leave, by a party, or a witness, due to attending a hearing, or staying away from home so as to attend a hearing;
6. not more than £750 in respect of an expert's fees;
7. such further costs as the court may summarily assess and order to be paid by a party who has "behaved unreasonably";
8. fixed costs prescribed by Tables 10 and 11 in PD 45 in respect of Stage 1, and where relevant Stage 2, where:
   a. the claim was within the scope of the Pre-Action Protocol for Low Value Personal Injury Claims in Road Traffic Accidents, or the Pre-Action Protocol for Low Value Personal Injury (Employers' Liability and Public Liability) Claims,
   b. the claimant reasonably believed that the claim was valued at more than the small claims track limit, in accordance with [4.1(4)] of the relevant protocol, and
   c. the defendant admitted liability under the process prescribed in the relevant protocol, but did not pay those Stage 1, and where relevant, Stage 2, fixed costs; and
9. the reasonably incurred cost of any approved transcript.

"Behaved unreasonably" does not necessarily include a party who has rejected an offer in settlement. The court may take this fact into consideration, however, when assessing (un)reasonableness.

These limits also apply to any fee, or reward, charged by a person exercising rights of audience as a lay representative.

iii. Re-allocation

When re-allocated from the small claims track to another track, costs in relation to the other track are allowable (CPR 27.15(1)).

Where a claim is re-allocated, from the multi-track to the small claims track, CPR 27.14 applies to the period before, as well as after, re-allocation (CPR 27.15(2)). The exception is where a court order directed, or a CPR or PD prescribes, otherwise.

2. Overriding objective

The overriding objective is to enable the court to deal with cases *justly* and at *proportionate cost* (CPR 1.1(1); and appendix A).

This includes six *factors*. One is to deal with the case in ways that are proportionate. This, in turn, includes four *aspects*.

When an application is heard, or a case management decision must be made, the following can be used to frame submissions.

a. Duty

The CPR imposes *different* duties on the court, and the parties.

i. Court

The *court* must seek to give effect to the overriding objective when exercising any power, or interpreting any rule (CPR 1.2).

This includes actively managing cases, so as to further the overriding objective (CPR 1.4(1)); and appendix B).

ii. Parties

The *parties* must help the court to further the overriding objective (CPR 1.3). This is *not* a duty to help another party.

A party ("A") does not have to assist another party ("B") to remedy B's procedural mistake, unless there is a genuine misunderstanding, relating to a material matter, to which A has contributed.

A is entitled to take a good procedural point. In doing so, A should act "in a proper professional manner in researching the position, advising the client and taking their instructions". It should not be capable of being recast as "technical games" (*Woodward & Anor v Phoenix Healthcare Distribution Ltd* [2019] EWCA Civ 985 at [50]).

In *Piepenbrock v Associated Newspapers Ltd & Ors* [2020] EWHC 1708 (QB) at [64], Nicklin J said that: "Providing s/he has done nothing to mislead or obstruct, a [party] could hardly be criticised if s/he decided to follow Napoleon's advice not to interrupt an enemy when s/he is making a mistake."

There is an important distinction, however, between a good procedural point and *adverse authority*. Advocates are under a duty to draw the court's attention to an authority that: undermines the case that she is advancing; and has not been cited by the other party.

b. Factors

Dealing with a case justly and at proportionate cost, so far as is practicable, includes considering six factors (CPR 1.1(2)).

First, ensuring that the parties are on an equal footing, and can participate fully in proceedings, and that parties and witnesses can give their best evidence. Secondly, saving expense. Thirdly, dealing with the case expeditiously and fairly.

Fourthly, allotting an appropriate share of the court's resources to the case, while taking into account the need to allot resources to other cases. Fifthly, enforcing compliance with CPRs, PDs, and court orders. Sixthly, dealing with the case in proportionate ways.

They are not: exhaustive (which is clear from the word 'includes'); expressed to be hierarchical; or absolute requirements (which is demonstrated by the caveat 'so far as is practicable').

i. Equal footing

There are two important components.

First, recognising that a person without a representative may justify such procedure as the court considers appropriate to further the overriding objective. Secondly, procedural and substantive correspondence with the court should be served on the other side.

1. Person without a representative

A person who does not have legal representation is also known as a "litigant in person" or an "unrepresented party". It is, however, better to use the term "person without a representative".

Where a person is without a representative, the court *must* have regard to this fact when *exercising any power of case management* (CPR 3.1A(2)).

The court must adopt such procedure at any hearing as it considers appropriate to further the overriding objective (CPR 3.1A(4)).

This includes the following (*Equal Treatment Bench Book*, July 2024, p 11 at [17]; and CPR 3.1A(5)).

First, ensuring that the process is explained in a manner that they can understand. Secondly, ensuring that they are informed about what is expected of them in ample time to prepare and comply with any CPRs, PDs, or court orders. Thirdly, whenever possible, ensuring that they are given sufficient time for their needs.

Fourthly, ascertaining from a person without a representative the matters about which a witness may be able to give evidence, or ought to be cross-examined. Fifthly, putting, or causing to be put, such questions as may appear to the court to be proper.

There is an important distinction, however, between ensuring that *case management directions* are clear, understandable, and achievable, and *lowering the standard of compliance.*

The former is in accordance with, and the latter is contrary to, authority. CPRs, PDs, and court orders, apply to *all* parties.

This is clear from *Barton v Wright Hassal LLP* [2018] UKSC 12, [2018] 3 All ER 487 at [18], where Lord Sumption (with whom Lords Wilson and Carnwath agreed) said (with emphasis added):

> "... Their lack of representation will often justify making allowances in making *case management decisions* and in conducting hearings. But *it will not usually justify applying to litigants in person a lower standard of compliance with rules or orders of the court.* The overriding objective requires the courts so far as practicable to enforce compliance with the rules: CPR rule 1.1(1)(f). *The rules do not in any relevant respect distinguish between represented and unrepresented parties.* ... Unless the rules and practice directions are *particularly inaccessible or obscure*, it is reasonable to expect a litigant in person to familiarise himself with the rules which apply to any step which he is about to take."

Lord Briggs (with whom the then President of the Supreme Court agreed) said at paragraph 42 (with emphasis added):

> "... Save to the very limited extent to which the CPR now provides otherwise, *there cannot fairly be one attitude to compliance with rules for represented parties and another for litigants in person*, still less a general dispensation for the latter from the need to observe them. ..."

The court must approach non-compliance by a person *without* a representative in the *same* way as non-compliance by a person *with* a representative.

Otherwise, there would be an unjustifiable disturbance in the balance struck by CPRs, PDs, and court orders.

The exception to which Lord Sumption referred does *not* carve out a general exception for claims allocated to the small claims track.

Relevant CPRs and PDs are unlikely to be inaccessible or obscure.

2. Correspondence

As a general rule, any communication with the court on a matter of *substance* or *procedure* must (CPRs 27.2(1)(h) and 39.8): be disclosed to, and served on, the other party; and state on its face that it has been copied to the other party, their identity and capacity.

Failure to do so, so as to deprive the other party of an opportunity to respond, amounts to "a serious procedural irregularity" (*National Westminster Bank Plc v Rushmer & Anor* [2010] EWHC 554 (Ch), [2010] 2 FLR 362 at [35]).

It may also, subject to hearing from the parties, result in sanctions, or the exercise of other case management powers.

Unless the court orders otherwise, any communication that does not state on its face that it has been copied to the other party, their identity and capacity: must be returned to the sender, without consideration, and with a brief explanation (CPR 38.8(5)).

"It is inappropriate, and unjust, to seek to communicate with the Court without this transparency. This cardinal principle is clearly recorded in CPR 39.8. Observance of it is important" (Fordham J in *Bell & Anor v Brabners LLP* [2021] EWHC 560 (QB) at [4]).

ii. Proportionality

Consideration should be given to the following, so that a case is dealt with in ways that are proportionate (CPR 1.1(2)(c)).

First, the amount of money involved. Secondly, the importance of the case. Thirdly, the complexity of the issues. Fourthly, the financial position of each party.

In cases arising out of road traffic collisions, for example, insurers are often named parties, in which case, their financial position cannot usually be described as modest. The first three, however, are always likely to be modest for the following reasons.

First, the amount of money involved is usually not more than £10,000.

Secondly, the importance of the case to the *parties* will likely be modest because: harassment or unlawful eviction claims will not be allocated to the small claims track; disputed allegations of dishonesty will not usually be suitable for allocation to the small claims track; and the value of a claim for damages for personal injuries will not be more than £5,000, £1,000, or £1,500.

Thirdly, the importance of the claim to *persons other than the parties* is likely to be modest because, in general, county court authority may not be cited.

Fourthly, the complexity of the issues is likely to be modest because: if the facts, law, or evidence, are complex, the claim is unlikely to be allocated to the small claims track; and it will not normally be allocated to the small claims track if it is likely to take more than a day (PD 26 at [15(5)]).

3. Court's duty to actively manage cases

The court must further the overriding objective by actively managing cases (CPR 1.4(1) and appendix B).

There are 12 prescribed considerations.

They are not exhaustive, or expressed to be hierarchical.

First, encouraging the parties to co-operate with each other. Secondly, identifying the issues at an early stage. Thirdly, deciding promptly which issues need full investigation, and a final hearing, and disposing summarily of those that do not.

Fourthly, deciding the order that issues are to be resolved. Fifthly, encouraging and facilitating the parties to use alternative dispute resolution. Sixthly, helping the parties to settle (part of) the case.

Seventhly, fixing timetables, or otherwise controlling the progress of the case. Eighthly, considering whether the likely benefits of taking a particular step justify the cost. Ninthly, dealing with as many aspects of the case as it can on the same occasion.

Tenthly, dealing with the case without the parties needing to attend court in person. Eleventhly, making use of technology. Twelfthly, giving directions to ensure that a final hearing proceeds quickly and efficiently.

They can be deployed whenever the court has to exercise a discretion, so as to persuade the court that: the way in which you invite the court to exercise that discretion is in accordance with the court's duty to *actively manage cases;* and, therefore, the *overriding objective,* which the court *must* seek to further.

a. Encouraging co-operation

Where there is no pre-action letter, a party fails to reply to sustained correspondence over a prolonged period, or unreasonably refuses to consider an offer of alternative dispute resolution, the court should take it into consideration.

Failure to do so is incompatible with the court's duty to actively manage cases, so as to further the overriding objective, which the parties are obliged to help the court to further.

These submissions can usually be best deployed when the court is invited not to award (all of) the fixed costs claimed, or applying for costs on the basis that a party has behaved unreasonably.

The court may direct the parties to cooperate in preparation for a remote, telephone or audio-visual, hearing. For example, so as to agree, and file with the court, an electronic bundle of documents.

Failure to comply may result in the hearing not going ahead, the claim being decided in the absence of one or both of the parties, or some other (likely costs) sanction.

b. Early identification of issues

The *key* documents should be disclosed *before* a claim is issued (PD – Pre-action Conduct and Protocols at [6(c)]; and appendix E).

Particulars of claim must set out the claim in a clear, coherent way. They must conform to PDs (CPRs 27.2(2); and 16.4(1)(e)).

In a claim based upon a written agreement, this includes attaching a copy of the contract (or documents constituting the agreement), and any incorporated general conditions of sale, or serving them with, the particulars of claim (PD 16 at [7.3]).

Where a party ("A") fails to do so, an application should be made by the other party ("B") to strike out A's statement of case. The basis is failure to comply with CPRs and PDs (CPR 3.4(2)(c)).

In the alternative, the application should invite the court to make an unless order. That is, unless the written agreement is provided within a specified time period, the claim will automatically be struck out.

The submission is that: the court is under a duty actively to manage the case; the issues have not been identified at an early stage; so that the court has been unable to further the overriding objective, which includes enforcing compliance with CPRs and PDs.

c. Summary disposal

Where particulars of claim disclose no reasonable grounds for bringing a claim, or a defence discloses no reasonable grounds for defending against them, an application should be made for strike out and / or summary judgment (CPRs 3.4(2)(a) and 24.3).

The issues in these statements of case do not need to be decided at a final hearing. They do not even need full investigation.

If allowed to proceed, they would be bound to fail. The case would not be dealt with expeditiously. An *in*appropriate share of the court's resources would be allocated to the case. Summary disposal is appropriate. It is also required by the overriding objective.

In a claim for credit hire, for example, if there is no evidence of basic hire rates, it is hard to foresee a need to cross-examine on the issue of impecuniosity, so as to establish whether or not the claimant was impecunious. The court will award the credit hire rate, as there is no alternative evidence (of the basic hire rate).

As it is unlikely to affect any judgment, there may be no need to resolve the "issue" of impecuniosity. The defendant may accept that the claimant was impecunious, so that this issue falls away, court time is saved, and the case is dealt with expeditiously.

d. Order of resolution

The obvious example is that liability should be decided before quantum. If liability is not established, quantum is academic.

In the credit hire example, where disputed, whether or not there was a need to hire should be resolved first. This is because, if there was no need to hire, a claim for credit hire should be dismissed. The question of quantum in respect of credit hire is academic.

e. Alternative dispute resolution

Where the parties agree to mediation, the claim will be referred to the Small Claims Mediation Service (CPR 26.6(4)).

Form N180: Directions Questionnaire (Small Claims Track) ("the questionnaire"), however, provides (with italicised emphasis added) that:

> You may seek to settle the claim either by direct discussion with the other party or by private or court mediation. If settlement is reached, parties may enter into a binding agreement which can be enforced if the terms of the agreement were to be breached.
>
> Mediation is a way of resolving disputes without a court hearing, where the parties are assisted in resolving their dispute with the help of an impartial mediator. Mediation is usually carried out by telephone in one hour time limited appointments.
>
> As part of your case, **HMCTS will provide a free, confidential Small Claims Mediation Service.** *For all money claims for £10,000 or less, parties are required to attend a mediation appointment organised by the Small Claims Mediation Service.*

> If you do not attend mediation, you may be subject to penalties. These could include the Judge ordering you to pay costs, or the Judge automatically ruling in favour of the other party(ies).
>
> If the claim is settled at this stage the parties can avoid further court fees, costs and time involved in preparing and attending a hearing. If you are unable to reach agreement with the other party at mediation, the claim will proceed to a small claims hearing.

The questionnaire also confirms that: 'Mediation does not apply to claims for Personal Injury or Road Traffic Accident [sic] or those started using Online Civil Money Claims.'

This is consistent with CPR 26.6, which prescribes that the rule in respect of referral to the Small Claims Mediation Service does not apply to claims following a road traffic accident, personal injury, or housing disrepair.

A party may request a stay in the questionnaire to attempt a settlement (CPR 26.5(1)). If the parties agree, the court will notify them that the claim has been stayed for a month (CPR 26.5(2)).

Otherwise, the court may direct that (part, or the whole, of) the case is stayed for an appropriate period (CPR 26.5(3)).

In the event of a stay, the claimant must inform the court if there is a settlement. At the end of a stay, if the claimant doesn't inform the court that a settlement has been reached, the court will give appropriate case management directions.

In *Churchill v Merthyr Tydfil County Borough Council & Ors* [2023] EWCA Civ 1416, [2024] 3 All ER 771 at [74], Sir Geoffrey Vos MR (with whom Carr LCJ and Birss LJ agreed) said:

> "...ii) The court can lawfully stay proceedings for, or order, the parties to engage in a non-court-based dispute resolution process provided that the order made does not impair the very essence of the claimant's right to proceed to a judicial hearing, and is proportionate to achieving the legitimate

aim of settling the dispute fairly, quickly and at reasonable cost.

iii) I decline to lay down fixed principles as to what will be relevant to determining the questions of a stay of proceedings or an order that the parties engage in a non-court-based dispute resolution process. Many of the factors mentioned at [61]–[63] above and the nature of the process contemplated will be relevant, as will other circumstances. …"

f. Helping settlement

On the day of the final hearing, where the parties consider that there is a real prospect of settling the claim, or even narrowing the issues, the court should grant an appropriate amount of time.

This is in accordance with the overriding objective to allot an appropriate share of the court's resources to the case, while taking into account the need to allot resources to other cases.

g. Controlling progress

Where a statement of case does not have a statement of truth, for example, the court should make an 'unless' order. That is, unless verified by a statement of truth, and filed and served by a certain date, it will automatically be struck out.

This is an example of the court fulfilling its duty to actively manage cases, through fixing a timetable, so as to control the progress of the case, without waiting for a party having to make (and pay the issue fee in respect of) an application. In this way, the court ensures that a case progresses expeditiously towards disposal.

h. Cost / benefit analysis

Where the claimant fails to attend a final hearing without giving written notice in accordance with CPR 27.9, or a good reason for failing to attend, the court should consider whether the likely benefits of adjourning the case justify the cost.

Where the amount in dispute is modest, and a barrister for each party has attended, the court will weigh up the following.

Unfairness to the defendant occasioned by granting an adjournment, including: the expense of attending *that* hearing; the additional expense of attending a *further* hearing; and that the case is *not* being dealt with expeditiously.

Balanced against this, the court will weigh any unfairness to the claimant if an adjournment is not granted: liability may be admitted; the defendant may have a substantial counterclaim; and the financial circumstances of the claimant may be relevant (she may be an impecunious individual, as opposed to an affluent insurer).

Also, the court will factor in the need to allot an appropriate share of the court's resources to the case, while taking into account the need to allot resources to other cases.

i. Efficiency

Special directions may be needed to ensure a fair hearing.

If so, the court may order a preliminary hearing where it is necessary for a party to attend court, so as to ensure that she understands what she must do to comply with the directions (CPR 27.4).

The court must, however: have regard to the desirability of limiting the expense to the parties of attending court; and make use of technology, in the form of remote hearings.

At a preliminary hearing, the court will deal with as many aspects as it can. This includes considering whether to fix a date for the final hearing (if it has not done so already), and giving any other, appropriate directions (CPR 27.6(5)).

j. Technology

The COVID-19 pandemic necessitated the use of remote hearings, so as to minimise the risk of transmission.

Whatever the (dis)advantages, remote (final) hearings appear to have been largely a temporary measure during the pandemic.

k. Directions

The court has a general power to add to, vary, or revoke, directions (CPR 27.7). This should be used to further the overriding objective by actively managing cases.

A party may invite the court to make a particular direction (PD 27A at [2.4]). This includes an order that, unless a statement of case is verified by a statement of truth, within a prescribed period of time, it should automatically be struck out (CPR 22.2(3)).

4. Pre-Action protocols & PD – Pre-Action Conduct

Pre-action protocols explain the conduct, and set out the steps, that are normally expected before commencing proceedings.

There are 15 pre-action protocols currently in force.

Where no specific pre-action protocol applies, however, as is the case in most claims that are allocated to the small claims track, the parties are expected to comply with the Practice Direction – Pre-action Conduct ("the Practice Direction") (appendix E).

a. Objectives

The parties must exchange sufficient information before proceedings, so that the following objectives are achieved.

First, to understand each other's position. Secondly, to make decisions about how to proceed. Thirdly, to try to settle the issues without proceedings.

Fourthly, to consider a form of alternative dispute resolution to assist with settlement. Fifthly, to support the efficient management of proceedings. Sixthly, to reduce the costs of resolving the dispute.

b. Reasonable & proportionate

Reasonable and proportionate steps should be taken to identify, narrow, and resolve, the legal, factual, or expert, issues.

Costs incurred in complying with the requirements of pre-action conduct should be proportionate. This includes the cost of correspondence, and information, that is exchanged. Proportionate steps before issuing a claim usually include the following.

First, the claimant writing to the defendant, setting out concise details of her claim. Secondly, the defendant responding to the claimant within a reasonable period. Typically, no more than 14 days in a straightforward claim. Thirdly, the parties disclosing key documents that are relevant to the issues in dispute.

c. Non-compliance

The court will take into account non-compliance in *substance* with the terms of the relevant pre-action protocol, or the Practice Direction. The court is not likely to be concerned with "minor or technical infringements" (Practice Direction at [13]).

Non-compliance will be taken into account when deciding what order, if any, to make as to costs (Practice Direction at [13]; and CPRs 3.1(4)-(6) and 44.2(5)(a)).

The court may decide that there has been a failure to comply in the following circumstances (Practice Direction at [14]).

First, failing to provide sufficient information to enable the objectives of pre-action conduct to be met. Secondly, failing to act within a relevant time limit, or otherwise within a reasonable period. Thirdly, unreasonably refusing to use a form of alternative dispute resolution, or failing to respond to an invitation to do so.

d. Contempt of court

A person who knowingly makes a false statement in a document prepared in anticipation of legal proceedings may be subject to proceedings for contempt of court (Practice Direction at [2]).

5. Statements of case

Statements of case set out (plead) a party's position. They should enable the other party to know what is alleged against them.

They are *formal* documents. Formalities *must* be followed.

Statements of case plead the material facts, what the claim or defence is, and the key law (where it is unusual).

a. Types

A "statement of case" includes the following.

Claim form. Particulars of claim (where not in the claim form). Defence. Counterclaim. Additional claim under CPR 20. Reply to the defence.

b. Rules & practice directions

CPRs and PDs apply (CPR 27.2(2)).

There are two reasons to be familiar with their requirements.

First, to ensure that the party who you represent has complied. Secondly, to identify another party's substantial non-compliance.

The following provide an insight into considerations when drafting statements of case following a road traffic collision.

It is not intended to be comprehensive. There are other, excellent professional texts on drafting statements of case with which this guide does not seek to compete, but rather to complement.

i. Legible & intelligible

When completing any court form by hand, use capital letters and black ink. This is for two reasons.

First, so that the original is legible. Secondly, if the original is scanned and photocopied, copies will be legible.

Most statements of case are typed. All the necessary elements to establish a claim, or defence, must be pleaded. Facts should be limited to those necessary to understand the claim, or defence.

ii. Heading

A statement of case must have a heading.

In general, the name of the court should be in the top, left-hand corner. It should be capitalised, emboldened, and underlined.

The claim number should be in the top, right-hand corner. It should also be capitalised, emboldened, and underlined.

Underneath, on the left-hand side, '**BETWEEN:**' should appear.

Below this, the names of the parties should be capitalised, centralised, and emboldened.

A party's status should appear in the line underneath their name. This should be underlined, and aligned to the right-hand side.

'And' is used in civil cases to separate the parties.

Following the name of the parties, between horizontal tram lines, the form of the statement of case should be stated, capitalised, centralised, and emboldened.

For example: '**DEFENCE AND COUNTERCLAIM**'.

iii. Numbers & figures

Pages, paragraphs, and lists, should be numbered consecutively.

Numbers and dates must be expressed as figures.

iv. Authority & evidence

Statements of case *may* do any of the following (PD 16 at [12.2]).

First, refer to any point of law on which the claim, or defence, is based. Secondly, give the name of any witness who that party proposes to call. Thirdly, attach a copy of any document or expert report that that party considers to be necessary.

v. Particularity

Statements of case are *fundamental.*

Often, they are too general, or too detailed.

Too general means a failure to set out the material details of law and fact that are necessary for a claim, or defence, to succeed.

Overly detailed, repetitive and encumbered with unnecessary authority, and, the court is unlikely to carefully consider it.

The art is in finding a balance.

Allegations must be particularised. For example, after a road traffic collision, an allegation of negligence should list the ways in which a party is alleged to have been negligent.

If it is claimed that the defendant was negligent in that she drove too fast for the road conditions, it should be pleaded.

vi. Contributory negligence

Where contributory negligence is alleged, often in a defence, or as an alternative in the particulars of claim, following a road traffic collision, it should be pleaded.

This assists the court to further the overriding objective by actively managing cases. This issue will be identified early on.

There is no need to put a percentage on the alleged negligence.

If relied on in closing submissions, a percentage can be given. This will take into account any oral evidence. Usually, one-half, one- / two-thirds, or one- / two- / three-quarters.

vii. Endorsement

If drafted by a legal representative, it should bear her signature.

If drafted by a legal representative as a member, or employee, of a firm, it should be signed in the name of that firm (PD 5A at [2.1]).

viii. Statement of truth

It *must* be verified by a statement of truth (CPR 22.1(1)(a)).

Where particulars of claim are not included in the claim form, they *must* be verified by a statement of truth (PD 16 at [3.2]).

1. Form

The form of the statement of truth is prescribed (PD 22 at [2.1]):

> [I believe / The claimant / The defendant believes] that the facts stated in [these particulars of claim / this defence (and counterclaim) / this reply to the defence and counterclaim] are true. [I un-

> derstand / The claimant / The defendant understands] that proceedings for contempt of court may be brought against anyone who makes, or causes to be made, a false statement in a document verified by a statement of truth without an honest belief in its truth.

When signed by a party, the first sentence begins: 'I believe'. The second sentence begins: 'I understand'.

When signed by a legal representative, the first sentence begins: 'The claimant / The defendant believes'. The second sentence begins: 'The claimant / The defendant understands'.

A statement of truth must be dated with the date on which it is signed (PD 22 at [2.7]).

2. Who

It must be signed by one of the following (PD 22 at [3]).

First, a party, or her litigation friend. Secondly, the legal representative of the party, or litigation friend.

The full name of the individual who signs must be printed clearly beneath her signature (PD 22 at [3.8]).

Entering a name on an online form satisfies the requirement for a statement of truth to be signed (PD 7C at [10]).

a. Legal representative

Where a party is legally represented, the "legal representative" may sign the statement of truth on her client's behalf. It will refer to *her client's* belief. She must state the capacity in which she is signing, and the name of her firm (PD 22 at [3.6]).

A "legal representative" includes a barrister, solicitor, solicitor's employee, or authorised person for the purposes of the Legal Services Act 2007 (CPR 2.3(1); and PD 3.10(2)).

A legal representative *must* use her own name (PD 22 at [3.9]).

A legal representative's signature will be taken by the court as her confirmation of the following three circumstances (PD 22 at [3.7]).

First, her client has authorised her to do so.

Secondly, before signing, she explained to her client that, in signing the statement of truth, she would be confirming her client's belief that the facts stated are true.

Where necessary, explanation may be through an interpreter.

Thirdly, before signing, she informed her client of the possible consequences to her client if it subsequently appears that her client did not have an honest belief in the truth of those facts.

b. Companies & partnerships

For a registered company / corporation, a director, treasurer, secretary, chief executive, "manager," or other officer, may sign (PD 22 at [3.2(1)]).

A "manager" should hold a senior position, and have knowledge of the content of the statement of case, or be responsible for managing those who do. The size and nature of the claim, and company, are relevant considerations (PD 22 at [3.10(1)]).

For a partnership, a partner, or a person having control or management of the partnership, may sign (PD 22 at [3.3]).

c. Insurers

An insurer may sign on behalf of a party where the insurer has a financial interest in the result of proceedings brought by, or against, that party. A director, treasurer, secretary, chief executive, manager, or other officer of the insurer, may sign (PD 22 at [3.4]).

3. Default

If a party fails to verify her statement of case with a statement of truth, the *court* may act on its *own initiative.*

First, by striking it out (CPR 22.2(2)). Secondly, by making an unless order (CPR 3.3; and PD 40B at [8.1] and [8.2]). That is, unless the statement of case is verified by a statement of truth before a certain date, it will automatically be struck out.

A *party* may also make an application for the statement of case to be struck out (CPR 22.2(3)), or an unless order.

A party's statement of case *remains effective* until it is struck out, however, that party cannot rely on it as evidence of any of the matters set out within it (CPR 22.2(1)).

In practice, where a statement of case is not verified by a statement of truth, the court will make an unless order.

If the issue arises on the day of the final hearing, however, the court has two options. First, require the party to verify the statement of case before, or during, the hearing. Secondly, strike it out.

6. Claim form

There are two methods for commencing proceedings.

Generally, it depends whether there is a *substantial dispute of fact.*

a. Substantial dispute of fact

In general, where there is no substantial dispute of fact, the *alternative* method of commencing proceedings may be used: CPR 8. Form N208 is the claim form.

In principle, there is nothing to stop a CPR 8 claim being allocated to the small claims track. In practice, however, it is uncommon.

Where there is a substantial dispute of fact, CPR 7 usually prescribes the procedure for starting a claim. Form N1 is used. Form N1A provides guidance.

To commence proceedings, a claim form is issued. This is sealed by the court with an official seal.

Unless there is an extension, the claim form must be served within four months of the date of issue (CPR 7.5).

b. Court

The name of the court should be on page one, in the top, right-hand corner. It is automatically completed when using Money Claim Online ("MCOL"). If not, it is the 'Civil National Business Centre'.

i. Money Claim Online

MCOL is an internet-based service. It purports to be a convenient, simple and secure way of making, or responding to, a money claim.

The 'Money Claim Online (MCOL) User Guide' (9 November 2021) is available at https://www.gov.uk/government/publications/money-claim-online-user-guide/money-claim-online-mcol-user-guide.

ii. Online suitability

MCOL is suitable on the following conditions (PD 7C at [4]).

First, the only remedy claimed is a specified sum that is less than £100,000 (excluding any interest or costs). Secondly, the procedure under CPR 7 is used.

Thirdly, the claimant is not a child, protected party, or in receipt of legal aid. Fourthly, the claimant's address for service is within the UK. Fifthly, the claim is against a single defendant, or two defendants if the claim is for a single amount against each of them.

Sixthly, the defendant is not the Crown, a person known to be a child or protected party, and her address for service is within England and Wales.

To use MCOL, you need the following.

First, a valid credit or debit card to pay court fees. Secondly, an address in the United Kingdom. Thirdly, an email address. Fourthly, regular internet access.

MCOL cannot be used in any of the following circumstances.

First, the claimant is under 18 years old. Secondly, the claimant is eligible for legal aid, or help with fees. Thirdly, the claim is for compensation following personal injury.

Fourthly, the claimant has been prevented from making claims by the court because she is a "vexatious litigant". That is, someone who uses court cases to harass other people. Fifthly, the claimant intends to issue a joint warrant of control.

Sixthly, a defendant is a child under 18. Seventhly, a defendant is someone who lacks "mental capacity". That is, someone who is unable to make their own decisions. Eighthly, a defendant is a government department or agency. Ninthly, a defendant is an individual or company as a result of a tribunal award. Tenthly, the claim relates to the tenancy deposit scheme.

iii. Steps

There are eight steps.

First, guidance. The claimant is required to confirm that she has read the guidance before issue.

Secondly, confirmation of claimant's details. This includes a correspondence address, and a reference number, if requested.

Thirdly, confirmation of a correspondence address, if the address that the claimant has already provided is outside the UK.

Fourthly, the details of the defendant(s). This includes the usual or last known residential address for individuals, the place of business for defendants who are individuals using a trading alias, or the registered address for corporations and companies.

Fifthly, the claim particulars. This is a statement confirming what money is owed, and why, in no more than 1,080 characters. If this is not possible, the claimant can tick a box after the statement that 'you may also send detailed particulars direct to the defendant'.

If so, an N215 Certificate of Service must be filed with the court within 14 days of the claim being issued, to confirm that the detailed particulars have in fact been served on the defendant.

Confirmation is needed as to whether interest is claimed, and, if so, under which act or agreement. Legal representatives enrolled with MCOL may also enter costs.

Sixthly, summary and statement of truth. Claims that are not issued immediately may be saved as a draft for 28 days, and revised at any time. Thereafter, they will be deleted.

Seventhly, payment of the issue fee using a credit or debit card.

Eighthly, the claim will be issued within two working days of the date that the claim was submitted. A notice will be sent by post to the person issuing the claim to confirm the same. The date of issue can also be seen under the 'Claim Overview' part of MCOL.

c. Parties

The *identity* and *capacity* of the parties must be clear.

i. Individuals

For individuals, title, and full name, *must* be provided.

For a recent name change, '(formerly …)' should follow.

A protected party should include the name of her litigation friend. For example: 'Ms Sarah Smith (by Mrs Helen Smith, her litigation friend)'.

ii. Companies & partnerships

For a partnership, the name of the partnership, followed by '(a firm)' should be used. For example: 'Smith & Smith (a firm)'.

For sole traders, the title and full name of the individual, followed by 'trading as …' should be used. For example: 'Ms Sarah Smith, trading as Smith's Bakery'.

Limited companies should include the word 'limited'.

To check whether a company has limited liability, search the website of 'Companies House' at https://find-and-update.company-information.service.gov.uk.

Company number, registered office address, and type (private or public limited company), are publicly available.

iii. Insurers

The European Communities (Rights against Insurers) Regulations 2002 (SI 2002/3061) allows claimants to bring proceedings arising out of road traffic collisions against the insurer of the defendant vehicle. This does not extinguish the right of the claimant to bring an action against the defendant.

d. Address

Postal addresses, including postcodes, *must* be used.

i. Individuals

For individuals, this is the *residential* address. Even with legal representation, a residential or business address *must* be provided.

ii. Businesses

For businesses, the *business* address can be used.

The *registered office* address of a limited company *must* be used. Companies House can be used to identify this.

e. Detail

Concise details of the claim always include the following.

First, the nature of the claim. Secondly, the remedy sought.

For example: 'The claimant claims damages and other losses arising from a road traffic collision on 1 September 2024 caused by the negligent driving of the defendant.'

In principle, particulars of claim can be pleaded on page three of the paper claim form. In practice, they are usually attached separately. If so, the words 'to follow' should be crossed out.

f. Value

There are three sets of rules.

i. Money

If claiming a fixed sum, this should be provided to the right of the box, entitled 'Amount claimed', in the bottom, right-hand corner.

Otherwise, under the heading 'Value', one of the following should be provided. First, 'not more than £10,000'. Secondly, 'more than £10,000 but not more than £25,000'.

Thirdly, when it is not possible to put a value on the claim, 'I cannot say how much I expect to recover' should be pleaded.

This is for allocation. The small claims track is not the "normal" track for a claim with a value of more than £10,000.

ii. Personal injury

For personal injury, the following must be pleaded: 'My claim includes a claim for personal injuries and the amount that I expect to recover as damages for pain, suffering and loss of amenity is'. This should be followed by one of the following (CPR 16.3(3)).

First, 'not more than £1,000'. Secondly, 'more than £1,000'. Thirdly, 'not more than £1,500'. Fourthly, 'more than £1,500.' Fifthly, 'not more than £5,000'. Fourthly, 'more than £5,000'.

This is for allocation. The small claims track is not the "normal" track where a claim for personal injuries is more than £5,000, £1,500, or £1,000, depending on the circumstances (CPR 26.9(1)).

iii. Housing disrepair

In a claim for not more than £5,000 in respect of housing disrepair to residential premises, the following must also be pleaded.

First: 'My claim includes a claim against my landlord for housing disrepair relating to residential premises. The cost of repairs or other work is estimated to be'. This should be followed by one of the following (CPR 16.3(4)).

Secondly, 'not more than £1,000', or 'more than £1,000'.

For unrelated damages, you must also plead: 'I expect to recover as damages'. This should be followed by one of the following.

First, 'not more than £1,000'. Secondly, 'more than £1,000'.

You must also plead whether 'the value of any other claim for damages' is 'not more than £1,000', or 'more than £1,000'.

This is necessary for allocation. The small claims track is not the "normal" track for a claim by a tenant of residential premises against a landlord where the cost of repairs, or other work, is estimated to be more than £1,000.

g. Interest

Interest must be particularised (CPR 16.4(2)).

Where a claim for interest is pursued at a final hearing, but that claim has not been pleaded, the following submissions are likely.

First, there has been a breach of a CPR. Secondly, the defendant has not had the opportunity to respond to the claim for interest in the defence. Thirdly, allowing the claim for interest will not further the overriding objective for the following reasons.

The parties are not on an equal footing because the defendant has been ambushed. The case must be dealt with fairly. The court must enforce compliance with court rules.

h. Preferred hearing centre

Contact details for county court hearing centres can be found at https://www.gov.uk/find-court-tribunal.

i. Individual

Where the defendant is an individual, the claim will be sent to the defendant's home court in two circumstances (PD 7B at [5.4]).

First, the defendant applies to set aside, or vary, judgment. Secondly, any party makes an application, which cannot be disposed of without a hearing.

ii. Not an individual

Where the defendant is not an individual, and either of the above circumstances apply, the claim will be sent to the county court hearing centre which serves the claimant's address for service (PD 7B at [5.5]).

If the claimant has legal representation, the claim will be sent to the county court hearing centre which serves the legal representative's address.

iii. Transfer

Page two of the claim form must be completed, including the claimant's preferred County Court Hearing Centre for hearings.

If a different preferred court is specified by the claimant or defendant in the respective directions questionnaire, the claim will be transferred to that court.

In the event of a conflict, the judge will decide. Otherwise, the claim will be transferred to the claimant's preferred court.

i. Vulnerability

If the claimant believes that they, or a witness who will give evidence on their behalf, is vulnerable, details should be pleaded.

Does the court need to consider whether additional support should be given?

In practice, this means a physical, mental, or learning disability, or long-term health condition. If so, details should be pleaded of the way(s) in which a party or witness is vulnerable, and what steps, support, or adjustments, should be given.

j. Human rights

Issues under the Human Rights Act 1998 are unlikely.

k. Address for service

The address for service of both parties must be pleaded.

i. Claimant

Where a claimant is represented, the address for service is that of the legal representative. This must be in the UK. It must include postal address and postcode. DX, fax, and email, may be provided.

Where an individual has conduct of a case for a company that is not represented, the business address of that person should be used. This is so that correspondence is received by that individual.

ii. Defendant

This is where the defendant is (last) known to live, or carry on business. The defendant can provide an address for service. This may be the name of her legal representative.

If the following apply, CPR 6.9 prescribes the rules for service.

First, personal service is not required. Secondly, the defendant or her solicitor has confirmed the latter's address for service. Thirdly, the defendant has not given an address for service.

l. Issue fee & costs

The issue fee and legal representative's costs should be inserted into the bottom, right-hand corner.

A legal representative's costs may only be claimed if one has been instructed. Appendix H shows the relevant amounts.

m. Remission

A claimant can apply for help with fees for a court hearing.

This is called "fee remission". Form EX160A provides detailed guidance. In summary, only individuals can apply.

For eligibility, a claimant must have no savings, investments, or only a small amount of the same, and satisfy one of the following.

First, in receipt of certain benefits. Secondly, on a low income.

If successful, there will either be no fee, or it will be reduced.

n. Issue

If using the Civil National Business Centre ("the CNBC"), the postal address is St Katherine's House, 21-27 St Katherine's Street, Northampton NN1 2LH.

Copies of the completed claim form should be posted to the CNBC.

The number of copies depends on the number of defendants. If there is one defendant, then two copies should be posted. One for the court, and one for the defendant.

A copy of the claim form should be retained. This is so that the claimant has a copy.

There are two main methods to pay a court fee.

First, by telephone, with a debit or credit card.

Secondly, online. The issue fee must be paid online for MCOL.

When in receipt of the issue fee, the court will "issue" the claim.

The claimant can elect to "serve" proceedings herself, however, generally the court will serve the defendant by First Class post.

o. Civil National Business Centre

The CNBC is not open to the public visiting in person.

It can be contacted by telephone, or email.

The telephone numbers are 0300 123 1372 for paper money claims and 0300 123 1057 for MCOL.

There are a number of email addresses, depending on the purpose of the enquiry. All are available at https://www.find-court-tribunal.service.gov.uk/courts/civil-national-business-centre-cnbc.

7. Particulars of claim

Not all statements of case are equal.

If a *defence* is struck out, the claim may still fail. If the *particulars of claim* ("particulars") are struck out, however, the claim cannot succeed. The burden is on the party bringing the claim.

a. Persons jointly entitled to a remedy

All persons who are jointly entitled to the remedy claimed by a claimant must be parties, unless the court orders otherwise.

If any such person does not agree to be a claimant, she must be a defendant, unless the court orders otherwise (CPR 19.3).

b. Within claim form or separate document

Particulars may be within the claim form or a separate document.

Whether the form is paper or electronic, there is limited space.

If separate particulars are filed and served, the claimant must do the following (CPR 7.4(1)-(4)).

First, serve the particulars on the defendant within 14 days after service of the claim form, and no later than the latest time for serving the claim form.

If MCOL is used, a certificate of service in the form of Form N215 must be filed at the Civil National Business Centre, within 14 days of serving the particulars on the defendant. This may be by email to ccbc@justice.gov.uk with the claim number in the subject line.

Secondly, file a copy of the particulars with the court within seven days of serving them on the defendant, unless a copy has already been filed, or the claim has not been transferred to a County Court Hearing Centre.

Separate particulars must contain the following (PD 16 at [3.3]).

First, the name of the court in which the claim is proceeding. Secondly, the claim number. Thirdly, the title of proceedings. Fourthly, the claimant's address for service.

If not contained in, or served with, the claim form, the claim form must state that the particulars of claim will follow (CPR 16.2(2)).

c. Contents

Particulars must contain the following (CPR 16.4).

First, a concise statement of the facts on which the claimant relies. Secondly, details of any interest claimed. Thirdly, 'other matters' that are prescribed in a PD. For example, personal injury claims.

d. Personal injury

The following *must* be pleaded (PD 16 at [4]).

First, the claimant's date of birth. Secondly, brief details of personal injury. Thirdly, that a schedule detailing claimed past and future expenses and losses is attached. Fourthly, where the evidence of a medical practitioner is relied on, it is attached to, or served with, the particulars.

e. Contract

Where based upon an agreement, the following must be pleaded.

i. Written

Written agreements require the following (PD 16 at [7.3]).

First, a copy of the contract, or documents constituting the agreement, should be attached to, or served with, the particulars. Secondly, the original(s) should be available at the hearing. Thirdly, any general conditions of sale incorporated into the contract should be attached. Where bulky, the relevant parts suffice.

ii. Oral

Oral agreements require the following (PD 16 at [7.4]).

First, the contractual words used. Secondly, by whom. Thirdly, to whom. Fourthly, when. Fifthly, where they were spoken.

iii. Conduct

Agreements by conduct require the following (PD 16 at [7.5]).

First, the conduct relied on. Secondly, by whom. Thirdly, when. Fourthly, where the acts constituting the conduct were done.

f. Statement of facts

In a claim following a road traffic collision, where there is no counterclaim, the defendant does not have to prove that the mechanism of the collision was as pleaded in the defence.

The burden is for the claimant to prove, on a balance of probabilities, that the collision occurred as pleaded in the particulars.

If a defendant proves that the mechanism of the collision pleaded in the particulars is wrong, the claim should fail.

Accordingly, particulars can be particularly helpful to *defendants*. Especially if the claimant's evidence is inconsistent with what is pleaded in the particulars. Where this is the case, it will form the substance of closing submissions.

g. Hire of a replacement vehicle

The following must be pleaded (PD 16 at [6.3]).

First, the need for the replacement vehicle at the relevant time. Secondly, the period (start and end dates) of hire claimed. Thirdly, the rate of hire. Fourthly, the reasonableness of the period, and rate, of hire.

Fifthly, in a claim for credit hire, whether the claimant could afford to pay in advance to hire a replacement car, and, if not, why. This is known as "impecuniosity".

In practice, the latter is usually the main issue in a claim for credit hire. It is often the difference between an award based on the credit hire, or the basic hire, rate.

Addressing impecuniosity in a witness statement is insufficient.

In *Zurich Insurance Plc v Umerji* [2014] EWCA Civ 357, [2014] RTR 23 ("*Zurich*") at [37], Underhill LJ (with whom Robin Jacob and Moses LJJ agreed) said the following (with emphasis added):

> "… The correct analysis would appear to be as follows. A claim for the cost of hire of a replacement vehicle is, strictly, a claim for expenditure incurred in mitigation of the primary loss, namely the loss of use of the damaged vehicle … *The burden is thus on the claimant to prove (and therefore plead) that such expenditure was reasonably incurred* … But in this kind of case it is clearly right that a claimant who needs to rely on his impecuniousness in order to justify the amount of his claim should *plead* and prove it. …"

Zurich was applied in *Mr Abdirahim Ali Diriya v Ms Kaltrina Bojaj & Anor* [2020] EWCA Civ 1400, [2021] 1 WLR 1277. Coulson LJ gave the leading judgment (with whom Nicola Davies and Rose LJJ (as she then was) agreed). At paragraph 7, Coulson LJ said (with emphasis added):

> "… In my view, the [claimant] ought to have provided the necessary pleading in respect of impecuniosity at the outset of the proceedings so that, in the absence of that information, the Unless Order was entirely proper. If … such orders are not uncommon, then that can only be because claimants in these sorts of cases are taking too lax an approach to *the obligation to plead* and prove *impecuniosity* so clearly spelt out in *Zurich*. That is a point to which I return below."

Coulson LJ returned to *Zurich* at paragraph 53:

> "… [defendants] are entitled to know the case they have to meet. They should not be expected to have to prepare for a trial where the critical item of claim depends on a one line assertion, and hoping that, as a result of the cross-examination of the [claimant], the judge will reject the claim. That is not how civil litigation is supposed to work post-CPR. …"

h. Considerations following a road traffic collision

Not every consideration will be relevant to every claim; different considerations will be relevant to different claims.

Particulars should plead only those facts that are *necessary* for the claim to succeed. Written evidence can set out other relevant facts.

i. When, where & who

What was the date, time and location of the collision? Who (or what company) is responsible for each vehicle? Is the claim subrogated? That is, does an insurance company have a right to pursue a third party who caused an insurance loss to the insured?

ii. Road layout

What was the name of the road, junction or roundabout? How many lanes were there? Were there traffic lights? Signage? Road markings? Were the lanes on the roundabout clearly separated?

iii. Traffic

Light traffic? Gridlocked? What were the types of vehicles on the road? Personal cars only, heavy goods vehicles, or slow-moving tractors, and farm machinery? Was this usual for the time of day?

iv. Weather

What were the weather conditions? Light or dark? Was there any street lighting? If so, was it on? Was it snowing, hailing, or raining? Was the road wet? What was the visibility like?

v. Vehicles

What were the makes, models, and vehicle registration plates, of the relevant vehicles? What direction(s) were they traveling in? Southeast, towards Reading, or in different directions?

vi. Speed

What was the speed limit? How fast were the relevant vehicles travelling? Were these speeds appropriate for the traffic, and weather, conditions? Was the claimant's vehicle stationary at the time of the collision? If so, was the engine off, and the handbrake on? If it was a manual transmission, was the gear stick in neutral?

vii. Proximity

Where were the relevant vehicles in relation to each other? Was the claimant's vehicle in front of, level with, or behind, the defendant's vehicle? How many metres behind the claimant's vehicle was the defendant's vehicle? If there were multiple lanes on the approach to a junction, which lane was the claimant in? Which lane was the defendant in?

viii. Perception

When did the claimant first see the defendant's vehicle before the collision (if at all)? When did the defendant first see the claimant's vehicle? Was a visual (hand) or audible (horn) signal used to notify the defendant of the claimant's vehicle?

ix. Objective intention

What were the parties' objective intentions? Were both vehicles indicating right? Was the claimant's vehicle positioned to the left of the lane, broadcasting an intention to turn left? Or, in the centre of the lane, showing an intention to go straight on? What (if any) mirrors were checked before changing speed, or direction? Was the left blind spot checked for cyclists before turning left?

x. Subjective intention

Where was the claimant's destination? Was it the workplace? If so, was it a routine journey? Was the claimant familiar with the road layout? What about the traffic conditions for that time of day?

xi. Mechanism

What was the mechanism of collision?

Was the claimant's vehicle hit by the defendant's vehicle when the latter was emerging from a side road? Was it a rear-end shunt? Was the claimant's vehicle parked?

Was the collision in a car park, on a roundabout, or did it involve vehicles changing lanes? Was it a concertina collision? Did the defendant swerve into the claimant's lane?

xii. Mitigation

Was there time to take defensive action, so as to avoid the collision? Was it possible for the claimant to steer, brake, or sound the horn, so as to avoid the defendant's vehicle entirely, or at least warn the defendant of the claimant's presence? If not, why?

xiii. Damage

Where was the damage to the relevant vehicles? Modest scratch, moderate dent, or heavy impact? Was there damage to the tailgate of the claimant's vehicle, causing the bonnet of the defendant's vehicle to crumple severely? Is there an engineers' report commenting upon the damage? Is there an estimate for repair? Or just an invoice for the repairs? If so, does it particularise the repairs that were in fact undertaken?

i. Interest

The following *must* be pleaded to claim interest (CPR 16.4(2)).

Whether it is under the terms of a contract, another enactment, or on some other basis. If it is under another enactment, the name of it must be pleaded. If it is on some other basis, what?

A claim for a specified amount of money requires the following.

First, the percentage rate at which interest is claimed. Secondly, the date from which it is claimed. Thirdly, the date to which it is calculated. This must be no later than the date on which the claim form is issued.

Fourthly, the total amount of interest claimed to the date of calculation. Fifthly, after that date, the daily rate that interest accrues.

i. Contractual

An agreed contractual term for interest should be pleaded.

In *Chaplair Ltd v Kumari* [2015] EWCA Civ 798, [2015] HLR 39 ("*Chaplair*"), it was held that a county court judge could make an award of costs in favour of a landlord in a claim for rent arrears. The terms of the lease / contract allowed recovery of the costs of legal proceedings.

The same principle applies to a contractual entitlement to interest.

ii. Statutory

There are two relevant statutory provisions.

A contractually agreed rate of interest is likely to be greater. In a business-to-business contract, a term for interest is implied.

1. County Courts Act 1984

Section 69 of this Act prescribes that the court has a *discretion* whether to make an award. It reflects the fact that a claimant has been denied use of a sum that the court has found due.

The *rate* and *period* that interest accrues is also discretionary. The annual rate of eight percent is often claimed. In practice, two (and increasingly three) percent is often awarded.

Interest is not recoverable in respect of credit hire charges that have not been paid (*Pattni v First Leicester Buses Ltd* [2011] EWCA Civ 1384, [2012] RTR 17 at [70]).

2. Late Payment of Commercial Debts (Interest) Act 1998

This Act implies three terms in business-to-business contracts.

First, *at least* eight percent interest a year on the price of goods or services. Secondly, a fixed sum is payable. Thirdly, reasonable costs of recovering the debt are payable.

The first implied term is for *simple* interest. It is at a fixed rate. This is set twice a year by adding eight percent to the Bank of England's official base / bank rate.

This can be found at https://www.bankofengland.co.uk/monetary-policy/the-interest-rate-bank-rate.

The rate that was current when interest started to run is claimable. This depends on when the contract was made. Interest ceases on payment of the principal sum.

For a debt below £1,000, the fixed sum is £40. For a debt of at least £1,000, but less than £10,000, the fixed sum is £70. For a debt of £10,000 or more, the fixed sum is £100.

Reasonable costs of recovering a debt are likely to include instructing a legal representative, and reasonable pre-action costs.

iii. Personal injury

Where general damages are awarded in claims following personal injury, interest is awarded at two percent from the date of service of the claim form (*Birkett v Hayes* [1982] 1 WLR 816, [1982] 2 All ER 710 (CA)).

j. Costs

A contractual right to costs should be pleaded.

Following *Chaplair* (see above), where a party has a contractual right to costs, she is not restricted to fixed costs.

That is, provided that there has been no conduct on behalf of that party disentitling her to the exercise by the court of its discretion in accordance with that entitlement.

8. Defence (& counterclaim)

To defend against a claim started using the procedure in CPR 7, a defence *must* be filed and served (CPRs 15.1, 15.2 and 15.6).

The time limit is either, within 14 days of service of the particulars of claim, or 28 days if the defendant has acknowledged service.

a. Response

A defence *must* respond to each allegation in the particulars of claim. There are three responses (CPR 16.5(1)).

First, denied. Secondly, unable to admit or deny, but which the claimant must prove. Thirdly, admitted.

There are two rules relating to denied allegations (CPR 16.5(2)).

First, reasons *must* be pleaded. Secondly, if a defendant has a different version of events to that set out in the particulars of claim, it *must* be pleaded.

Where a specific allegation has not been dealt with, but the nature of the defence in relation to that allegation has been pleaded, the court will require the claimant to prove the allegation.

In a money claim, the claimant must prove any allegation relating to the amount of money claimed, unless it is expressly admitted by the defendant.

Subject to this, the court will take any allegation that is not dealt with in a defence to be admitted (CPR 16.5(3), (4) and (5)).

Admitted facts do not need to be proved. Authority and evidence supporting them is irrelevant. The court will not consider them.

b. Address for service

If the defendant has not filed an acknowledgment of service, she *must* give an address for service, including a full postcode (CPRs 6.23(1) and 16.5(8)).

This must be, either, a business address within the UK of a solicitor acting for the defendant, or an address in the UK where the defendant resides, or carries on business.

c. Limitation

In *Ketteman & Ors v Hansel Properties Ltd & Ors* [1987] AC 189, [1987] 2 WLR 312 (HL), it was held that limitation is a procedural defence that *must* be pleaded. Lord Griffiths (with whom Lords Templeman and Goff agreed) said at 219 (with emphasis added) that:

> "A defence of limitation permits a defendant to raise a procedural bar which prevents the [claimant] from pursuing the action against him. It has nothing to do with the merits of the claim which may all lie with the [claimant]; but as a matter of public policy Parliament has provided that a defendant should have the opportunity to avoid meeting a stale claim. The choice lies with the defendant and *if he wishes to avail himself of the statutory defence it must be pleaded.*"

In general, the limitation period for breach of contract is six years from the date that the contract was breached.

For negligence, in general, the limitation period is six years from the date that physical damage was suffered; not when the act or omission complained of occurred.

For personal injury, in general, the limitation period is three years from the date of injury, or, if later, the date of knowledge of the person who was injured. For example, if a person develops concussion some days or weeks after a road traffic collision, the date of knowledge of injury may be later than the date of the collision.

d. Counterclaim

A counterclaim is a separate claim.

CPRs and PDs for particulars of claim apply.

Where there is a defence to the claimant's claim, and a counterclaim against the claimant, the statement of case is known as a "defence and counterclaim".

A counterclaim should follow the defence. If the facts pleaded in the defence are relied on in the counterclaim, this should be succinctly stated in a single sentence.

Where a counterclaim is filed with the defence, the court's permission is not required (CPR 20.4(2)(a)).

Issuing a counterclaim will attract an issue fee. This is based on the amount claimed in the counterclaim (see appendix F).

To defend against a counterclaim, the claimant *must* file and serve a defence to the counterclaim (CPRs 15.2, 15.6 and 20.2).

9. Reply to the defence (& counterclaim)

Reply to a defence is *optional.* Defence to a counterclaim is *not.*

Where a counterclaim is not defended, the defendant may be able to request that default judgment is entered on the counterclaim.

a. Reply

There are three rules (CPR 15.8).

First, any reply to the defence *must* be filed with the claimant's directions questionnaire. Secondly, it *must* be served on all other parties at the same time. Thirdly, it should form one document with any defence to the counterclaim, with the latter following the former, unless the dates on which they are due to be filed differ.

b. Defence

There *must* be a defence to a counterclaim to defend against it.

CPRs and PDs relating to defences apply.

Where there is a reply to a defence, and a defence to a counterclaim, the statement of case is known as a "reply to the defence and counterclaim".

A party's statements of case must not be incompatible.

For example, particulars of claim that are irreconcilable with a reply to the defence. To this extent, they risk being struck out.

10. Directions questionnaires

The *court* must further the overriding objective by actively managing cases. This includes three considerations (CPR 1.4(2)).

First, appropriate encouragement, and facilitation, of alternative dispute resolution. Secondly, fixing timetables, or otherwise controlling the progress, of the case. Thirdly, giving directions, so as to ensure that the final hearing proceeds quickly, and efficiently.

The *parties* are under a duty to help the court to further the overriding objective. This includes ensuring that the case is dealt with expeditiously and fairly (CPR 1.1(2)(d)).

This is why a directions questionnaire ("a questionnaire") is vital.

a. Notice of proposed allocation

If a defence is filed, the court *will* do two things (CPR 26.4(1)(a)).

First, provisionally decide the track that appears to be most suitable. Secondly, serve a notice of proposed allocation on each party. This is Form N149A (SCT).

This notice *will* do four things (CPR 26.4(1)(b)).

First, specify any matter to be complied with by the date prescribed in the notice. Secondly, require the parties to file completed questionnaires with the court, and serve copies on all other parties.

Thirdly, state the address of the court, or court office, to which the questionnaire must be returned. Fourthly, inform the parties how to obtain the questionnaire.

b. Filing

The questionnaire is Form N180. It will *always* be served by the court on a person without a representative (CPR 26.4(2)).

The questionnaire should be returned by the date in the notice of allocation. It cannot be extended by agreement (CPR 26.4(6)-(7)).

The name of the court to which the questionnaire must be returned may be different from that in which the claim was issued.

Ensure that the questionnaire is returned to the correct court.

c. Service

Questionnaires must be served on all parties (CPR 26.4(1)(b)(ii)).

d. Default

If a party fails to comply with the notice of proposed allocation by the specified date, the court will serve a further notice on that party. She *will* be required to comply within seven days.

If she *still* fails to comply, her statement of case will be struck out, *without* further order of the court (CPR 26.4(9)).

If a *claimant* fails to file a questionnaire, the court may strike out her claim. If a *defendant* fails, judgment may be entered against her (CPR 26.4(10)).

A party who was in default will not normally be entitled to an order for the costs of any application to set aside or vary that order, or the costs of attending a case management conference.

Unless the court considers that it is *unjust*, she *will* be ordered to pay any costs caused to any other party (CPR 26.4(11)).

e. Informing the court

The parties *must* let the court know immediately if there is no need for a final hearing. In practice, this will be due to settlement.

Both parties are under the same duty to help the court to allocate an appropriate share of the court's resources to the case, while taking into account the need to allot resources to other cases.

Reasonable and proportionate efforts should be made to settle.

Both parties are under a duty to consider whether the dispute can be settled without a hearing. This can be achieved by the parties having a discussion directly, negotiation between legal representatives, or mediation.

f. Small Claims Mediation Service

Mediation is a *confidential* process. It gives the *parties* control over any agreement. Settlement may be *facilitated.*

i. Details

The questionnaire requires the parties to provide the following information.

First, a telephone number. Secondly, dates to avoid within the next three months.

Thirdly, whether an interpreter will be used, and, if so, the type. In certain circumstances, the court will arrange for, and pay the cost of, an interpreter. In practice, this is where a party cannot pay for an interpreter herself, and does not have a friend, or family member, who can act as an interpreter.

Fourthly, whether the mediator needs to consider if additional support should be given, due to a vulnerability.

In practice, that means a physical, mental, or learning disability, or long-term health condition. If so, details of the way(s) in which a party or witness is vulnerable, and what steps, support, or adjustments are necessary, should be given.

ii. Features

A mediator may be able to assist with what the law says in a particular circumstance. This will be from a neutral perspective. It will be dispassionate. She will have no interest in any agreement.

Offers can be made without influencing what will happen if the claim is subsequently disposed of by the court.

This enables the parties to attempt to reach an agreement, *without* compromising their positions, should the claim continue to a final hearing. Positions are reserved in absence of agreement.

If an agreement is reached, reduced to writing, and signed, it is *binding*, like any other contract.

The terms of any agreement may be inserted into a "Tomlin" order. This is enforceable by the court. There is a remedy for breach.

As a mediated settlement is *voluntary*, however, freely agreed terms of settlement are usually honoured. There is seldom a need to enforce a freely-negotiated agreement in the courts.

Accordingly, the free and confidential Small Claims Mediation Service merits careful consideration. It is one of a number of options that can be explored without prejudice.

It is also *convenient.* A suitable time for both parties is agreed. The process is usually carried out over the telephone in under an hour.

It is also usually quicker than waiting for a final hearing.

iii. Procedure

If the claim is for £10,000 or less, and is not on the basis of losses following a road traffic accident, personal injury or housing disrepair, the court *will* organise mediation (CPR 26.6(2)).

If all parties agree to mediation in their questionnaires, the claim will *also* be referred to mediation (CPR 26.6(4)).

The parties will be contacted. A mutually convenient appointment will then be arranged by the Small Claims Mediation Service.

Contact will be made within normal working hours. Monday to Friday, from 09:00 to 17:00. This excludes bank holidays.

Further information can be obtained by sending an email to scmreferrals@justice.gov.uk, or over the telephone during normal working hours, on 0300 123 4593.

g. Track

The questionnaire asks if the small claims track is appropriate.

This is the opportunity to give reasons why it is not, if that is the case. In so far as they apply, the matters that are relevant to allocating a claim to a track should be addressed.

h. Determination without a hearing

Each party needs to confirm whether the claim is suitable for determination without a hearing.

That is, by a judge considering the pleadings and evidence, and serving the parties with a note of the reasons for her decision.

Claims may be disposed of without hearings in two circumstances.

First, if both parties agree (CPR 27.10). Secondly, until 1 December 2024 (unless it is extended), without the agreement of the parties in certain circumstances (PD 51ZC at [1]).

If the claim is not suitable for determination without a hearing, in so far as they apply, the matters that are relevant to allocating a claim to a track should be addressed.

i. Hearing centre

The hearing centre closest to the party who is completing the questionnaire is likely to be their preferred venue.

A party with a registered disability, childcare commitments, or acting as a carer, is a good reason to justify the claim being heard in the hearing centre that is nearest to that party.

If a claimant files a request for judgment in the county court, which includes an amount of money to be decided by the court in accordance with the procedure for obtaining default judgment, the claim will be sent to the preferred hearing centre (CPR 12.6(1)).

If so, further correspondence should be sent, and any further requests should be made, to that hearing centre (CPR 12.6(2)).

In certain circumstances, defended cases may be sent from one hearing centre, or court office, to another (CPR 26.1(1)(b)).

Money claims may be transferred within the court (CPR 26.3).

j. Experts

In claims following a road traffic collision, there are an increasing number of claims in which, although the vehicle has been repaired, it is nevertheless alleged to have suffered a diminution in value.

The evidence relied on is often in the form of a (main) report, or a number of (subsidiary) reports that are appended to the main report. The main report expresses that there is diminution in value.

Frequently, there is a similar statement to that required for expert reports. That is, the expert who is offering her opinion is aware of her duty to the court.

If so, the importance of section F2 of the questionnaire is second only to the notice of allocation.

If permission is sought to use the written evidence of an expert, the appropriate box should be ticked. The reason why, the name of the expert (if known), the area of expertise, and the likely cost if appointed, should also be stated.

Where there is *no* request to rely on expert evidence by a party in her questionnaire, and the court has *not* given permission, there is a robust argument that expert evidence should *not* be allowed.

The party seeking to rely on expert evidence has not discharged her duty to help the court to further the overriding objective.

This is because the court has been unable to actively manage the case, including by giving directions to ensure that the final hearing proceeds both quickly, and efficiently.

The questionnaire is used to assist the court in the management of the claim. If it has *not* been accurately completed, the court has *not* been assisted.

'The small claims track in the civil courts' (Form EX306) provides that: 'If you want to use an expert, you need the court's permission. Because of this, you should say so in the directions questionnaire.' This guidance will not have been followed.

Opportunities to further the overriding objective were missed.

First, to consider at an early stage whether the likely benefits of granting permission justify the cost. Secondly, to deal with it on the same occasion as making directions for the final hearing.

The notice of allocation is likely to include the following:

> If a party is aware of a reason why this [time] estimate might be substantially inaccurate, that party must notify the court immediately.
>
> ...
>
> No party may rely at the hearing on any report from an expert unless express permission has been granted by the court beforehand. Anyone wishing to rely on an expert must write to the court immediately on receipt of this Order and seek permission, giving an explanation why the assistance of an expert is necessary.
>
> ...
>
> Because this Order has been made without a hearing, the parties have the right to apply to have the Order set aside, varied or stayed. A party making such an application must send or deliver the application to the court (together with any appropriate fee) to arrive within seven days of service of this Order.

All three directions will have been breached.

An oral application for permission to rely on an expert was not contemplated when the time estimate for the final hearing was made. This is a reason that the time estimate might be substantially inaccurate. Yet, the party seeking to rely on an expert did not notify the court immediately, or, in fact, at all.

Furthering the overriding objective includes enforcing compliance with rules and court orders. In particular, the rule prescribing the duty of the parties to help the court to further the overriding objective, and the court order set out above, so as to ensure that the case is dealt with, both expeditiously, and fairly.

j. Witnesses

How many witnesses will attend the final hearing?

This includes the party completing the questionnaire, if that party will give evidence.

This question enables the court to allocate the claim. If oral evidence is likely to take more than a day, it will not normally be allocated to the small claims track.

Having done so, a time estimate for the final hearing can be made.
When a witness, or an expert, will be unavailable over the following six months, this should be set out. It may be due to a professional, or personal, commitment. For example, a holiday.

l. Interpreters

If a party or a witness requires an interpreter, the relevant box at section F4 should be ticked. The *type* should also be stated.

Otherwise, if the matter proceeds to a final hearing, the witness cannot sufficiently understand English, there is only one witness statement in

English, and there is no interpreter, the court is more likely to refuse to adjourn, and strike out that witness' evidence.

In some circumstances, the court will arrange, and meet the cost of, an interpreter. In general, however, cases that do not involve possession of property, or committal, do not qualify for legal aid.

In any event, there must be an inability to pay for an interpreter, and a lack of friends, or family, who can interpret.

Those who can only follow proceedings with a Welsh interpreter, however, are entitled to one.

If a party *subsequently* becomes aware of the need for an interpreter, the court, and the other party, should be notified *immediately*. This is likely *substantially* to affect the time estimate of the final hearing. Usually, there is a direction ordering the parties to notify the court immediately where this is the case.

m. Vulnerability

If a party believes that they, or a witness who will give evidence on their behalf, is vulnerable, details should be given.

Does the court need to consider whether additional support should be given?

In practice, this means a physical, mental, or learning disability, or long-term health condition. If so, details of the way(s) in which a party or witness is vulnerable, and what steps, support, or adjustments are necessary, should be given.

n. Other information

Whether a party has been advised of their right to give evidence in Welsh or English, whether anyone wishes to speak in either (or both) language(s), and whether documents are in either (or both) language(s), must be set out.

o. Stay

A party may request a stay in the questionnaire to attempt a settlement (CPR 26.5(1)). If the parties agree, the court will notify them that the claim has been stayed for a month (CPR 26.5(2)).

Otherwise, the court may direct that (part, or the whole, of) the case is stayed for an appropriate period (CPR 26.5(3)).

In the event of a stay, the claimant must inform the court if there is a settlement. At the end of a stay, if the claimant doesn't inform the court that a settlement has been reached, the court will give appropriate case management directions.

p. Signature

The questionnaire must be signed by a party, legal representative, or litigation friend.

q. Further information

The court may order a party to provide further information if it is appropriate (CPR 27.2(3)).

In practice, this is where a statement of case is unclear.

For example, where a statement of case is *so* incoherent that it makes no sense; or, if there *is* a coherent set of facts, *even* where those facts are true, they do *not* disclose any legally recognisable claim, or defence (PD 3A at [1]).

The court will usually be hesitant, however, before deciding to exercise this draconian power. It extinguishes a claim, or defence. This should be a last resort.

r. Other directions

A *party* may invite the court to make a direction (PD 27A at [2.4]).

The best place to do so is in the questionnaire.

The *court* also has a general power to make directions (CPR 27.7).

For example, there is no photograph, or sketch plan, of the location of a road traffic collision. The court may then make an order for further information, such as: 'Parties must agree and file a clear and legible plan, together with pictures, of the accident location, at least seven days before the final hearing.'

11. Allocation

Unless stayed, a claim will generally be allocated to track when all parties have filed their directions questionnaires (CPR 26.7(1)).

This will be with the benefit of the competing statements of case, and the completed directions questionnaires.

Once allocated, the case will be stayed for settlement discussions, mediation, or the court will give directions for a final hearing.

a. Generally suitable

The following are 'generally suitable' (PD 26 at [15(3)).

First, consumer disputes. Secondly, accident claims. Thirdly, disputes about the ownership of goods. Fourthly, most landlord and tenant disputes, other than opposed claims under CPR 56, disputed claims for possession under CPR 55, and demotion, or prohibited conduct standard contract order, claims.

A disputed allegation of dishonesty will usually mean that the case is *not* suitable for the small claims track (PD 26 at [15(4)]).

Claims by a tenant of residential premises against her landlord, alleging harassment or unlawful eviction, *must not* be allocated to the small claims track (CPR 26.12(2) and (3)).

b. Relevant matters

In general, the small claims track is the "normal" track for a claim with a value of not more than £10,000 (CPR 26.9(1) and (4)).

To decide whether to allocate to the normal track, the court 'shall have regard to' (CPR 26.12) the following (CPR 26.13(1)).

First, financial value (if any) of the claim. Secondly, nature of the remedy sought. Thirdly, likely complexity of the facts, law or evidence. Fourthly, number of (likely) parties.

Fifthly, the value of any counterclaim, or additional claim, and the complexity of any matter relating to it.

Sixthly, amount of oral evidence which may be required. Seventhly, importance of the claim to non-parties. Eighthly, views expressed by the parties. Ninthly, circumstances of the parties.

This list is not exhaustive. Neither is it hierarchical.

i. Financial value

It is for the *court* to assess the financial value of a claim.

The following will be disregarded (CPR 26.13(2)).

First, any amount not in dispute. Secondly, any claim for interest. Thirdly, costs. Fourthly, allegations of contributory negligence. Fifthly, any prescribed amount in respect of a claim for, or including, non-monetary relief.

1. Amount in dispute

The following are *not* in dispute (PD 26 at [14(7)]).

First, an amount in respect of which the defendant admits liability. Secondly, a sum in respect of an item forming part of a claim for which judgment has been entered.

Thirdly, a specific sum claimed as a distinct item, and which the defendant admits that she is liable to pay. Fourthly, a sum offered by the defendant, which has been accepted by the claimant, in satisfaction of any item which forms a distinct part of the claim.

A claim with a financial value of more than £10,000 *may* be allocated to the small claims track (PD 26 at [15(5)]).

2. Admissions

If an admission is made before allocation, reducing the amount in dispute to a figure of not more than £10,000, the *normal* track is the *small claims* track (PD 26 at [14(8)]).

a. Unequivocal

In *Pervez Akhtar v Jordan Boland* [2014] EWCA Civ 872, [2015] 1 All ER 644, Sir Stanley Burnton (with whom Gloster and Floyd LJJ agreed) said (with emphasis added) that:

> "[16] Where an allegation made by one party in proceedings is admitted by the other party in *unqualified* terms, that other party must not, seek to adduce evidence or raise arguments to the effect that that admission is not binding on him. *The court has no jurisdiction to investigate a fact that has been admitted*, unless the party making the admission obtains the permission of the court under [CPR 14] to withdraw the admission and does so.
>
> [17] This principle applies even more strongly to a judgment for all or part of a claim. Neither party may adduce evidence or make submissions that if accepted would lead to decisions or findings inconsistent with the judgment, unless there is a successful application to set the judgment aside.
>
> [18] Where a defendant admits part, and not the whole, of an unliquidated damages claim, the claimant is entitled to seek

> judgment on that admission, and to pursue the proceedings and seek and obtain judgment for the balance. ..."

Paragraph 16 above was cited by Lord Hodge (with whom Lords Lloyd-Jones, Briggs, Burrows and Stephens JJSC agreed) in *TUI UK v Griffiths* [2023] UKSC 48, [2023] 3 WLR 1204 at [41].

Lord Hodge continued: "The trial judge's role is normally limited to determining the disputed issues which the parties present and to determining those issues based on the evidence which the parties adduce."

For example, in a claim for £12,000, the defendant unequivocally admits that the claimant is entitled to judgment for £5,000, so that the *amount in dispute* is the balance of £7,000.

This may be allocated to the small claims track for three reasons.

First, the amount in dispute is not more than £10,000. Secondly, the court disregards any amount not in dispute (CPR 26.13(2)(a)). Thirdly, in any event, a claim of more than £10,000 may still be allocated to the small claims track (PD 26 at [15(5)]).

b. Equivocal

Where an admission is *equivocal*, or inconsistent with other allegations, there should be a request for clarification.

A *party* may do so in writing. They may also invite the court to make a direction for clarification (PD 27A at [2.4]).

The *court* may also order a party to provide further information, if the court considers that it is appropriate (CPR 27.2(3)).

3. None

A claim without a financial value will be allocated to the 'most suitable' track (CPR 26.4(1)(a)(i)).

The following matters are relevant (CPR 26.13(1)).

ii. Remedy

For example, a claim for personal injuries, where the value of the claim is not more than £10,000, but the value of the claim for damages for personal injury is *more* than £5,000, should *not* be allocated to the small claims track (CPR 26.9(1)(a)).

The remedy means that small claims is not the normal track.

The court may grant any final remedy that the court could grant if the claim were allocated to another track (CPR 27.3). The court has jurisdiction to grant the following.

First, damages and interest of any amount. Secondly, restitution. Thirdly, injunctions. Fourthly, declarations. Fifthly, specific performance. Sixthly, possession of property.

iii. Factual, legal or evidential complexity

Complex facts, law or evidence may mean that the *fast* track is the *normal* track. The following will be determinative (CPR 26.9(6)).

First, whether the final hearing is likely to last no longer than a day. Secondly, whether oral evidence is limited to one expert per party in relation to any expert field. Thirdly, whether expert evidence is limited to two fields.

If the answers to all of the above are 'yes', the fast track is the normal track.

iv. Counterclaim / Part 20 claim

Where the case involves more than one money claim, the court will not generally add the value of the claims together.

There may be a claim, counterclaim, and an additional claim. Generally, the court will regard the largest one of them as determinative of the financial value (PD 26 at [14(10)]).

v. Oral evidence

The court will not normally allocate a claim to the small claims track if it is likely to last more than a day (PD 26 at [8.1(2)]).

vi. Party view

This is 'an important factor'. It is not decisive (PD 26 at [14(9)]).

Even if it is not the normal track, the parties may agree that the case should be allocated to the small claims track.

In practice, this is common, due to fixed, modest costs.

c. Pre-allocation hearing

Where a hearing takes place before allocation, the court may treat that hearing as an allocation hearing (PD 26 at [5]).

For example, an application for summary judgment.

Otherwise, an allocation hearing will *only* be held on the court's own initiative if it considers that it is *necessary* (PD 26 at [13(1)]).

The parties will be given at least seven days' notice of the hearing. This will be in Form N153. It will contain a brief explanation of the decision to order an allocation hearing (PD 26 at [13(2)]).

Failure to attend may lead to an order that the party who did not attend must pay the costs of the party who did attend.

d. Challenging

A party who is dissatisfied with an order allocating the claim to a track may challenge it in one of two ways.

First, appeal. Secondly, an application for re-allocation.

If made at a hearing, and that party was present, represented, or gave notice that she would not attend, she should appeal.

In any other case, she should apply for re-allocation.

e. Standard directions

"Standard directions" includes the following (CPR 27.4(3)(a)).

First, 'a direction that each party shall, at least 14 days before the date fixed for the final hearing, file and serve on every other party copies of all documents (including any expert's report) on which he intends to rely at the hearing'.

Secondly, any other standard directions set out in PD 27A.

In practice, standard directions are made with two exceptions.

First, where the case has been stayed. Secondly, where the judge specifies other directions.

Standard directions are in PD 27A at Appendix B (see appendix D).

f. Witness statements

The court *must* have regard to five factors when deciding whether to order parties to exchange witness statements (PD 27A at [2.5]).

First, whether either, or both, parties are represented. Secondly, the amount in dispute. Thirdly, the nature of the matters in dispute. Fourthly, whether the need for any party to clarify her case can better be dealt with by an order requiring her to give further information. Fifthly, the need for the parties to have access to justice, without undue formality, cost or delay.

CPR 32 (the rules of evidence) does not apply (CPR 27.2(1)(c)). The exception is the rule permitting the court to control evidence.

In other words, the rules prescribing the form of, and consequences of failure to serve, witness statements, do not apply.

A separate rule, enabling the court to direct a witness statement that has not been verified by a statement of truth shall not be admissible as evidence, is not disapplied (CPRs 27.2(2) and 22.3).

In practice, where the notice of allocation provides for witness statements, it usually includes the following direction:

Witness statements must:

a) Start with the name of the case and the claim number;
b) State the full name and address of the witness;
c) Set out the witness' evidence clearly in numbered paragraphs on numbered pages;
d) End with this paragraph: 'I believe that the facts stated in this witness statement are true. I understand that proceedings for contempt of court may be brought against anyone who makes, or causes to be made, a false statement in a document verified by a statement of truth without an honest belief in its truth.'

g. Experts

An expert may not give evidence at a hearing, whether written or oral, without permission of the court (CPR 27.5).

The court is under a duty to restrict expert evidence to that which is reasonably required to resolve the proceedings (CPR 35.1).

Where required, the court usually directs that evidence is to be given by a single joint expert (CPRs 27.2(1)(e) and 35.7).

Form, content and duties are *not* prescribed by CPR 35 (the rule relating to experts). There are two exceptions (CPR 27.2(1)(e)).

First, the overriding duty is to the court (CPR 35.3). Secondly, the rules relating to instructions to a single joint expert (CPR 35.8).

The amount that a party may be ordered to pay for experts' fees is a sum not exceeding £750 for each expert (PD 27A at [7.3(2)]).

h. Special directions

"Special directions" means 'directions given in addition to or instead of standard directions' (CPR 27.4(3)(b)).

The information and documentation usually required for certain types of claim in PD 27A at Appendix A is informative.

Special directions are in PD 27A at Appendix C (see appendix D).

No later than 28 days after giving special directions, the court may consider what further directions are to be given (CPR 27.4(1)(c)).

In practice, the court will do one of the following.

First, vary standard directions. Secondly, add further special directions, and order a final hearing. Thirdly, order a preliminary hearing.

i. Preliminary hearing

A preliminary hearing may be held (CPR 27.6(1)).

When deciding whether or not to hold one, the court *must* have regard to the desirability of limiting the expense to the parties of attending court (CPR 27.6(2)).

The parties must be given at least 14 days' notice of the date of the preliminary hearing (CPR 27.6(3)).

It may only be held in three circumstances (CPR 27.6(1)).

First, special directions are needed to ensure a fair hearing, and it appears necessary for a party to attend a hearing, so as to ensure that she understands what she must do to comply.

Secondly, to dispose of the claim, on the basis that a party has no real prospect of success.

Thirdly, to enable (part of) a statement of case to be struck out, on the basis that it discloses no reasonable grounds for bringing, or defending, the claim.

If all parties agree, it may also be the *final* hearing (CPR 27.6(4)).

Otherwise, at, or after, a preliminary hearing, the court *will* do the following (CPR 27.6(5)).

First, fix the date of the final hearing (if the court has not done so already), and give the parties at least 21 days' notice of the same, unless they accept less notice.

Secondly, inform the parties of the amount of time allowed for the final hearing. Thirdly, give any other, appropriate directions.

j. Hearing fee

When a claim is allocated, a hearing / trial fee becomes payable.

Usually, it *must* be paid *28* days before the hearing.

If the action does not proceed on the *claim*, but merely on the *counter-claim*, the hearing fee is payable by the *defendant*.

See appendix G for hearing fees.

In practice, the notice of allocation usually contains the following:

> Unless the claimant does by 4.00pm on the [**date**] [**month**] [**year**] pay to the court the trial fee of £[amount] or file a properly completed application (i.e. one which provides all the required information in the manner requested) for help with fees, then the claim will be **struck out with effect from** [**date**] [**month**] [**year**] **without further order and, unless the court orders otherwise, you will also be liable for the costs which the defendant has incurred.**
>
> ...
>
> The trial fee is **non-refundable.** If the parties settle before the trial fee is due, the trial fee will not be payable. If a consent order settling the matter is requested after the trial fee has been paid, the consent order fee will still be payable.
>
> **Please note, unless you apply for help with fees, there will be no further correspondence from the court office regarding payment of the fee or warnings as to the consequences of non-payment.**

k. Disposal without a hearing

The court may dispose of the claim without a hearing.

The court may do so in two circumstances. First, if both parties agree (CPR 27.10). Secondly, until 1 December 2024 (unless the pilot scheme is extended), without the agreement of the parties in certain circumstances (PD 51ZC at [1]).

The court may still order a final hearing, however, even when the parties agree to disposal without a hearing.

12. Preparation

Everyone prepares in their own way.

The following are merely suggestions. Over time, rituals of preparation often mature, increasing time-efficiency, and effectiveness.

There are some timeless principles to prepare for a final hearing.

First, promptly check that you have all of the documents. Secondly, have a spare, unmarked copy of the documents. Thirdly, consider the relevant information and documentation checklist.

a. Contact

When a barrister is representing a party, the initial contact is likely to be a professional client (usually, a solicitor) contacting a barristers' chambers. They will try to book counsel. The professional client will speak to a "clerk" or "practice manager".

Sometimes, professional clients know who they want. On other occasions, they want a recommendation. If so, practice managers put forward counsel who are able to accept instructions.

If the names are not known to the professional client, an online search will likely follow. A selection will then be made.

This is one reason to keep online, professional profiles up to date, including: areas of practice; recent instructions; publications; and training and seminars.

The practice manager will request that the professional client send whatever documents there are, agree a fee, and enter the case into the selected barrister's professional diary.

The documents, often sent by email, may be printed off by the practice manager, and left in the barrister's pigeon-hole.

Increasingly, however, an electronic copy of the documents is forwarded via email by the practice manager to the barrister.

Counsel is notified. She can then scan the papers.

b. Scan

Upon receipt of the documents, scan them. Promptly.

Those instructing should be put on notice of the following.

First, a document that appears to be missing, or otherwise illegible. Secondly, if there appears to be a material breach of a CPR, PD or court order. Thirdly, if it becomes apparent that an application is necessary, or desirable.

Your professional client should then be able to act promptly.

The documents should contain the following.

First, written instructions. Secondly, statements of case. Thirdly, court orders and notice(s) of hearing(s). Fourthly, evidence.

Fifthly, relevant correspondence, including pre-action, evidence of filing and service, offers of settlement, and interim or final payments.

Instructions will state the documents that the representative should have. Ensure that you do, in fact, have those documents.

Often, a bundle has not been agreed. Or even directed. If so, the claimant's documents will be separate to those of the defendant.

Ensure that you have the documents in respect of every party.

i. Instructions

It is *always* preferable to have *written* instructions.

Professional clients will often have drafted statements of case, assisted with witness statements, and engaged in pre-action correspondence. They will likely have a view on the issues, merits, and compliance (or otherwise) with CPRs, PDs and court orders.

Without written instructions, a telephone call should be made to the professional client. Oral instructions can then be taken. These can be confirmed in writing via email to the professional client.

This may begin: 'Further to our telephone conversation this afternoon, just to put your instructions in writing …'

Written instructions are often in a similar format.

First, enclosed documents. Secondly, name of your professional client, their firm, and the name of any other party's legal representative (if they have representation).

Thirdly, material facts of the case. Fourthly, issues in dispute. Fifthly, evidence. Sixthly, agreements to extend a time limit.

Seventhly, any authority that is relied on, (ideally) including the neutral citation, where it is found in the law reports, and the relevant paragraph(s).

Eighthly, costs claimed. Ninthly, interim or final payments. Tenthly, the name, email address, and telephone number of your professional client.

1. Enclosures

The documents enclosed with your instructions are likely to include a final hearing bundle (if there is one).

Otherwise, there may be a bundle for each party, or just a collection of documents on which the parties seek to rely.

Although your professional client may have provided you with a paginated bundle of documents, it may not have been filed with the court, and / or served on the other party.

If so, you will not be able to rely on the page numbers in your bundle during the hearing because the court, and the other party, will not have the same pagination.

Relevant correspondence should also be enclosed. This includes offers, and agreements to extend the time for filing and service.

2. Clients

Instructions should confirm the following.

First, the name of the party who you are representing. Secondly, whether the hearing is a preliminary, disposal, or final hearing. Thirdly, the name of the court.

Fourthly, the date and time of the listing. Fifthly, the way in which the hearing will take place. For example, in person, telephone, or audio-visual. Sixthly, the time estimate.

The time of the hearing in your instructions, the notice of allocation, and / or the listing on CourtServe may be different. If so, the notice of allocation is authoritative.

If your case does not appear on CourtServe, there are two things that you can do.

First, if you are a legal representative, email your professional client to confirm whether they have received any correspondence from the court (adjourning / vacating) the hearing.

Secondly, (ask your professional client to) email the legal representative for the other side in case they have received any correspondence from the court.

The notice of hearing should specify whether it is in person, or remote. If remote, it should also state whether it will be telephone, or audio-visual, and the software. For example, BT MeetMe or CVP.

Final hearing time estimates range from an hour to a day. Most preliminary or "disposal" hearings are no longer than half an hour.

If the time estimate appears to be substantially inaccurate, advise your professional client. She can then notify the other party, and the court. If she does, ask for the correspondence doing so.

For example, it may be necessary, or desirable, to make an application for relief from sanctions, following breach of an unless order. If so, the time estimate may be substantially inaccurate.

3. Facts

For example: 'The claim arises out of a road traffic collision which took place on 1 September 2024'.

It should be clear whether or not there is a *counter*claim or *additional* claim. In any event, check the defence. If there is, there should also be a defence to the counterclaim / additional claim.

Is liability, quantum, or both, in dispute?

In a claim following a road traffic collision, duty of care and breach of duty may be admitted, but causation denied. Or, liability (including causation) may be admitted, but quantum is denied.

Alternatively, one head of loss may be admitted (such as a claim for repairs). Another (such as credit hire) may be disputed.

Quantum may even be agreed, subject to liability. If so, ensure that you have a breakdown of the agreed sums for each head of loss.

How many witnesses will give evidence?

For example, the defendant may not have a witness in a claim for credit hire where liability is admitted.

If the claimant has filed and served *two* witness statements, but the directions questionnaire provides that the claimant proposes to rely on *one* witness, the time estimate for the hearing may be substantially inaccurate. Especially, if there are also two witnesses for the defendant, so that there are *four* witnesses in total.

Finally, is interest claimed?

If so, on what head(s) of loss, at what rate, and for what period?

Eight percent is often claimed in respect of known sums of money. As opposed to general damages for a sum to be determined.

Two or three percent is usually awarded.

4. Issues

There may be a difference between the issues that are apparent from the statements of case, and the issues that you are instructed to cross-examine on, and then make submissions in respect of.

This may not only be because evidence will have been exchanged since the statements of case were filed and served.

a. Claim

Often, particulars of claim include heads of loss that are effectively irrecoverable at a hearing.

For an example of an irrecoverable head of loss, take the fee of an engineer's report. This is often pleaded. Especially in claims for credit hire. There are three reasons why it is not recoverable.

First, CPR 27.14 prescribes the only recoverable disbursements. An engineer's fee is not one of them. Secondly, the (obiter) authority of *Clark v Ardington* [2002] EWCA Civ 510, [2003] QB 36 at [155]-[156]. Thirdly, CPR 45.58 prescribes, under the heading 'Disbursements', that this is, in fact, a disbursement.

For these reasons, an engineer's fee is often not pursued.

Or, there may be a claim for the cost of repairs, but there is no invoice, or other evidence of the sum claimed, in respect of it. If so, although a claim for repairs may be pleaded, it is not likely to be pursued at the final hearing due to a lack of evidence.

Finally, there may be a claim for interest on special damages that have not been paid. For example, there may be a claim for interest on the cost of repairs. In fact, there is no evidence that the sum claimed for repairs has actually been paid. Accordingly, it is unlikely that this claim for interest will be pursued at a final hearing.

b. Defence

The defence may deny each and every allegation, putting the claimant to proof, and requiring the claimant to provide a repair estimate, evidence of impecuniosity, and a credit hire agreement.

If the claimant provides this evidence, the defendant may admit the cost of repairs, and the sum claimed under the credit hire agreement. If so, these issues will no longer be in dispute.

5. Evidence

If a party indicates in the directions questionnaire that she will rely on a witness, the notice of allocation usually orders any witness statements to be filed and served 14 days before the hearing.

Check whether the evidence has, in fact, been filed and served in accordance with these directions. *Proof* that the evidence on which a party seeks to rely has been filed and served is *invaluable.*

a. Filing & service

Often, another party, the court, or both, indicate that they do not have any evidence for the party who you represent. This appears to be the case especially for remote hearings. If so, filing and service is likely to form a preliminary issue.

If you are able to submit that you have proof that the evidence was filed and served, this often short-circuits such issues. If not, you can forward this proof to the relevant court actor by email.

Proof of filing and service thereby guards against strike out, summary judgment, or dismissal, due to want of evidence.

Proof may take the form of an email, with evidence clearly attached. Or, a cover letter, stating what evidence is enclosed.

The deadline for filing and serving evidence may appear to have been breached. The parties may have agreed to extend the deadline, however, so proof of this agreement would be helpful.

In practice, this would likely consist of an email chain. Your professional client should be able to forward this to you.

Proof of filing and service can also alert you to the fact that, for example, the key evidence (an invoice) in the counterclaim (for the cost of repairs) has not been filed and served at all.

You are then able to advise your professional client to file and serve the evidence ahead of the final hearing, and prepare to make submissions as to why you should be allowed to rely on it.

b. Experts

If a party has provided an expert report, check whether the notice of allocation has granted permission to rely on it. If not, check whether that party has requested permission to rely on expert evidence in her directions questionnaire.

Where permission has not been granted, but there is a request to rely on expert evidence in the directions questionnaire, the court may be more likely to grant permission, and allow it into evidence.

c. Absence

A party may have given notice that she would like the case to be decided in her absence. If so, check whether the requirements for doing so have been met.

6. Authority

Case law may be included in the documents that you receive.

If so, check that it conforms to PDs governing the citation of authority. If so, has it been subsequently considered, appealed, or distinguished?

There may be additional authority in the statements of case. If so, find the relevant law report. Does it conform to the PDs governing its citation? Has it been subsequently considered, appealed, or distinguished?

In any event, conduct a cost / benefit analysis of whether it is worth investing the time in citing and making submissions on it, or you can safely succeed without it.

7. Costs

You may be instructed to make an application for costs on the basis that the other party has behaved unreasonably. If so, why?

Is there a witness statement in support? If not, and your view is that one would be of assistance, is there enough time for your professional client to draft one?

In any event, if instructed to make an application for substantial costs, a statement of costs should have been filed and served. Proof of the same is helpful in case of dispute.

Your instructions may state that numerous requests for an invoice have been made. Yet there has been no response. If so, the requests themselves are invaluable, on which to base submissions.

8. Offers

You should have any offer, and any correspondence enclosing it.

In any event, speak to your professional client to confirm whether an offer has been made. If so, how many? When? What were the terms? Was there any response?

9. Payments

If a payment has been made in respect of a claim, it is either an interim, or a final, payment.

Where an interim payment is made, there is no admission as to liability, or quantum.

A final payment is an admission for that amount.

a. Interim

An 'interim payment' may be acknowledged in a statement of case.

Of course, if it was made subsequent to the statements of case, it cannot be acknowledged in them.

Ideally, however, it should also be acknowledged in the particulars of claim. If an interim payment is not credited in a statement of case, the advocate for the party who made the payment may only be able to invite the court to order that credit is given for any sum already paid.

Where an interim payment is not acknowledged in a statement of case, and the party who made it successfully defends against the claim, the court may decline jurisdiction to order repayment. This is why it is *crucial* to acknowledge interim payments.

If an interim payment is not acknowledged in a statement of case, is there any evidence of it? If so, you can seek to agree the interim payment with the other side before, or rely on it at the appropriate time during, the hearing.

b. Final

Where a final payment has been made in respect of a head of loss that is claimed, liability for that head of loss, and the sum paid towards it, cannot be disputed.

Where a final payment is made before a claim for the same has been issued, the paying party should be able to provide evidence of the date, amount, and recipient.

If so, the court will not order the paying party to pay the same sum again. The paying party will also have a strong argument that the other party has behaved unreasonably, or at least that any costs that may be payable should be reduced.

10. Contact details

If your professional client is out of the office for any period of time, this should be stated. Details should be given of a person to contact in her absence. If not, your practice manager may be able to assist.

In practice, when an email is sent to a professional client who is out of the office for a significant period of time, they are likely to have set up an automated "out of office" reply. If so, it will often include the email address of another person who can be contacted.

ii. Statements of case

Statements of case *must* comply with CPRs, PDs, and court orders.

1. Compliant

Check for compliance.

In particular, that they are verified by a *valid* statement of truth.

2. Names

The names of the parties should be correct.

If the claimant has a contract with a limited company, but the name on the claim form and particulars of claim do not end with 'limited', an application to amend should be made.

Ensure that you have written instructions before making an oral application for permission to amend the name on those statements of case, and, if appropriate, to dispense with the need for re-filing and re-service.

The relevant pages on the website of Companies House can be used to evidence the fact that a company is limited, as well as the company number. The court can take "judicial notice" of the same.

If you are attending an in-person hearing, copies should be printed for the judge, and the other party. Otherwise, the relevant page(s) of Companies House can be saved as a pdf, ready to be attached and sent via email upon request.

Where permission has been given to amend the name of a party, ensure that the operative part of the order provides for the amendment, and, if directed, the date by which amended statements of case must be re-filed and re-served.

iii. Evidence

Usually, whatever submission you are instructed to make can be made on the evidence that has been filed and served.

Sometimes, however, you may need to weigh up the benefit of relying on an *objective, public* document, from a *reputable* source, against the likelihood that the other party, or the judge, will object.

In any event, speak to your professional client.

Ensure that you act with instructions.

1. In the documents

The enclosed documents may not be arranged in the usual way.

That is, statements of case, court orders, evidence, then correspondence. There may be no rhyme or reason as to the ordering.

Ensure that you do not miss a defence to the counterclaim. There may be a reference to it in the documents. If there is a counterclaim, it is likely that there will be a (reply and) defence to it.

The documents may not be paginated. If there are page numbers, they may not be continuous. Or, if there are separate bundles for the claimant and the defendant, a document may appear at page ten of the former, and one of the latter.

If an original document was double-sided, the copy may be single-sided, so that your copy is missing every other page. Photocopies of written, or even typed documents, may be illegible, truncated, or cropped. Photographs may be in black and white, so that they are of little assistance.

Not all documents necessarily will be relevant. Especially this holds true with correspondence. Often, all (even irrelevant) correspondence relating to a case will be included.

Important correspondence includes evidence of filing, service, and offers to settle. Ensure that you have the same before the hearing.

2. Not in the documents

For example, in a claim following a road traffic collision, there may not be any images, or other evidence, of the road layout.

Where liability is in dispute, however, the court will likely be assisted by this evidence. The other party is unlikely to resist you being able to rely on it, provided that you ensure the following.

First, that any other party, and the court, are provided with copies before the hearing. Secondly, you explain to any other party, and to the court, what it is, where it is from, and the good reason that it assists. Thirdly, it is from an objective, public, freely available source. For example, Google Maps.

In the unlikely event that evidence can be rebutted using, for example, a printout from the website of Companies House, it is unlikely to be agreed by the other party.

The court, on the other hand, may well allow it to be adduced.

iv. Orders

Court orders are necessary to confirm whether or not the parties have complied with directions for the final hearing.

For example, whether the date for filing and service of witness statements has been complied with. If not, why?

Some notice is preferable to *no* notice.

If the other party has had a day to consider it, they may also have been able to take instructions. The prejudice of excluding it will be weighed against the prejudice of admitting it. That balance is likely to change if there is, *at least some,* notice.

v. Correspondence

Correspondence falls under five sub-headings.

First, pre-action. Secondly, evidence of filing and service. Thirdly, agreements. Fourthly, offers of settlement. Fifthly, payments.

1. Pre-action

Pre-action correspondence is relevant for the issue of costs.

2. Filing & service

Especially on an unassigned list, or where a claim has been transferred between courts, evidence of filing and service is *vital.*

All too often, the same is disputed. With evidence, you help the court to further the overriding objective by dealing with issues as to filing and service, expeditiously, and fairly.

3. Agreements

The parties may agree to extend a deadline. Or, there may be an agreement that a point will not be taken.

For example, where a witness statement is served after the deadline, the recipient may confirm that it is unnecessary to address the court on service, as a point will not be taken on service.

Where there is agreement, evidence of that agreement is invaluable. Without it, a submission on whether there was an agreement is hollow. If disputed, it is unlikely to succeed.

4. Offers

Offers, and any associated replies, are important for two reasons.

First, if an offer remains open for acceptance, there may have been a material change in circumstances since the offer was made. It may now be advisable to accept it. For example, a key witness is no longer able to attend the final hearing.

Secondly, offers are relevant when deciding what order for costs (if any) to make.

5. Payments

If there is an interim payment, and it has not been acknowledged in a statement of case, you should have evidence of it.

If there is no evidence, and the other party does not accept that there has been an interim payment, then, you can invite the court to add a paragraph in the operative part of the order, directing that credit is to be given for any sums already paid.

c. Analyse

Having confirmed that you have written instructions, statements of case, court orders, and evidence, a careful reading will enable you to confirm for yourself the *relevant* facts, issues, and evidence.

i. Agreed facts

Identify material facts that are *not* in dispute.

In a claim for an unpaid parking charge, for example, it may be possible to make a note that the following are *agreed* facts.

First, the defendant parked on the relevant land. Secondly, she did so for the time alleged by the claimant. Thirdly, the defendant was obliged to pay. Fourthly, the claimant was responsible for the management of the relevant land.

Agreed or *objective* facts are *important.*

They are the *anchor* from which the judge can build a picture as to what happened. From this, you must construct your client's case, using the evidence that *is* in dispute, so as to persuade the court that the claimant has (not) discharged the burden of proof.

ii. Disputed facts

Identify the facts that *are* in dispute, relevant, and therefore assist, or undermine, one of the competing cases.

Take that claim for an unpaid parking charge.

First, the sign notifying the defendant that payment was required was clear / confusing. Secondly, the claimant was / was not aware that she had to pay to park. Thirdly, there was / was not a way to make payment because the machine was / was not working.

If the likelihood of each of the conflicting cases are finely balanced, then, the burden of proof can effectively be deployed. A defendant can use it successfully to argue that the claim should be dismissed.

If there is a claim, and a counterclaim, following the same incident, however, the burden of proof is of less assistance. The *claimant* has the burden of proving the *claim*. The *defendant* has the burden of proving the *counter*claim. *Both* parties therefore have a burden.

iii. Issues

Identify the *real* issues in the case.

These are often more discrete than the statements of case suggest.

Once an issue has been identified, the opposing positions taken on that issue in the statements of case can be identified. Then, the disputed evidence going to that issue can be identified.

This focuses *cross-examination,* and *closing submissions.*

There is *no* need to ask questions on issues that are *not* in dispute.

d. Checklist of information & documents

Depending on the type of case, the court usually needs certain information and documentation (PD 27A at Appendix A).

i. Road traffic

First, witness statements (including statements from the parties themselves). Secondly, invoices, and estimates, for repairs. Thirdly, agreements, and invoices, for the cost of any car hire.

Fourthly, any police accident report. Fifthly, a sketch plan, which should, wherever possible, be agreed. Sixthly, photographs of the scene of the accident, and the damage.

ii. Building, repairs, goods sold & contract

First, any written contract. Secondly, photographs. Thirdly, any plans. Fourthly, a list of works complained of. Fifthly, a list of any outstanding works.

Sixthly, any relevant estimate, invoice, or receipt, including any relating to repairs to each of the alleged defects. Seventhly, invoices for work done or goods supplied. Eighthly, estimates for work to be completed. Ninthly, a valuation of work done to date.

iii. Landlord & tenant

First, a calculation of the amount of any rent alleged to be owing, showing amounts received, preferably in the form of a schedule. Secondly, details of any alleged breaches of an agreement which are said to justify withholding any deposit itemised, showing how the total is made up, with invoices, and estimates, in support.

iv. Breach of duty

First, what it is said by the claimant that is alleged to have been done negligently by the defendant. Secondly, why it is said that this negligence is the fault of the defendant. Thirdly, what damage is said to have been caused.

Fourthly, what injury, or losses, have been suffered, and how any (and each) sum that is claimed has been calculated. Fifthly, the response of the defendant to each of the above.

e. Telephone

If a document appears to be missing, evidence appears not to conform to CPRs, PDs or court directions, or you just wish to confirm your instructions, *speak* to your professional client.

There may be important context that has not made its way into your written instructions. Perhaps, due to time constraints.

Your professional client may feel at ease with confirmation that her chosen counsel has received the documents, understands her instructions, and is grateful for them.

f. Spare copies

Ensure that you have *un*marked, *colour* copies of the documents.

All too often, evidence is filed and served, but the court and the other side do not have it before a hearing.

Take *hard* copies to an in-person hearing. *In any event,* have electronic copies to hand. A tablet can be used as a last resort.

13. Authority

In *Parr v Keystone Healthcare Ltd & Ors* [2019] EWCA Civ 1246, [2019] 4 WLR 99 at [26], Lewison LJ opined that "it is a matter of considerable regret that the practice direction on the citation of authorities … has been almost wholly ignored."

This paragraph was cited in *Artcrafts International Spa v Mou Limited* [2024] EWHC 1558 (KB) at [4], where Bryan J said that:

> "The parties have also provided me with no less than 98 authorities occupying 4 lever arch files. Such over citation of authority is to be deprecated … The applicable principles … are well established, and well-known, and were ultimately common ground before me."

Whether you are in the Court of Appeal, the High Court, or the county court, the parties are under an obligation to help the court to further the overriding objective when relying on authority.

a. Legal principle

In *Kaur & Anor v Secretary of State for the Home Department* [2019] EWCA Civ 1101, [2019] 4 WLR 94 at [48], Floyd LJ endorsed a warning from over one hundred years ago:

> "Cases, so far as regards the law, are most useful, but when they are applied to particular facts, they, as a rule, are of little service. Each case depends on its own particular facts, and the facts of almost every case differ …"

The lesson is that, as a general rule, authority should be relied on for a statement of *legal principle*. A previous case is unlikely to be so factually similar that it can be relied on to dispose of a new case.

Most claims are decided on the facts. This is usually with the benefit of oral evidence. So, it is unlikely that an authority that will dispose of a case can be found in advance of a final hearing.

b. Practice directions

There are four PDs prescribing when authority may (and may not) be cited, and the procedure for doing so.

i. Citation of Authorities [2012] 1 WLR 780

In 2012, the then Lord Chief Justice issued the above PD.

The preamble provides that it was "issued in order to clarify the practice and procedure governing the citation of authorities and applies throughout the ... county courts".

Under the heading 'Citation of authority', it prescribes that: "When authority is cited, whether in written or oral submissions, the following practice should be followed."

1. Official Law Reports

Where a judgment is reported in any of the four, *official* Law Reports ("the Law Reports"), *that* report *must* be cited.

They are as follows: Appeal Cases ("AC"); Queen's Bench ("QB"); Chancery ("Ch"); and Family ("Fam").

This is for two reasons.

First, these are the most authoritative. Secondly, they contain a summary of the arguments.

2. Weekly Law Reports & All England Law Reports

Until a case is reported in the Law Reports, if it is reported in the Weekly Law Reports ("WLR"), or the All England Law Reports ("All ER"), the WLR or the All ER should be cited.

There is no hierarchy. Either may be used.

3. Specialist series

If three conditions are satisfied, a specialist report may be cited.

First, the case is not reported in the Law Reports, WLR, or All ER. Secondly, it contains a headnote. Thirdly, it was made by individuals holding a Senior Courts qualification.

4. Other reports

When not reported in any of the above, other reports may be cited.

5. Transcripts

Only when a case has not been reported may the official transcript be used. This may be found on the website of the British and Irish Legal Information Institute: www.bailii.org.

It should not usually be cited, "unless it contains a relevant statement of legal principle not found in reported authority."

In *The King (on the Application of YR) v London Borough of Lambeth* [2022] EWHC 2813 (Admin), [2023] HLR 16 at [119], Paul Bowen KC said (with emphasis added):

> "Also referred to was one case … an unreported judgment dismissing a renewed application for interim relief made prior to the grant of permission. This should not have been cited: as the *Practice Direction (Citation of Authorities) (Senior Courts)* makes clear, at paragraph 10, 'an unreported case should not usually be cited unless

> it contains a relevant statement of legal principle not found in reported authority'. It did not. I would add that *this principle holds true to an even greater extent in relation to judgments on unreported interlocutory applications.*"

6. Format

Authority must be in one of two formats.

First, a photocopy of the published report. Secondly, a copy of a reproduction of the case in electronic form, which has been authorised by the publisher of the relevant reports.

In any event, it must be easily legible, ideally with a 12-point font.

ii. Citation of Authorities [2001] 1 WLR 1001

With the substantial growth in the number of cases that are available, reported in a number of different law reports, and transcripts that are freely available online, the court has limited the *nature,* and the *amount*, of authority, that may be relied upon.

Increasing efficiency and proportionality of litigation, so as to reduce cost, must be balanced against the interests of justice.

It is in conformity with the overriding objective to deal with cases justly and at proportionate cost.

Accordingly, the then Lord Chief Justice issued the above PD prescribing three rules governing the use of authority.

1. Relevant & useful

The overriding objective will be compromised if the court is burdened with a weight of *in*appropriate, *un*necessary authority, and advocates are *un*certain as to when it is necessary to use authority.

Accordingly, this PD limits citation of authority to cases that are both *relevant,* and *useful to the court.*

The latter is a reference to the duty to cite adverse authority.

2. Adverse authority

The duty of an advocate to draw the court's attention to adverse authority applies if two conditions are satisfied.

First, it undermines the case that she is advancing. Secondly, it has not been cited by the other party.

In the context of a claim for credit hire, for example, where enforceability is in dispute, this may include *Irving v Morgan Sindall Plc* [2018] EWHC 1147 (QB), [2018] RTR 23.

In this case, it was held that the claimant, who had been assured by a credit hire company that she would never be personally responsible for hire charges, had a *contingent* liability to the hire company. She was not getting a free hire car. The defendant was liable to pay these charges.

3. County court authority

It may *not* be cited unless one of the following is satisfied.

First, it *clearly* indicates that it purports to establish a *new* principle. Secondly, it *clearly* indicates that it purports to *extend* the present law.

It *must* be in the form of an *express statement* to that effect.

There are two exceptions.

First, to illustrate the conventional measure of damages in a *personal injury* case. Secondly, to demonstrate current, county court authority, on an issue where there is *no higher-level authority.*

In practice, then, before relying on county court authority, you should be able positively to submit that there is no binding (High Court, Court of Appeal, or Supreme Court) authority on the point.

iii. Judgments: Form and Citation [2001] 1 WLR 194

In 2001, the arrangements for the preparation, distribution and citation of judgments were modernised.

A PD prescribed rules for the formatting of judgments, including the requirement for numbered paragraphs.

The main reason was to facilitate the publication of judgments on the internet. It was hoped that it would also assist those searching for judgments on electronic databases.

The neutral citation is the "official number attributed to the judgment". It "must always be used on at least one occasion when the judgment is cited in a later judgment."

After EWCA, 'Civ' is the reference used for 'Civil Division'. The reference for 'Criminal Division' is 'Crim'.

The tenth Civil Division case of the year, for example, has the same official number as the tenth case of the Criminal Division. So, it is important to include the reference 'Civ'.

When a judgment is reported, the neutral citation "will appear in front of the familiar citation from the law report series."

The paragraph number of a judgment should remain consistent, whichever report of the case is used.

If more than one paragraph of a judgment is cited, each numbered paragraph should be enclosed with a square bracket.

iv. Judgments: Form and Citation [2002] 1 WLR 1346

In 2002, the practice of neutral citation was extended to all judgments handed down by the High Court in London. Ever since, a unique number has been given to these judgments.

After 'EWHC' and the unique number, High Court judgments have the following descriptive words: (Ch) Chancery Division; (Pat) Patents Court; (QB) Queen's Bench Division; (Admin) Administrative Court; (Comm) Commercial Court; (Admlty) Admiralty Court; (TCC) Technology and Construction Court; and (Fam) Family Court.

Unlike Court of Appeal judgments, however, it is unnecessary to include the descriptive words when citing the paragraph number of a High Court judgment. This is because each High Court judgment has a *unique* number. Court of Appeal judgments do not.

c. Citation

When a case is cited, the full case name should be used.

When written, *italics* should be used for the names of the parties.

This should be followed by the neutral citation (if there is one), and a comma, followed by where it is cited in the law reports.

By convention, if two conditions are satisfied, the name of the court should appear in brackets after the first page of the report.

First, no neutral citation. Secondly, decided after 1865.

The most frequently used references include: (HL) House of Lords; (CA) Court of Appeal; and (QB) Queen's Bench Division.

When a particular paragraph is cited, the number can be encompassed within square brackets. For example: *Barton v Wright Hassal LLP* [2018] UKSC 12, [2018] 3 All ER 487 at [18].

d. Marked

The relevant paragraph(s) can be marked.

When marking a hard copy, black pen should be used. Then, where the authority is scanned, or photocopied, it remains legible.

A vertical, straight line can be drawn down the side of the page encompassing the relevant paragraph(s).

Or, PDF software can be used to draw the line.

e. Copies

At an in-person hearing, ensure that you have hard copies of any authority that you rely on. For the court, and any other party.

After signing in with the usher, a copy of any authority should be handed to that usher. She will pass it on to the judge. Any authority handed to an usher *must* also be handed to the other party.

This should be as soon as practicable. The other party should have as much time as possible to consider it. Both the legal principle that decided the case, and the relevant paragraph(s), should be communicated to the other party.

At a remote hearing, ensure that you have an electronic copy. You may be requested to email it to the court, and the other party.

If the authority has been filed and served before the hearing, print off copies of the email filing and serving it. That can be stapled to the front of the authority, so as to short-circuit any dispute over whether the authority has, in fact, been filed and served.

f. Cost / benefit

Claims are usually determined by findings of fact. The relevant legal principles are usually trite.

Accordingly, authority should be the *exception.* Not the norm.

If you know that the other side is a person without a representative, balance the benefit of an authority, against the perception that you are intimidating a person without a representative.

Lengthy, appellate analysis, on trite law, is unlikely to be read.

g. Context

Using a professional legal database, check for three material circumstances before deciding to rely on an authority.

First, whether it has been *positively considered* in later cases. Secondly, whether it has been *successfully appealed.* Thirdly, whether it is subject to a *pending appeal.*

If the answer to any of these questions is "yes", it *must* be communicated to the other *party*, and to the *court.*

i. Subsequent consideration

If the legal principle that decided a case has been *applied* to *decide* a later case, this is likely to indicate that it is *good* law.

Especially if the latter is an *appellate* court, the paragraph that you rely on is cited *word-for-word*, or the reasoning behind that principle is approved by *express* words.

It may also indicate, however, that the legal principle is trite. This will call into question whether it is necessary to cite any authority.

If a case has been negatively considered, criticised, or confined to its facts, this *weakens* any general authority that it may have.

Especially if this was by a higher court.

These facts would need to be communicated to the court, and to the other party. It follows that, on balance, an authority of questionable weight may not be worth relying on.

ii. Determined appeal

Check for the following.

First, whether the appeal was *successful*. Secondly, whether the *legal principle* on which you rely was endorsed. Thirdly, whether the *reasoning applying that principle* was endorsed.

For example, in *Stevens v Equity Syndicate Management Ltd* [2014] EWHC 689 (QB), [2014] RTR 34 at [21], Burnett J (as he then was) held that the court was entitled to find a lack of impecuniosity:

> "It is striking that the bank statements showed very little activity at all. In other words, the money passing through the bank account could not conceivably reflect the totality of economic activity of a man, still less a family man. …"

On appeal ([2015] EWCA Civ 93, [2015] 4 All ER 458 at [7]), Kitchin LJ (as he then was, with whom Floyd and Jackson LJJ agreed) said that: "Burnett J upheld the Recorder's findings on impecuniosity and there is no further appeal against that decision".

Accordingly, the judgment of Burnett J was appealed. His judgment on *impecuniosity,* however, was not.

Burnett's J reasoning on impecuniosity remains *good* law.

It was not expressly endorsed by the Court of Appeal. As High Court authority binds a (deputy) district judge, recorder, and circuit judge, however, this is of no consequence.

iii. Pending appeal

If there is an *application* for permission to appeal, or permission to appeal has been *granted,* this is a relevant fact that should be communicated to the other party, and to the court.

In principle, these circumstances *weaken* the authority upon which you intend to rely. There is a prospect of the following.

First, the judgment will be *reversed.* Secondly, the legal principle upon which you intend to rely will be *criticised.* Thirdly, *different* reasoning surrounding the principle will be endorsed.

The benefit of this authority should therefore be considered.

14. Skeleton arguments

The purpose of a skeleton argument 'is to assist the court by setting out as concisely as practicable the arguments upon which a party intends to rely' (PD 52A at [5.1(1)]).

a. Assist the court

Skeleton arguments are usually *un*necessary. Often, the applicable law is trite. The issues, facts, and evidence, are straightforward.

Judgment usually turns on oral evidence.

When instructed to make an application to strike out a statement of case because it is an abuse of process, however, a skeleton argument is likely to assist the court.

It will set out the key facts, relevant legal principles on misuse of the court's procedure, and submissions as to why allowing proceedings to continue would be manifestly unfair, or otherwise bring the administration of justice into disrepute.

Skeleton arguments also provide an opportunity to get the judge onboard with your submissions before the hearing.

b. Requirements

A skeleton argument has six requirements (PD 52A at [5.1(2)]).

First, concision. Secondly, define and confine areas of controversy. Thirdly, numbered paragraphs (and pages).

Fourthly, cross-reference relevant documents. Fifthly, self-contained. Sixthly, excluding extensive quotations.

i. Concision

Words, sentences, and paragraphs, should be *short.*

Headings, sub-headings, and lists, can all be used for ease of navigation, organising content, and reducing word count.

Skeleton arguments before substantive appeals in the Court of Appeal should be less than 25 pages.

There should be a *very* good reason to go beyond five pages.

1. Headings & sub-headings

Typical headings may include facts, issues and submissions.

Sub-headings can also be used to make arguments.

When resisting an application for relief from sanctions, for example, under the heading 'submissions', the sub headings may be as follows: breach is serious and significant; no good reason; and all the circumstances weigh in favour of refusing relief.

2. Lists & punctuation

Lists enable *brevity.* They reduce the number of necessary words.

Punctuation can aid *pithiness.*

For example: appropriate use of the Oxford comma; semi-colons to separate two, closely related, but independent sentences; and full colons before a list, or where a semi-colon will not do.

Paragraphs should be *short.*

3. Layout

Concision does *not* mean that the font, size of font, and space in between each line, should be reduced.

The objective is *not* to cram content onto each page.

Content should be well-spaced, so that it is clear. Free space can then be used for notes in the margins, and in between sentences.

Times New Roman, font size 12, and 1.5-line spacing, is often used.

ii. Define & confine areas of controversy

Identify the issues that are in dispute, and the issues that are not in dispute. The scope of each should be set out.

In a claim for credit hire, for example: 'Liability is admitted. Quantum is disputed. There are three heads of loss: repairs are admitted in the sum of £2,000; and credit hire and the engineer's fee are denied. The credit hire issues are need, period and rate.'

iii. Numbering

Pages and paragraphs should be numbered, for ease of navigation.

There are advantages to single-sided skeleton arguments.

First, blank pages, so that lengthy, handwritten notes may be written on these pages, where there is insufficient space in the margin, or in-between lines.

Secondly, should the skeleton argument need to be photocopied, or scanned, there is a greater prospect that all of the pages will, in fact, be photocopied, or scanned.

iv. Cross-referencing

Where there is an admission in a statement of case, the name of the document, and the paragraph, should be precisely identified.

Often, a paginated bundle does not exist.

If so, for example, 'paragraph 7 of the Defence', or 'page 2 of the claimant's engineers' report', provide workarounds.

Authority should conform to the PDs.

When an authority is cited, set out the following.

First, the *legal principle* for which it is authority. Secondly, the *paragraph(s)* of the authority where it is found. Thirdly, if more than one authority is relied on to establish this principle, *the reason.*

For example:

1. When a claim is issued, a claimant must bring forward her whole case. She cannot subsequently open the same litigation in respect of matters which ought to have been brought forward, but, in fact, were not.

2. This is "Henderson abuse". It has been well-established law since Wigram V-C set out the rule in the case of *Henderson v Henderson* [1843-60] All ER Rep 378 at 381, in these terms:

> "... where a given matter becomes the subject of litigation in, and of adjudication by, a court of competent jurisdiction, the court requires the parties to that litigation to bring forward their whole case, and will not (except under special circumstances) permit the same parties to open the same subject of litigation in respect of matter which might have been brought forward as part of the subject in contest, but which was not brought forward only because

> they have, from negligence, inadvertence, or even accident, omitted part of their case. …"

State the consistent shorthand used for pages and paragraphs.

For example: 'References in square brackets are to paragraph numbers.' If so, don't also use square brackets for page numbers.

v. Self-contained

Key submissions should be set out.

For example, an argument that is *not* self-contained may state that: 'The first submission is in paragraph four of the Defence'; and 'the second submission is in paragraph twelve of the Defence'.

Footnotes should be unnecessary.

vi. Quotations

As a general rule, only the *key* sentence should be quoted.

Occasionally, there will be more than one key sentence. There should be a *good* reason to quote more than a paragraph.

Do *not* quote out of any material context.

c. Content

Few strict rules exist. There is flexibility to find your own style.

i. Headings

The header should be similar to a statement of case.

The sole exception is, of course, the *title* of the document.

This should also be within tramlines, capitalised, and emboldened. In contrast to a statement of case, it should start with the status of the party, followed by the name of the document.

The name of an application can be used. For example: '**DEFENDANT'S SKELETON ARGUMENT RE ABUSE OF PROCESS**'.

The electronic file name may be the same, albeit with the addition of the claim number. That way, if it is filed and served via email, the file name can be copied and pasted in the subject of the email.

ii. Reading time

How long will it take to read? This should follow the heading.

It enables the court to gauge how long it will take to consider. This in turn permits the court to actively manage the case.

It is likely to take no more than five minutes.

iii. Invitation

What is the court being asked to do? A sentence should suffice.

For example, 'strike out this claim as an abuse of process under CPR 3.4(2)(b) because there is a binding settlement.'

Cite the relevant CPR, PD, or court order that you are relying on.

iv. Facts

Set out only the *necessary* facts.

In the above example, the salient facts may be as follows:

1. This claim arises out of a road traffic collision, which occurred on 10 July 2023.

2. Liability is not in dispute.

3. On 12 August 2023, the claimant submitted a Claim Notification Form ("CNF") under the MOJ Portal.

4. Section E of the CNF was completed relating to provision of an alternative vehicle. The claimant indicated that she required an alternative vehicle, but also that she had not been provided with one. No details of hire were provided.

5. No request was made to the defendant insurer to provide an alternative vehicle.

6. From 5-20 August 2023, the claimant hired a vehicle on credit hire terms.

7. On 29 October 2023, the claimant submitted the Stage 2 Settlement Pack, claiming personal injury, and physiotherapy charges.

8. On 12 November 2023, the defendant made a final offer of £3,500. On 3 December 2023, this was accepted.

9. On 4 February 2024, proceedings were issued against the defendant to recover the following:

    a. credit hire in the sum of £4,545.53; and

    b. repairs, in the sum of £4,210.12.

10. This was two months after settlement.

v. Costs

Are costs sought because a party has behaved unreasonably?

For example:

If the court strikes out this claim as an abuse of process, it follows that the claimant has behaved unreasonably in bringing this claim for the purposes of CPR 27.14(2)(g).

Accordingly, the defendant invites the court to award the reasonable costs of defending the claim. This is set out in the Defendant's Statement of Costs that was attached to, and filed and served via, an email dated 1 September 2024.

vi. Sign & date

The name of the legal representative who has drafted the skeleton argument should appear at the bottom.

By convention, it is capitalised, emboldened, and aligned to the right-hand side of the page.

The date that it was drafted should follow.

These are the last words before the back sheet.

vii. Back sheet

Skeleton arguments should have a back sheet.

The heading is identical to the first page. The text is on the right-hand side of the page only. The left-hand side is blank.

The name, professional address, and status of the legal representative who has drafted the skeleton argument, should be stated. For example, 'Counsel for the Defendant'.

The name, professional address, and status of the legal representative who is instructing counsel, should also be stated. For example, 'Solicitor for the Defendant'.

If printed off and stapled, the *back* sheet should face the *back*.

When the skeleton argument is picked up, you should be able to see the front page. When you turn it over, you should be able to see the back sheet. This is for ease of reference.

viii. Spelling, grammar & punctuation

This may indicate that the necessary time has not been invested in researching, drafting and proofreading.

If so, the ability to persuade will diminish.

Avoid the judge forming a negative view of you, or your client's case, before you have even opened your mouth.

d. Form

Substance is important. So is *form.*

A skeleton argument should look aesthetically pleasing.

This demonstrates that time has been invested in proofreading.

Font, size, and spacing, is consistent. Shorthand is consistent.

For example: 'paragraph 4', 'para. 4', or '[4]'; and 'Particulars of Claim', 'PoC', or 'particulars of claim'.

Define abbreviations.

In practice, brackets and quotation marks are used: ("...").

e. Notice

If there is a need for a skeleton argument, there is likely to be factual, legal, or evidential, complexity.

Accordingly, the judge, and the other party, should have sufficient notice of it. This provides them with an opportunity to read, process, and conduct their own research into the relevant complexity.

If a party has sufficient notice of your submissions, and remains unable to counter them effectively, they become more powerful.

The court will then be more likely to exercise a draconian power of case management. This includes early termination. For example: striking out a claim; or granting summary judgment.

i. File & serve

A court order may include a direction as to how and when.

If so, follow this direction. If there is no such direction, skeleton arguments should be filed and served no less than three days before a hearing. Some notice, however, is better than no notice.

The afternoon before a hearing is preferable to on the day.

Ensure that you have evidence that the skeleton argument has been filed and served. This may be disputed.

It may be by way of an email with an attachment, or cover letters.

ii. Springboard

Skeleton arguments are not statements of case, or evidence.

If it has not been filed and served, the *court* may not read it.

If so, *you* may still decide to use it as a framework. The judge may be inclined to find a reason to give judgment against your client if you read it word-for-word. It should not be used as a script.

Use it as a springboard into the law, facts and evidence.

f. General advice

There are five pieces of general advice on skeleton arguments.

First, your audience is the judge; not your lay / professional client.

Secondly, be optimistic; not unrealistic.

Thirdly, when using an authority, use the actual quote from the paragraph of the judgment. Not the headnote. Only quote the headnote if it more succinctly summarises the ratio.

Fourthly, apply the legal principle that you have quoted to the facts of the case that the judge has to decide. Why does it mean that you should win; and the other side should lose?

Fifthly, in an appeal skeleton: use the first paragraph to introduce what the appeal is about; and then summarise each ground of appeal, followed by why each ground should succeed / fail.

15. Arrival

On arrival, sign in with the usher.

Have a conference with your client, and any witnesses for the party who you represent.

Then, have a discussion with the other party.

a. Sign in

There are three reasons for signing in.

First, the hearing should not then proceed without you.

Secondly, if you have any witnesses, when they sign in, the usher will be able to inform them that you are at court, so that you can have a conference.

Thirdly, when (the legal representative for) the other party signs in, the usher will inform them that you are at court, so that you can have a discussion.

b. Note

Note the courtroom that the matter will be heard in. This is because a transcript may be requested in the case of an appeal.

Note the title, and surname, of the judge. For example: 'Deputy District Judge Smith'.

Note the title, surname, and status of any other legal representative. They may be counsel, solicitor, or solicitors' agent.

c. Listing

Many claims are listed at 10:00, or 14:00.

This does not mean that your case will be called on before, or even at, this time. It is the time before which you must have signed in.

You may be waiting an hour, a morning, or even a day, before your case is adjourned due to lack of judicial time. If this appears to be a realistic prospect, ensure that your witnesses are aware of it.

Your case may not have an assigned listing. This means that there may not be a fixed courtroom in which the matter will be heard, judge who will hear it, or time before which the matter will be called on.

If so, it is on an "unassigned" or "floating" list.

i. Managing expectations

Often, lay clients equate listing with a professional appointment. They may need to make childcare arrangements, renew their parking, or otherwise make additional arrangements.

ii. Spare copies

When the claim is on a floating list, the prospect that the court will have all of the documents, and that a witness bundle has made its way to the courtroom in which the hearing will take place, is often *drastically* reduced.

This is a good reason to take at least one *spare, un*marked, *hard* copy of the documents to any in-person hearing.

Evidence of filing and service is also *invaluable* in case of dispute.

iii. County Court at Central London

When you sign in, you will be asked for your name, and often your mobile telephone number.

When a courtroom, and a judge, becomes available, the parties will be notified. This may be via text message if you give your mobile telephone number.

The parties may be released for the luncheon adjournment by the same means. If you wish to speak to the other side, you can request a text message to be sent, inviting them to return to the reception area, so as to facilitate a discussion.

iv. Alternative dispute resolution

You may be waiting for some time.

The duty to assist the court to further the overriding objective requires you to attempt to narrow the issues, if it is not possible to settle (part of) the case.

If you do not have authority to do so, ask your professional client. You can call them on the telephone, or send them an email.

You may have to explain why it is a good use of time. It will save costs in the event that the matter is adjourned.

The Small Claims Mediation Service is also likely to be available.

In practice, if both sides have legal representation, and have instructed counsel, authority to use this service may not be given. If this is the case, the parties should at least be able to narrow the issues to only those which are properly arguable.

The phrase "let's let the judge decide" is often the sign of weakness. It usually reveals that the legal representative does not think that the point will succeed, but considers that she must pursue it.

It may demonstrate that authority, or evidence, weighs against it.

Never agree that a point is doomed to fail. If it is, explain why it is unarguable to your professional client, and get their instructions to drop it.

It is useful to hear what the other party says about their case before the hearing. You will often learn the following.

First, how the other party will *present* their case. Secondly, perceived *strengths*. Thirdly, perceived *weaknesses*.

v. Subsequent listing

If adjourned, request a *fixed* listing on the return date. That is, not to be listed in a back-to-back / floating list.

d. Non-attendance of witnesses

If it appears as though one of your witnesses is not going to attend, telephone your professional client. Failing that, send an email.

There may be a good reason why they have not attended.

For example, they may have had to attend an accident and emergency department of a hospital.

Instructions from your professional client, confirming the same, will often secure an adjournment.

They will also go some way to defending an application for the costs of the adjournment.

Especially where the matter has been transferred from one court to another, a witness may have gone to the wrong court.

Act *promptly*. Do not wait until the last minute.

e. Late attendance of legal representative

If you are likely to be late, act *promptly.*

First, send an email to your professional client. Copy in your practice manager. Relay that you are likely to be late, the reason, and your estimated time of arrival.

Your professional client may email the other party to convey the same. Especially if she is represented.

Secondly, ask your practice manager to email the court, copying in both you, and your professional client. The email should relay that you are likely to be late, the reason, and your estimated time of arrival.

Thirdly, ask your professional client to forward that email on to the legal representative for any other party.

Other claims may be able to be called on before you arrive.

Parties and witnesses will be grateful to be kept informed.

It is also a professional courtesy.

Public transport is often delayed. It may even be cancelled. It is *what you do about it* that matters.

Failure promptly to communicate with court actors is avoidable.

f. Conference

If the issues in dispute do not require oral evidence, you may not have a witness. If so, a conference is unnecessary.

Especially where liability is in dispute, however, you will likely need a conference. This will be with the party who you represent, and any of her witnesses.

g. Speak to the other party

There are five reasons to speak to the other party.

First, to confirm that the parties have the relevant documents. Secondly, to agree the issues in dispute. Thirdly, to attempt to agree quantum, subject to liability. Fourthly, to exchange any authority. Fifthly, to agree costs and witness expenses, subject to liability.

i. Papers

If a legal representative has not got a copy of a document that you seek to rely upon, you should be able to provide them with a copy.

If they say that they have not seen the document before, or otherwise dispute service, request evidence of service from your professional client via email.

Then, forward it on.

It is also worth requesting evidence that the document has been filed with the court. If the other party does not have a document, it is possible, if not likely, that the court will not have it.

Evidence of filing and service can be shown to the other party, so that these potential issues can be resolved before the hearing.

Documents are often filed and served via email.

The size of a document may mean that the email to which it is attached does not reach its recipient. Ask your professional client to confirm to you, via email, that they have *not* received an "undelivered" response to the email filing and serving a document.

Often, when an email is sent to the court, an automated email is received to effect that the court has received an email. If so, ask your professional client to forward it on to you.

ii. Issues

In a credit hire claim, if evidence of impecuniosity has been served, the defendant may decide not to dispute it.

This means that one *significant* issue will no longer be in dispute.

The need to cross-examine a claimant on her wage slips, bank and credit card statements, therefore falls away.

The claimant will likely be reassured to hear this.

It will also enable the parties to state the issues that are in dispute at the outset of the hearing, so as to focus oral evidence, and then submissions, on the real issues. These are likely to be different, or at least narrower, than the statements of case may suggest.

iii. Quantum

If there is an invoice, subject to liability, it may be possible to agree the head of loss to which it relates. This saves court time.

For a claimant, it can be reassuring to agree quantum subject to liability. If she succeeds on liability, a known amount will follow. There is no uncertainty that the court will award a different sum.

The estimated length of the hearing may also reduce. In an unassigned list, your case is then more likely to be called on.

If quantum can be agreed, subject to liability, in principle, so can interest, and the period for payment. For example, within 21 days.

In absence of agreement, the normal order is within 14 days.

If you are representing a party who does *not* have a burden of proof, be aware that, if you admit an issue, or a head of loss, then, if a witness for the party with the burden of proof does *not* turn up, the advocate for her can submit that she is *not* needed to prove that issue, or head of loss. This is because it has been *admitted.*

For example, if need to hire a credit hire car is admitted, and the claimant does not attend to confirm her statement, the advocate for the defendant cannot then decide to dispute need due to the inability of the claimant to confirm her statement at the hearing.

The practical reality for the defendant is that a submission that the credit hire claim should be dismissed because need has not been proven can*not* be made. The credit hire claim will *not* be dismissed for want of evidence because need has been *admitted.*

iv. Authority

Authority that is relied upon should be provided to the other side.

This includes rules of the Highway Code.

Do not assume that the other party is familiar with an authority.

The *legal principle* for which it is authority, and the *paragraph* at which it is found, should both be clearly communicated.

This is especially important for a party without a representative.

v. Costs, disbursements & witness expenses

These can usually be agreed, subject to liability.

Where witness expenses appear to be unreasonably high, the paying party may request to cross-examine on it. This will usually take place after judgment. If so, ensure that you do not agree to a witness being released before she is cross-examined on expenses.

16. Conference

Where liability is in dispute, a conference is often necessary.

Even where only quantum is in dispute, a witness may be needed to give evidence. For example, in a claim for credit hire, where the defendant wishes to cross-examine on the need to hire.

In these circumstances, a conference is useful for three reasons.

First, to build rapport. Secondly, to outline the procedure. Thirdly, to confirm whether a witness statement requires amendment.

a. Venue

If the hearing is in person, the conference will usually be in person.

If remote, it will often take place over the telephone.

i. In person

Instructions usually request counsel to attend court up to an hour before the time that the hearing is listed. This is for a conference.

If not, do not assume that any witnesses will attend court before the hearing is listed. Contact your professional client. Request that any witnesses attend court before the hearing for a conference.

ii. Remote

Instructions may request counsel to telephone a witness before the time that the hearing is listed. This is for a conference.

In any event, you may email your professional client during working hours the day before the hearing to confirm the following.

First, any witnesses giving evidence. Secondly, their telephone numbers. Thirdly, that they have a copy of the documents. Fourthly, the time that you intend to start a conference. Fifthly, that they have a separate electronic device, connected to the internet, and access to email.

A witness may not have been told that you would like a conference. She may not have the relevant documents.

She may intend on participating in the hearing, and being taken to the documents in oral evidence, using one electronic device. Often, a mobile telephone.

She may need to receive additional documents on the day.

b. Build rapport

To fill in gaps in the evidence, you need rapidly to build rapport.

The witness is then more likely to have trust and confidence in you. Answers will be given to the questions that have been asked.

You will then be in a position to advise, take instructions, and to represent the best interests of your client during the hearing.

It is often easier to build rapport during in-person conferences.

i. Greeting

This varies depending on the form of the conference.

Briefly introducing yourself often puts a witness at ease.

1. In person

A genuine smile, appropriate eye contact, and a sincere greeting, assist to build rapport. Open body language can also help.

Stating that you have told the usher that you are here, and that you will try to find a private room, will both put a witness at ease.

Finding a private conference room is often easier if you arrive early. In many courts, they are limited. If you find one, let the usher, and the other side, know which room you are in.

If possible, sit next to the witness. Not opposite.

The latter can appear adversarial, as though you are interviewing them. Sitting next to a witness, however, so that you can both look at a document, is often perceived as *collaborative*, thereby assisting to put a witness at ease.

A cup of water from a water fountain can also help.

2. Remote

The majority of communication is non-verbal. Gestures, facial expressions, posture, and eye contact are all lost using a telephone.

The importance of the *actual words* used is therefore likely to increase. Volume, tone and intonation are the only tools that you can use to build trust, confidence and rapport.

ii. Break the ice

Some small talk is often preferable before questions.

Once the ice is broken, and a level of trust and confidence has been established, you can progress to outline the procedure.

iii. Note

You may wish to briefly explain that you will be taking a note.

First, so that, if your lay client has any questions about what was said, there is a contemporaneous note. Secondly, so that your lay client's legal representative can read what was discussed. Thirdly, if necessary, to advise on prospects of appeal.

It can also put a witness at ease to confirm that the note is *confidential.* It will *not* be shown to the other party, or to thc court.

c. Outline the procedure

What is the agenda for the conference? What will happen in court?

i. Before

The agenda for the conference will likely be as follows.

First, outline the procedure that the court is likely to adopt. Secondly, questioning, so that you understand your lay client's case and version of events, and to fill in any gaps in the evidence. Thirdly, advice on prospects, if necessary.

ii. During

Imagine that you have not been to court before.

Who sits where? Who speaks first? How do you address the judge?

The hearing will be recorded by the court. It must not be recorded by anyone else. It is a criminal offence to do so.

1. In person

Wait for the usher to announce the case.

It is etiquette to bow when entering, and exiting, the courtroom.

This is more than merely a nod, but less than a full bow / curtsy.

If the judge greets the parties, respond appropriately. It is unusual to speak to the judge first. If the judge greets the parties with "good morning", it is appropriate to repeat that greeting.

As one faces the judge, usually the claimant sits on the left. The defendant sits on the right.

There is no need to stand.

2. Remote

No person, other than a court actor, may take part in the hearing without the permission of the judge. Parties, legal representatives, witnesses, interpreters, and the judge, are court actors.

Before joining, you should be in a private, and quiet, area. Another person should not be able to hear you. Reduce background noise.

Treat the hearing as though you were going to court.

If uncertain about how to join the hearing, or what to do if there is a technical problem, check the notice of hearing.

a. Telephone

Usually, the court will call the telephone numbers that have been provided. Often, this is five minutes before the hearing starts.

The call may be from an unknown number.

On answering, you will usually be invited to join a conference call.

You will be asked to press 'star' and '1' to join.

You will be asked to give your full name. You may also be asked to press the 'hash key' afterwards.

Upon joining, press 'star' and then '6' to mute. Repeat to unmute.

b. Audio-visual

Dress as if it was an in-person hearing.

Often, audio-visual hearings are via Cloud Video Platform ("CVP").

If there is a problem using CVP, the court may be contacted.

Details will be provided in the notice of hearing.

Joining using a computer and Google Chrome is recommended.

Close all browsers and tabs. Open a new window. Maximise it.

Copy the address from the email arranging the hearing. Paste it into the address bar of your browser. Click: 'Enter'.

Type your full name into the box, entitled: 'Your name'. This should be followed by your role. For example: 'Counsel for the Defendant'.

Click the downward arrow on the bottom right. Click the top option. Click: 'Connect'.

Check that 'Microphone' and 'Camera' are set to 'Default'. Test and adjust your video and sound. Click: 'Start'.

Enter the 'PIN'. This is usually in the email arranging the hearing. If not, check the notice of hearing. Click: 'Connect'.

If you do not have a PIN, click: 'Guest' then 'Connect'.

You will enter a digital waiting room. Mute your microphone and turn off your camera. The buttons are in the bottom of the window.

The 'chat room' should be used to report technical issues. For example, inability to hear, or see, another court actor.

To leave the hearing, click the red telephone button.

3. Giving evidence

When giving evidence, the following guidance may assist.

First, speak clearly, loudly, and slowly. The judge, and any legal representative, will be taking a note.

Secondly, answer the question. If the question misses an important detail, answer the question, *then* add that detail.

Thirdly, if possible, answer "yes" or "no". A *short* answer is usually more persuasive.

Fourthly, if the question is not understood, ask for it to be repeated. If it remains unclear, ask for it to be put in other words.

Fifthly, it is not a memory test. For example, if a relevant date is in your statement, you can look at it. If you cannot remember the answer to a question, just say so.

4. Submissions & judgment

The advocate for the claimant does not usually open a case, unless requested to do so by the judge. Claims are usually straightforward. It is unusual to have complex issues of law, fact, or evidence.

The court will often be assisted by the claimant outlining the documents, the issues in dispute, and who is in the hearing.

Salient parts of the evidence that assist, or undermine, the competing cases, may be briefly summarised before judgment.

The claim will likely be allowed, or dismissed, in an oral judgment.

iii. After

After the hearing, you will have a brief conference with your *lay* client, so as to explain the result, and outline any next steps.

You will also speak to your professional client, outline the order, and email your attendance note to your *professional* client.

d. Questioning

What evidence relates to the issues in dispute?

Fill in gaps. Clarify any material ambiguities.

You should then be in a position to provide summary advice on prospects, and go on to represent your client's best interests.

i. Ethics

When questioning, be careful *not* to lead, or otherwise suggest, answers, to questions on issues that are *in dispute.*

This includes verbal, *and* non-verbal, communication.

Confirming, and filling in gaps, in your instructions, are different skills to cross-examination. You are *not* determining liability. You are advising on what *the court is likely to find* on the evidence.

ii. Active listening

Often, people feel more comfortable relaying *their* version of events, in the way that *they* wish to do so.

Then, once they are happy that they have been *understood,* they are usually comfortable answering questions.

Often, the quicker that you build rapport using *active listening skills,* the quicker you are able to progress to collecting full instructions, effectively, and time-efficiently.

iii. English

If the statement of a witness is in English, that witness *must* be able to understand *written,* and *spoken,* English.

The exception is where an interpreter is present.

Witnesses *must* be able to answer questions in English under cross-examination.

If it becomes apparent that the witness is unable to do so, or you are otherwise not able to take full instructions in conference, *promptly* call your professional client.

Check whether an interpreter has been booked. If not, was there any indication that an interpreter was needed in the directions questionnaire? If not, an application to adjourn will be difficult.

It will be *even more* difficult, however, where you have *not* confirmed the need for an adjournment *before* the hearing.

First, you can explain the need for an adjournment to the other party. This provides an opportunity to make a *joint* submission that the matter ought to be adjourned.

Secondly, an application to adjourn is more likely to succeed if it is *voluntarily* made *before* a witness is called, so that you are on the front foot, as opposed to being *forced* to make it *during* oral evidence, when it is clear that a witness cannot sufficiently understand English.

Thirdly, as there is a real risk that the evidence of that witness will be struck out, and therefore the party who you represent will be unsuccessful, put your *professional* client on notice of these risks.

Fourthly, if you are unable to take instructions in conference, this will become clear during the hearing. You might also be reprimanded by the court for failing *promptly* to flag up this problem.

iv. Confirm written evidence

A witness should have an opportunity to read her statement.

This should be an *un*marked copy of the same document that has been filed, served, and in the bundle (if there is one).

Having read the statement, invite a response as to whether or not there is anything to be amended.

If so, take a *word-for-word* note as to which *paragraph* is to be amended, and the *words* to be substituted.

Repeat this to the witness to confirm that your note is accurate.

If there is no request to amend, enquire whether the statement is true and accurate. Record the answer in your attendance note.

This is so that, if under cross-examination, the witness agrees that her statement is *in*accurate, or has otherwise *changed* her evidence, you have a contemporaneous note of the above.
Ask the witness whose signature appears at the end of her statement. Take a note of the answer.

Ask *open* questions on issues that are likely to be in dispute.

Even if the witness is giving evidence against the case theory of the party who has called her, or the bulk of the evidence, you have an ethical duty *not* to coach, or otherwise to *train,* a witness.

Routine witness preparation, however, is ethical.

v. Fill in gaps

If a head of loss is not evidenced in a party's statement, or otherwise evidenced in the documentation that has been filed and served, ask *open* questions to find out about it.

For example, where 'miscellaneous expenses' are claimed, but they are not evidenced in the documents, there may be evidence in the form of receipts that that party has brought to the hearing.

Or, the witness may be able to state *what* those expenses were, *when* they were incurred, and *why* they were necessary.

If permitted, you could ask a couple of open questions in examination-in-chief. This evidence would then be taken into account.

If you propose to ask questions in examination-in-chief, it is good etiquette to relay what those questions are, and why you are asking them, to the legal representative for another party.

This is for two reasons.

First, if the court asks whether there is any objection to you asking the questions, it is more likely that another party will say: " No".

Secondly, if they object, you can at least submit that you have put your opponent on notice of the questions that you seek to ask, and why you are asking them, so that it is more likely that the court will, nevertheless, allow you to ask them.

vi. Loss of earnings & expenses

Loss of earnings and expenses can be claimed, should the party for whom a witness gives evidence succeed.

They should be noted.

Ideally, they will be agreed with the other party before the hearing. If not, you will be able swiftly to relay them at the relevant time at the end of the hearing.

e. Advising

If required to advise, you should now be in a position to do so.

If an issue is *not* properly arguable, this should be *stated.* The reason should be briefly *explained.* Both should be *understood.*

Counsel must *not* let her professional discretion be fettered.

Of course, there is a *qualitative* distinction between a point that is *not properly arguable*, and one that is *merely weak.*

The former is a *legal* question. It is *binary.* It involves *professional* ethics. The latter is often grounded in the facts and evidence.

f. Time management

Usually, you will have up to half an hour if you have one witness.

With multiple witnesses, you will have to manage your time carefully. Ensure that you have full instructions before the hearing.

Once you have advised, if necessary, you can answer any questions that your lay client, or any of her witnesses, have.

17. Applications

The court may act on the application of a party, or under the court's general powers of case management (CPR 3).

In general, applications should be made by issuing an application notice. The procedure is prescribed in CPR 23.

Form N244 should be used. This is an "application notice".

Applications for summary judgment, or other disposal before a final hearing, should be made before, or when filing, directions questionnaires (PD 26 at [11(2)]).

In any event, any application should be made as soon as it appears that it is *necessary* or *desirable* (PD 23A at [2.5]).

It may only become apparent that an application should be made on the day of a hearing. If so, speak to your professional client. Explain the need for the application. Get instructions to make it.

Some judges will refuse to hear an application unless an application notice has been filed and served. To guard against this possibility, you can take the following instructions.

Your professional client undertakes to file and serve an application notice promptly. In any event, within, say, three working days.

These instructions should be in writing. They may be in the form of an email: 'Further to our conversation, I instruct you to …'

In receipt of these instructions you have two options.

First, invite the court to exercise the court's general powers of case management to grant the application on the *court's own motion.*

Secondly, if the court refuses to act on its own motion, you can make an application *on behalf of a party* on instructions.

Counsel should never undertake to file and serve an application, or to pay court fees. *Professional clients* may give undertakings.

a. Default judgment

"Default judgment" means judgment without a hearing.

Where a defendant in a claim, or a claimant in a counterclaim, fails to file and serve a defence before the relevant date, default judgment may be entered.

It is in accordance with the overriding objective to deal with an undefended claim, or counterclaim, for two reasons.

First, it is *just* because it is undefended. Secondly, as there is no need for directions, full investigation, or a final hearing, early termination disposes of the matter at *proportionate cost.*

It is also in accordance with the court's duty of active case management for two reasons.

First, it is an example of promptly deciding which issues need full investigation, followed by a final hearing, and disposing summarily of those that do not. Secondly, it considers whether the likely benefits of allowing the case to continue justify the cost.

i. Administrative

A party merely has to file a *request* for judgment to be entered.

Administrative staff can enter judgment. It does not need to be a judge. There is no consideration of the merits of the claim.

ii. Excluded claims

Judgment cannot be entered in the following types of claim.

First, for delivery of goods, subject to an agreement regulated by the Consumer Credit Act 1974 (CPR 12.2(a)). Secondly, Part 8 claims (CPR 12.2(b)). Thirdly, where the defendant has applied for strike out, or summary judgment, and that application has not been disposed of (CPR 12.3(3)(a)).

Fourthly, where the defendant has satisfied the whole claim, including any claim for costs, on which the claimant is seeking judgment (CPR 12.3(3)(b)). Fifthly, the claimant is seeking judgment on a claim for money, and the defendant has admitted to pay all of it, but has requested time to pay (CPR 12.3(3)(c)).

iii. Default of acknowledgement of service

To obtain judgment in default of an acknowledgment of service, the following conditions must be satisfied (CPR 12.3(1)).

First, the defendant has not filed an acknowledgment of service, or defence to (any part) of the claim. Secondly, the relevant time period has expired.

iv. Default of defence

To obtain judgment in default of (documents intended to be) a defence, the following conditions must be satisfied (CPR 12.3(2)).

First, an acknowledgment of service has been filed, but not a defence; in a counterclaim, a defence to that counterclaim has not been filed. Secondly, the relevant time limit has expired.

Acknowledgement of service (CPR 10) does not apply to a counterclaim (CPR 30.4(3)).

v. Procedure

In general, default judgment is obtained by making a request using the relevant form in the following claims (CPR 12.4(1)).

First, a specified amount of money. Secondly, an amount of money to be decided by the court. Thirdly, delivery of goods, where the claim form gives the defendant the alternative of paying their value. Fourthly, any combination of these remedies.

Forms are prescribed for (un)specified, and non-money, claims.

vi. Set aside

There are two rules. One is *mandatory.* The other is *discretionary.*

1. Must

Default judgment wrongly entered *must* be set aside (CPR 13.2).

There are three grounds.

First, in case of a judgment in default of an acknowledgement of service, there has not in fact been such default. Secondly, in case of a judgment in default of a defence, there has not in fact been such default. Thirdly, the whole of the claim was satisfied before judgment was entered.

2. May

There are two grounds on which a court *may* exercise its *discretion* to set aside default judgment (CPR 13.3).

First, the defendant has a *real prospect of successfully defending* the claim. Secondly, it appears to the court that there is *some other good reason* why the judgment should be set aside, varied, or the defendant should be allowed to defend the claim.

There is no *right* to set aside. Even where a ground is satisfied.

The court *must* take into account whether or not the party seeking to set aside made the application *promptly* (CPR 13.3(2)).

An application must be supported by *evidence* (CPR 13.4(3)).

Default judgment may be set aside on an *application* by a party, or the court acting on the *court's own motion.*

In *FXF v English Karate Foundation Ltd & Anor* [2023] EWCA Civ 891, [2024] 1 WLR 1097 at [72], Sir Geoffrey Voss MR (with whom Nicola Davies and Birss LJJ agreed) said that the Court of Appeal "is now clearly stating that the *Denton* tests apply in their full rigour to applications to set aside default judgments."

As HHJ Cadwallader subsequently set out in *Thiscompany Ltd & Ors v Welsh & Ors* [2024] EWHC 2159 (Comm) at [17]:

> "... The Court should first consider the matters set out in CPR 13.3 (the merits of the case and the delay in making the application). Whether the defendant has a real prospect of successfully defending the claim is a threshold condition ... If that threshold is crossed, whether to grant the application is a discretionary question, and the *Denton* test is engaged. That involves (a) identifying and assessing the seriousness and significance of the breach, (b) considering why the default occurred, and (c) evaluating all the circumstances of the case, including the factors set out in CPR 3.9."

b. Transfer

An application can be made, to the court in which the case is being heard, for it to be transferred to another court.

There should be a *good* reason in support. For example: distance to the court; disability; or childcare commitments.

This should have been set out in the directions questionnaire, however, before the case was initially transferred. Accordingly, the good reason is likely to be consequent upon a *change in circumstances* since the directions questionnaire was completed.

c. Consent

Where the parties agree the terms in which a judgment should be given, or order that the court is invited to make, it may be entered and sealed if three conditions are met (CPR 40.6).

First, none of the parties is a person without a representative. Secondly, the approval of the court is not required by a CPR, PD, or other enactment. Thirdly, the judgment or order is prescribed.

There are eight prescriptions (CPR 40.6(3)).

First, the judgment or order is for the payment of money (which may still need to be decided by the court), or the delivery up of goods with, or without, the option of paying the value of the goods, or the agreed value.

Secondly, dismissal (in whole or in part) of proceedings.

Thirdly, stay (and disposal) of proceedings on agreed terms.

Fourthly, stay of enforcement of a judgment, either unconditionally, or on condition that the money due is paid by instalments specified in the order.

Fifthly, setting aside a default judgment, which has not been satisfied. Sixthly, payment out of money which has been paid into court. Seventhly, discharge from liability of any party.

Eighthly, payment, assessment, waiver or other provision for costs as may be agreed.

If these conditions are met, there are three further requirements (CPR 40.6(7)).

First, the agreed order must be drawn up by the parties. Secondly, it must be expressed to be "By Consent".

Thirdly, it must be signed by the legal representative acting for each of the parties to whom the order relates, or, if a person without a representative successfully applies for a judgment or order in terms which are agreed, by that person.

Where a hearing date has been fixed, the parties must inform the court immediately (PD 23A at [8.5]).

d. Summary judgment

The jurisdiction is closely related to strike out (PD 3A at [1.5]).

Summary judgment prescribes a wider scope, however, for dismissing a claim, or a defence.

In *Swain v Hillman & Anor* [2000] PIQR P51 (CA) at P52-P53, Lord Woolf MR (as he then was) (with whom Pill and Judge LJJ agreed) said that:

> "Clearly, there is a relationship between r. 3.4 [strike out] and r. 24.2 [summary judgment.] However the power of the court under Part 24, the grounds are set out in r. 24.[3], are wider than those contained in r. 3.4. The reason for the contrast in language between r. 3.4 and r. 24.[3] is because under r. 3.4, unlike r. 24.[3], the court generally is only concerned with the statement of case which it is alleged discloses no reasonable grounds for bringing or defending the claim.
>
> ... The words 'no real prospect of being successful or succeeding' ... direct the court to the need to see whether there is a 'realistic' as opposed to a 'fanciful' prospect of success. ..."

It is a procedure by which the court may decide a claim, or a particular issue, without a final hearing (CPR 24.1(a)).

Summary judgment may be granted on an *application* by a party, or the *court's own motion* (PD 26 at [11]-[12]).

i. When

Any application should be made before, or when filing, the applicant's directions questionnaire (PD 26 at [11(1)]).

If an application is not made before directions questionnaires must be filed, the intention to make an application should be included in the applicant's directions questionnaire.

This is likely to help the court because it is relevant to allocation and case management (PD 26 at [10] and [11(3)]).

Where an application is made, the court will not normally allocate the claim before hearing the application.

Where a party files a directions questionnaire, stating that she *intends* to make such an application, but has *not* yet done so, the court will usually direct an *allocation hearing* to be listed.

ii. Allocation hearing

An application may be heard at the allocation hearing, if the application notice has been issued, and served, in sufficient time (PD 26 at [11(4)]).

If summary judgment is granted before allocation, the general rule is that the successful party can apply for costs.

Where costs are assessed on the standard basis, following the conclusion of a claim that has not been allocated, costs may be restricted to those that would have been allowed on the track to which the claim would likely have been allocated (CPR 46.13(3)).

iii. Grounds

Two grounds must be satisfied (CPR 24.3).

First, *no real prospect of succeeding* on the claim, defence, or issue. This means that it must carry some *degree of conviction.* In other words, it is not *merely fanciful.* It is more than merely arguable.

The standard is therefore *not* on a balance of probabilities.

Secondly, there is *no other compelling reason* why the case, or issue, should be disposed of at a final hearing.

The burden of proof is on the applicant.

e. Strike out

The jurisdiction is related to summary judgment (PD 3A at [1.5]).

In general, where properly arguable, an application should be made for strike out and / or summary judgment.

The court may treat an application for strike out as one for summary judgment. This is to dispose of issues, claims, or defences, that do not deserve full investigation, and a final hearing (*Three Rivers District Council & Ors v Governor & Company of the Bank of England (No 3)* [2001] UKHL 16, [2003] 2 AC 1 at [88]).

i. When

Any application should be made before, or when filing, the applicant's directions questionnaire (PD 26 at [11(1)]).

If an application is not made before directions questionnaires must be filed, the intention to make an application should be included in the applicant's directions questionnaire.

This is likely to help the court because it is relevant to allocation, and case management (PD 26 at [10] and [11(3)]).

Where an application is made, the court will not normally allocate the claim before hearing the application.

Where a party files a directions questionnaire, stating that she *intends* to make such an application, but has *not* yet done so, the court will usually direct an *allocation hearing* to be listed.

Where a statement of case is not verified by a statement of truth, a party may apply to the court for an order that (*unless* it is verified by the service of a statement of truth, within a certain period) it will *automatically* be struck out (CPR 22.2(3); and PD 3A at [1.6]).

ii. Grounds

The court may strike out (part of) a statement of case if one of the following conditions are satisfied (CPR 3.4(2)).

First, it discloses *no reasonable grounds* for bringing, or defending, the claim. Secondly, it is an *abuse* of the court's process, or otherwise *likely to obstruct the just disposal* of proceedings. Thirdly, there has been a *failure to comply* with a CPR, PD, or court order.

The court has a *separate* power to strike out a statement of case that is not verified by a statement of truth (CPR 22.2(2)).

1. No reasonable grounds

Where a statement of case satisfies one of the following, it discloses no reasonable grounds (PD 3A at [1.2] and [1.4]).

First, it sets out no facts indicating what the claim is about. For example: 'Money owed £5,000'.

Secondly, it is incoherent and makes no sense.

Thirdly, those which contain a coherent set of facts, which, even if true, do not disclose any legally recognisable claim, or defence.

Fourthly, in the case of a defence, it consists of a bare denial.

2. Abuse of process & obstructing just disposal

In *Hunter v Chief Constable of the West Midlands Police & Ors* [1982] AC 529 (HL) at 536, Lord Diplock (with whom Lords Russell, Keith, Roskill and Brandon agreed) defined an "abuse of process" in these terms (with emphasis added):

> "It concerns the inherent power which any court of justice must possess to prevent misuse of its procedure in a way which, although not inconsistent with the literal application of its procedural rules, would nevertheless be *manifestly unfair to a party* to litigation before it, or would otherwise *bring the administration of justice into disrepute* among right-thinking people."

a. Unlawful conduct

Unlawful conduct is not a necessary condition.

In *JSC VTB Bank v Skurikhin & Ors* [2020] EWCA Civ 1337, [2021] 1 WLR 434 at [51], Phillips LJ (with whom Sir Keith Lindblom and Lewison LJ agreed) said (with emphasis added) that:

> "… proceedings can be struck down as an abuse of process where there has been no unlawful conduct, no breach of relevant procedural rules, no collateral attack on a previous decision and no dishonesty or other reprehensible conduct. Indeed, *the power exists precisely to prevent the court's process being abused through the lawful and literal application of the rules*, and most likely would not be needed or engaged where a party was acting unlawfully or in breach of procedural rules, where established rules of law or procedural sanctions would usually suffice to protect the court process. …"

b. Forms

The most common forms of abuse are as follows.

First, a *collateral attack* on a factual issue decided in another court of competent jurisdiction.

Secondly, *res judicata*. That is, where there has already been a *final* decision, on the *same* cause of action, between the *same* parties, in which the issue in dispute in the earlier, decided claim, and the latter, undecided claim, are *identical*.

Thirdly, where a later claim *could*, and *should*, have been made in *previous* proceedings (*Henderson v Henderson* [1843-60] All ER Rep 378 at 381).

Fourthly, where the claim has already been settled, or compromised. For example, through a binding settlement agreement.

c. Fact-sensitive

In *Yearwood v Yearwood (Antigua and Barbuda)* [2020] UKPC 26 at [31], Lady Black reflected on previous authority from the House of Lords: "This makes clear that a broad, merits-based judgment, taking into account all of the circumstances, is involved in determining whether there has been an abuse of the court's process."

3. Default

Material default frequently takes the following forms.

First, failure to verify a statement of case, or a witness statement, with a statement of truth. Secondly, failure to comply with an unless order. Thirdly, where a party, who is unable to read or sign a statement of truth, nevertheless purports to do so.

a. Statement of truth

The consequence of failure to verify a statement of case, or witness statement, are often different.

In *Mark Damian Clarkson v Future Resources FZE & Eight Ors* [2022] EWCA Civ 230 at [47], Simler LJ (with whom Lewison and Snowden LJJ agreed) said that:

> "The signing of a statement of truth is no empty formality. Its importance is emphasised by the potential liability for contempt of court if signed without an honest belief in its truth. …"

It must be dated with the date that it was signed (PD 22 at [2.7]).

i. Statement of case

Two consequences follow failure to verify a statement of case with a statement of truth (CPR 22.2(1)).

First, it remains effective, unless it is struck out. Secondly, a party may *not* rely on it as *evidence* of any of the matters pleaded in it.

ii. Witness statement

The statement of truth in a witness statement *must* be signed by the *witness* (CPR 22.1(6)(b)).

That is, *not* by a legal representative, or anyone else.

The statement of truth must be in the witness' own language (PD 22 at [2.6]).

There will usually be two reasons that witness statements need to be verified with a statement of truth.

First, the *rule* prescribing that witness statements *must* be verified by a statement of truth, the PD prescribing the form that it must be in, and the CPR prescribing the consequences of default.

CPRs 27.2(2) and 22.1(1)(b) prescribe that witness statements must be verified by a statement of truth.

PD 22 at [2.2] prescribes that it should be in the language of the witness statement, and as follows (PD 22 at [2.2]):

> I believe that the facts stated in this witness statement are true. I understand that proceedings for contempt of court may be brought against anyone who makes, or causes to be made, a false statement in a document verified by a statement of truth without an honest belief in its truth.

CPR 22.3 prescribes the consequence of default is that 'the court may direct that it shall not be admissible as evidence'.

Secondly, a *court order* prescribing that witness statements *must* be verified by a statement of truth, the form that it must be in, and the consequence of default.

This is often found in a notice of allocation, directing that:

> Witness statements must:
>
> ...
>
> d) End with this paragraph: 'I believe that the facts stated in this witness statement are true. I understand that proceedings for contempt of court may be brought against anyone who makes, or causes to be made, a false statement in a document verified by a statement of truth without an honest belief in its truth.'
>
> ...

> The court may decide not to take into account a document or the evidence of a witness if these directions have not been complied with.

In practice, whether the CPRs / PDs and / or a court order bites, it is unlikely that there will be any material difference in outcome.

Both provide the court with a *discretion.*

Where a witness statement is not admitted into evidence, it will likely mean that the party who she is giving evidence for has no evidence. If so, that party's case may be struck out.

b. Unless order

Failure to comply with an unless order will mean that the sanction in that order will take effect. The exception is where the party in default applied for, and in fact obtains, relief (CPR 3.8(1)).

An application must be supported by evidence (CPR 3.9(2)).

Take the following example.

The court directs a claimant to fully particularise the allegations in the particulars of claim. This must be done within a certain period of time. The sanction for default is specified in the order: the statement of case will automatically be struck out.

c. Inability to read or sign

A court order and PD usually prescribes what must be done where a person cannot read or sign a document that must be verified by a statement of truth.

i. Court order

The notice of allocation will usually include this direction:

> If a witness is unable to read the statement in the form produced to the court, the statement must include a certificate that it has been read or interpreted to the witness by a suitably qualified person. If a witness who has made a statement is to give evidence or be cross-examined and is unable to do so in spoken English (or Welsh if the hearing is in Wales), the party relying on that witness must ensure that a suitable independent interpreter is available.
>
> The judge may refuse to hear the evidence or consider any statement of any witness whose statement has not been prepared and copied to the other party and the court in accordance with the paragraphs above.

Where the direction for a certificate, or suitable independent interpreter, is applicable, but has *not* been complied with, the judge may *refuse* to take into account any evidence to which it relates.

ii. Practice direction

Where a statement of case or witness statement containing a statement of truth is to be signed by a person who is unable to read or sign it, other than by reason of language alone, there are three requirements (CPR 22.1(9)).

First, it must contain a certificate made by an authorised person. That is, someone who is able to administer oaths, and take affidavits. She need not be independent of the parties or their representatives.

Secondly, the authorised person must certify the following.

The document has been read to the person approving it. That person appeared to understand it, and approved its contents as accurate. The declaration of truth has been read to that person. That person appeared to understand the declaration, and the consequences of making a false declaration. That person signed, or made their mark, in the presence of the authorised person.

The form of the certificate is prescribed (PD 22 at [2.4]):

> I certify that I [name and address of authorised person] have read over the contents of this document and the declaration of truth to the person approving the document [if there are exhibits, add 'and explained the nature and effect of the exhibits referred to in it'] who appeared to understand (a) the document and approved its content as accurate and (b) the declaration of truth and the consequences of making a false declaration, and made their mark in my presence.

Failure to follow these requirements will mean that the document is *not* verified by a *valid* statement of truth.

f. Amendment

After a statement of case has been served, it may *only* be amended, *either* with the written consent of all other parties, *or* with the court's permission (CPR 17.1(2)).

For the latter, a formal application *should* be made, in accordance with CPR 23.6 and PD 23A at [2]. A draft amended statement of case *should* be attached (PD 17 at [1.2(2)]).

In *Shiji Sivaji v Ministry of Defence* [2020] EWHC 2006 (QB) at [29], HHJ Allan Gore QC said that:

> "… It is one thing to permit without a draft a proposed amendment that is self-evident and uncontroversial such as an erroneously pleaded date or reference to the wrong document or even sometimes as to a name. It is quite another thing to amend upon an issue known to be controversial and going to the very core question of whether a liability in law arises."

If permission is given, the applicant should file, and serve, the amended statement of case within 14 days, or such other period as the court directs (PD 17 at [1.3] and [1.5]).

It should be verified with a statement of truth (CPR 22.1(2); and PD 17 at [1.4] and [2.1]).

g. Adjourn

Contact the other side to see whether the parties agree to adjourn.

If the other side is *not* contacted before a formal application is made, which is *not* resisted, the court will be *un*likely to award the cost of it. This is because it will have been *un*necessary.

Absent agreement, a *formal* application must be made.

This will need a *good* reason (PD 27A at [6.2]).

The court may adjourn a hearing (CPR 3.1(2)(b)).

When exercising this power, the court will discharge its duty.

First, to give effect to the overriding objective (CPR 1.2(a)). Secondly, by actively managing cases (CPR 1.4).

i. Overriding objective

The overriding objective includes the following (CPR 1.1(2)).

First, saving expense. Secondly, dealing with the case in a way which is proportionate to the: amount of money involved; importance of the case; and financial position of each party. Thirdly, ensuring that the case is dealt with expeditiously and fairly.

Fourthly, allotting an appropriate share of the court's resources to the case, while taking into account the need to allot resources to other cases.

ii. Court's duty to manage cases

Active case management includes the following (CPR 1.4(2)).

First, deciding which issues need full investigation and a final hearing, and accordingly disposing summarily of others. Secondly, fixing timetables, or otherwise controlling the progress of the case. Thirdly, considering whether the likely benefits of taking a particular step justify the cost of taking it.

Fourthly, dealing with as many aspects of the case as it can on the same occasion. Fifthly, giving directions to ensure that the final hearing proceeds quickly and efficiently.

iii. Health

Success will likely depend on the following.

1. Material difference

Where a witness can*not* attend, but the evidence that she would be able to give would make *no* material difference to the outcome of the case, the court should *refuse* an adjournment.

Where the witness is *key,* her evidence is likely to be *material.*

In a claim where liability is in dispute, and both witness accounts are wholly inconsistent, the court will seek to place the parties on an equal footing. To do so, an adjournment may be granted.

Where a key witness can show *genuine* ill-health, the court will usually grant (at least) a *first* adjournment.

2. Evidence

To establish genuine ill-health, medical evidence may be expected.

Ideally, this will satisfy the following criteria in *General Medical Council v Hayat* [2018] EWCA Civ 2796 at [38].

First, the medical professional should be identified. Secondly, she should give details as to her familiarity with the party's medical condition. This includes detailing recent consultations.

Thirdly, the party's medical condition should be identified, with the features of that condition, which, in the medical professional's opinion, prevent that party attending the final hearing. Fourthly, there should be a reasoned prognosis. That is, likely course of the medical condition.

The court is *not* bound to accept medical evidence.

If it is rejected, however, there should be a *good* reason.

A person without a representative suffering stress is insufficient.

In *Forrester Ketley v Brent & Anor* [2012] EWCA Civ 324 at [25], Lewison LJ (with whom Longmore LJ agreed) said (with emphasis added) that:

> "… Judges are often faced with late applications for adjournment by litigants in person on medical grounds. *An adjournment is not simply there for the asking.* While the court must recognise that litigants in person are not as used to the stresses of appearing in court as professional advocates, nevertheless something more than stress occasioned by the litigation will be needed to support an application for an adjournment. *In cases where the applicant complains of stress-related illness, an adjournment is unlikely to serve any useful purpose* because the stress will simply recur on an adjourned hearing."

3. Accommodation, representation & merits

The court should consider if reasonable accommodation is possible, a representative can deal with the case, and the merits.

In *Michael Decker v Geoffrey William Hopcraft* [2015] EWHC 1170 (QB), Warby J (as he then was) said (with emphasis added) that:

> "27. … the question of whether the litigant can or cannot participate in the hearing effectively does not always have a straightforward yes or no answer. *There may be reasonable accommodations that can be made to enable effective participation.* … But the court needs evidence in order to assess whether this can be done or not and, if it can, how.
>
> 28. … If the issues are straightforward and their merits have already been debated in correspondence, or on previous occasions, or both there may be little more that can usefully be said. If the issues are more complex *but the party concerned is capable,* financially and otherwise, *of instructing legal representatives in his or her place and of giving them adequate instructions* their own ill-health may be of little or no consequence. …
>
> 29. … sometimes, it may appear to the court at the outset or after hearing some at least of the rival arguments that *in truth the matter before it is one on which one or other side is bound to succeed.* The closer the case appears to one or other of these extremes the less likely it is that proceeding will represent an injustice to the litigant. Thus, in *Boyd & Hutchinson (A Firm) v Foenander* [2003] EWCA Civ 1516 the Court of Appeal proceeded with the hearing of an appeal on the basis that it would refuse an adjournment if it concluded, as it did, that the appeal had no real prospect of success. This appears consistent with the conclusions of Neuberger J in *Fox v Graham* that where the court refuses a litigant in person an adjournment it may proceed in his absence if satisfied either (a) that it is right to grant the applicant the relief sought or (b) that the application is plainly hopeless."

4. Directions

Notwithstanding the above, if a party, or other witness, is *needed for the case to be dealt with justly*, but is unable to be present *through no fault of her own*, the court will usually grant an adjournment, however disproportionate that may appear.

The obvious example is where a party has been abruptly admitted to an accident and emergency department of a hospital.

If the court has reservations, it may give directions (CPR 27.7).

For example, that (further) medical evidence is filed and served before a specified time and date.

In default, the issue of costs may be specified, or reserved.

h. In-person / remote hearing

A remote, telephone or audio-visual, hearing may be suitable.

i. Court order

If so, this may be set out in a notice of allocation, or a notice of hearing / trial date.

Usually, it will contain the following direction:

> If any party considers that the hearing cannot proceed by way of [Cloud Video Platform] they must **within 48 hours** of receipt of this Order send to the Court office by email to … and send to the other party a full explanation of why they say that a hearing by [Cloud Video Platform] should not take place. Such written communication will be treated as an application to adjourn the [Cloud Video Platform] hearing and will be placed before the Judge on the papers for decision and any further directions.

If a party considers that a remote hearing would *not* further the overriding objective, they *must* follow the prescribed procedure.

Vulnerability, as set out in a statement of case, or directions questionnaire, may form the foundation of a request.

ii. Rules

There is no *right* to an in-person, or a remote, hearing.

The court *must* seek to further the overriding objective by actively managing cases.

Relevant factors of the *overriding objective* include the following.

First, saving expense. Secondly, dealing with the case in ways that are proportionate to the importance of it. Thirdly, ensuring that it is dealt with expeditiously and fairly. Fourthly, allocating an appropriate share of the court's resources to it, while taking into account the need to allot resources to other cases.

Active case management includes the following considerations.

First, whether the likely benefits of taking a particular step justify the cost. Secondly, dealing with the case without the parties needing to attend court. Thirdly, making use of technology. Fourthly, giving directions to ensure that the final hearing proceeds, both quickly, and efficiently.

i. Set aside

A party may apply for an order that judgment is set aside, and that the claim is reheard, provided the following (CPR 27.11(1)).

First, she was neither present, nor represented, at the hearing. Secondly, she did not give written notice to the court, requesting that the claim be decided in her absence.

The application must be made not more than 14 days after the day on which notice of the judgment was served on her.

It may only be granted if two conditions are met (CPR 27.11(3)).

First, the applicant had a *good* reason for not attending, *being represented* at the hearing, or *giving written notice* to the court. Secondly, she has a *reasonable prospect of success.*

An application can*not* be made where the parties agreed to deal with the claim without a hearing (CPR 27.11(5)).

If the application is successful, the court *must* fix a new date for hearing the claim. This may take place *immediately*. It may also be dealt with by the judge who set aside judgment (CPR 27.11(4)).

j. Relief from sanctions

Where there has been a failure to comply with a CPR, PD, or court order, any sanction has effect. That is, unless the defaulting party applies for, and in fact obtains, relief (CPR 3.8(1)).

Unless the court orders otherwise, however, the deadline for complying with a CPR, PD or court order, may be extended by *prior written agreement* of the parties, up to a *maximum of 28 days,* unless it would put a hearing date at risk (CPR 3.8(4)).

i. Need

Before making a formal application, check whether the CPR, PD, or court order, *specifies* a sanction.

If not, and there is *no* automatic sanction, then, there is *no* need to apply for relief. This is because no sanction will have taken effect.

Sometimes, a notice of hearing makes, what *appear* to be, formal directions. For example: 'You must submit a request to adjourn in writing, by post or email to enquiries.bournemouth.countycourt@justice.gov.uk.' If this is *not* followed, a court "order" has *not* been breached because this is merely a *notice* of hearing.

In practice, an *order* will recite the name of the judge who made it, and include the word "Order" in the top, left-hand corner. Whereas a *notice* will not recite the name of a judge, and will include the word "Notice" in the top, left-hand corner.

1. Discretion

The notice of allocation usually includes a direction that the judge 'may refuse to hear' evidence that has not been prepared, filed and served, in accordance with it.

There is a material difference between *may* refuse to hear, and, for example, breach of an unless *order.*

The former provides the court with a *discretion* as to whether or not to *impose* a sanction. An unless *order,* however, *specifies a sanction.* For example, 'shall stand automatically struck out'.

The latter therefore requires an application for relief from a sanction *that has taken effect.* This is an important distinction.

2. Court order

Often, an application for relief is in respect of an unless order.

In credit hire claims, for example, the following direction is usually made in a notice of allocation (with emphasis added):

> Because the claim includes a claim for hire of a replacement vehicle:

a) the Claimant shall be *debarred* from relying upon the fact of impecuniosity for the purposes of determining the appropriate rate of hire *unless* the documents to be served by the Claimant includes the following documents which are in his control:

   i) copies of the Claimant's wage slips or equivalent documentation evidencing the approximate level of available income to the Claimant for the period of three months pre-accident and covering the period of hire; and

   ii) copy bank and credit card statements for a period of three months pre-accident and covering the period of hire.

This *unless order* requires the claimant to serve the relevant documents that are in her control. The *specified sanction* in default is that she is *debarred* from relying on a plea of impecuniosity.

The following recital may also be included in a notice of allocation:

> **Warning: You must comply with the terms imposed upon you by this order; otherwise your case is liable to be struck out or some other sanction imposed. If you cannot comply you are expected to make formal application to the Court before any deadline imposed upon you.**

Absent a formal application, the following may be submitted.

First, the notice of allocation recites that a written application is *expected* to be filed, and served. Secondly, it must be issued *before* the relevant deadline.

Both aspects in the recital have been breached.

The notice of allocation will also include the following direction:

> Because this Order has been made without a hearing, the parties have the right to apply to have the Order set aside, varied or stayed.

> A party making such an application must send or deliver the application to the court (together with any appropriate fee) to arrive within seven days of service of this Order.

If the application for relief is in respect of an unless order in the notice of allocation, the following submissions may be made.

First, if unable to comply, the court order directed that a *written* application to set aside, vary, or stay, the unless order, *must* be made, and the appropriate *fee* paid. Secondly, the application had to be made within *seven days* of service of the order.

Both recital and direction in the court order have been breached.

Absent a *good* reason, a claimant who has failed to make a formal application before the relevant deadline is in difficulty.

ii. Evidence

Applications *should* follow the procedure in CPR 23 (CPR 3.9(1)).

They *must* be supported by evidence (CPR 3.9(2)).

Often, by a witness statement, signed by a legal representative.

In *Margaret Nelson & Two Ors v Circle Thirty Three Housing Trust Ltd* [2014] EWCA Civ 106, [2014] 3 Costs LO 355 at [18], Sir Robin Jacob (with whom McFarlane LJ (as he then was) and Rimer LJ agreed) confirmed that, even if the party in default does not make an application, "the court can of its own motion consider whether there should be such relief".

Sir Robin Jacob clarified at [20], however, that there were:

> "... very special circumstances here: first of all, very, very substantial compliance with the disclosure order; and secondly the evidence which we now have that although it was late, the first defendant did make proper efforts to get the necessary documents

> and that it was not her fault that she did not get them, but the bank's. Further, she now has them and they have been served on the other side some time ago."

Sir Robin Jacob cited the earlier case of *Marcan Shipping (London Ltd) v George Kefalas & Anor* [2007] EWCA Civ 463, [2007] 1 WLR 1864 ("*Marcan Shipping*"), in which Moore-Bick LJ (with whom Pill and Keene LJJ agreed) gave the leading judgment.

Marcan Shipping, in turn, considered the earlier authority of *Keen Phillips v Field* [2006] EWCA Civ 1524, [2007] 1 WLR 686.

At paragraph 33 of *Marcan Shipping*, Moore-Bick LJ said (with emphasis added):

> "*Keen Phillips v Field* was a *very unusual* case. The only question for decision was whether the court had jurisdiction to grant relief from sanctions under rule 3.8 in the absence of an application by the party in default. This court held that despite the wording of rule 3.8, which naturally assumes that the party in default will make an application for relief, the court has jurisdiction to act of its own initiative in an appropriate case. However, *the jurisdiction is one which is likely to be exercised only rarely because it will usually be necessary for evidence to be placed before the court to enable it to consider the various matters to which rule 3.9 refers.* In that case, however, there was no dispute relating to the manner in which the judge had exercised his discretion, and rightly so, because it was accepted that the claimant's failure to comply with the order had resulted from matters wholly outside its control, had caused no prejudice of any kind to the defendant and had had no adverse effect on the course of the proceedings."

Absent an application, "very special" or "very unusual" circumstances are needed before the court will "only rarely" grant relief.

The following circumstances have been held to qualify.

First, "very, very substantial compliance".

Secondly, "proper efforts to get the necessary documents and that it was not her fault that she did not get them ... and they have been served on the other side some time ago".

Thirdly, that there is "no dispute [that relief should be granted] because it was accepted that [a party's] failure to comply ... resulted from matters wholly outside its control, had caused no prejudice of any kind to the [other party] and had had no adverse effect on the course of the proceedings."

iii. Three-stage test

The court will apply the following test when deciding whether or not to grant relief from sanctions (*Denton & Ors v TH White Ltd & Ors* [2014] EWCA Civ 906, [2014] 1 WLR 3926 ("*Denton*") at [24]):

> "... The first stage is to identify and assess the seriousness and significance of the 'failure to comply with any rule, practice direction or court order' which engages rule 3.9(1). If the breach is neither serious nor significant, the court is unlikely to need to spend much time on the second and third stages. The second stage is to consider why the default occurred. The third stage is to evaluate 'all the circumstances of the case, so as to enable [the court] to deal justly with the application including [the factors in CPR 3.9(1)]'. ..."

1. Seriousness & significance

Previous breaches are irrelevant ("*Denton*" at [27]):

> "The assessment of the seriousness or significance of the breach should not, initially at least, involve a consideration of other unrelated failures that may have occurred in the past. At the first stage, the court should concentrate on an assessment of the seriousness and significance of the very breach in respect of which relief from sanctions is sought. ..."

If *neither* serious, *nor* significant, the court *should* grant relief.

2. Good reason

The question is not whether there is *a* reason.

It is whether there is a *good* reason.

Authority provides that "good reasons are likely to arise from circumstances outside the control of the party in default" (*Andrew Mitchell MP v News Group Newspapers Ltd* [2013] EWCA Civ 1537, [2014] 1 WLR 795 ("*Mitchell*") at [43]; and *Denton* at [30]).

A legal representative's failure will rarely amount to a good reason (*Mitchell* at [41]; and *Denton* at [12]):

> "… Solicitors cannot take on too much work and expect to be able to persuade a court that this is a good reason for their failure to meet deadlines. They should either delegate the work to others in their firm or, if they are unable to do this, they should not take on the work at all. …"

One of the following is usually necessary, but *not* sufficient.

First, failure to consult. Secondly, lack of authority.

The leading authority is Peter Gibson LJ in *Training in Compliance Ltd (t/a Matthew Reed) v Dewse (T/A Data Research Co)* [2001] CP Rep 46 (CA) ("*Training*") at [66] (with emphasis added):

> "… It seems to me that, in general, *the action or inaction of a party's legal representatives must be treated under the Civil Procedure Rules as the action or inaction of the party himself.* So far as the other party is concerned, it matters not what input that party himself has made into what the legal representatives have done or have not done. The other party is affected in the same way; and dealing with a case justly involves dealing with the other party justly. It would not in general be desirable that the time of the court should be taken up in considering separately the conduct of the legal representatives

> from that which the party himself must be treated as knowing, encouraging, or permitting. …"

Training was quoted in *Mullock v Price T/ A The Elms Hotel Restaurant* [2009] EWCA Civ 1222, [2010] CP Rep 10 ("*Mullock*") at [22].

In *Mullock,* Ward LJ (with whom Sedley and Smith LJJ agreed) said that: "I respectfully agree. It seems to me wrong that a party should shield behind his representatives."

Mullock concerned an application pursuant to CPR 13.3. That is, whether default judgment should (as opposed to must) be set aside. As that application is an application for relief, however, *Mullock* is also relevant authority for CPR 3.9.

Ward LJ continued in *Mullock* (with emphasis added):

> "23. I say that it is wrong essentially for two reasons. *First, the language* of CPR 13.3 is explicit: it requires 'the person seeking to set aside the judgment' to make the application promptly. So it *focuses on that person's action. Secondly, the Civil Procedure Rule in fact impose duties on the parties to the litigation, and it seems to me that must mean the parties themselves irrespective of the help and advice they are or are not receiving.* Their duty under CPR 1.3 is this:
>
> > 'The parties are required to help the court to further the overriding objective.'
>
> One of those objectives is of course to ensure that the case is dealt with expeditiously, and *I am therefore quite satisfied that it was* the duty of Mr Price, *a personal duty,* to ensure that the case was dealt with expeditiously and in the particular circumstances of this case to act promptly to set aside any judgment entered in default of his having put in his appearance."

Training was also recently quoted in *Gladwin v Bogescu* [2017] EWHC 1287 (QB), [2017] 4 Costs LO 437 at [30]. In the next paragraph, Turner J said (with emphasis added) that:

> "... since the introduction of the Jackson reforms, *the general approach of the courts is likely to be less rather than more indulgent of legal advisors* as a justification for granting forbearance to the litigants themselves. ..."

Training was followed by Julian Knowles J in *Deutsche Leasing (UK) Ltd v Zaskin College Ltd* [2018] EWHC 1977 (QB) at [73].

3. All the circumstances

An application following a serious, or significant, breach, for which there is no good reason, is *not* doomed to fail.

Where submissions on the first two stages are not properly arguable, on instructions, concede them.

You will gain credibility with the court.

You will also be able to invest more time in the third stage.

This is virtually always properly arguable.

The court will have regard to *all* the circumstances of the case.

The factors in CPR 3.9(1), however, are "of particular importance and should be given particular weight" (*Denton* at [35]).

First, that litigation is conducted efficiently, and at proportionate cost. Secondly, to enforce compliance with CPRs, PDs, and court orders.

Evidence in support of an application may *not* address these factors. If so, emphasise the *particular importance,* and *particular weight,* that *must* be placed on them, yet there is *no* evidence on these factors in support of the application for relief.

a. Proportionality

Is the sanction proportionate to the breach?

Take the following example.

The sanction means that the defendant has no evidence. The claim is for £10,000. The defence is fully particularised, and properly arguable. The sanction effectively extinguishes the defence.

On these facts, proportionality may weigh in favour of relief.

b. Compliance

This is where previous breaches are added to the scales.

Multiple breaches can be an *especially* weighty circumstance.

The court "must always bear in mind the need for compliance … because the old lax culture of non-compliance is no longer tolerated" (*Denton* at [34]).

c. Promptness

This may be *critical.*

If an application for relief is prompt, the other party may be under an obligation to consent to it, so as to discourage opportunism.

On the other hand, in *Oak Cash & Carry Ltd v British Gas Trading Ltd* [2016] EWCA Civ 153, [2016] 4 All ER 129 at [61], Jackson LJ (with whom King and Lindblom LJJ agreed) said (with emphasis added) that:

> "In my view the defendant's lack of promptness in applying for relief is *the critical factor.* When that delay is added to all the other factors, it can be seen that the defendant's default has *substantially disrupted the progress of the action.* Bearing in mind factors (a) and (b) in rule 3.9 (which under *Denton* must be given particular

weight) *there is really only one answer to the question which arises at stage 3. The court must refuse the application for relief.*"

d. Opportunism

Resisting an application that must succeed breaches the duty to help the court to further the overriding objective (*Denton* at [43]):

> "… It is as unacceptable for a party to try to take advantage of a minor inadvertent error, as it is for rules, orders and practice directions to be breached in the first place. Heavy costs sanctions should, therefore, be imposed on parties who behave unreasonably in refusing to agree extensions of time or unreasonably oppose applications for relief from sanctions. …"

Unreasonable opposition should form the basis of a submission that the *manner* in which that party has conducted her case demonstrates that she has behaved unreasonably. Accordingly, she should pay the consequential costs.

k. Error of procedure

Where there has been an error of procedure, CPR 3.10 *may* assist.

It is titled: 'General power of the court to rectify matters where there has been an error of procedure'.

Where there has been an error of procedure, such as a failure to comply with a rule, or practice direction, it prescribes two powers.

First, that the error does *not* invalidate any step taken in the proceedings, *unless* the court so orders. Secondly, the court *may* make an order to *remedy* the error.

Errors relating to *service* of proceedings can*not* be rectified.

The rule enables the court to take one of three courses of action.

First, *in*validate the step which was taken in error. Secondly, *correct* the error by way of an order. Thirdly, *waive* the error, by declaring it valid, because it has *caused no prejudice.*

If the error justifies strike out, the first course of action is likely. The second is likely where the error *has* caused prejudice, but it can be rectified by directions. If the error has *not* caused any prejudice, the third course of action is likely.

In *Integral Petroleum SA v SCU-Finanz AG* [2014] EWHC 702 (Comm) at [37], Popplewell J (as he then was) said that: "CPR 3.10 … prevents a triumph of form over substance."

This rule and authority can be used to persuade the court to simply waive a procedural error, because it has caused no prejudice, and the court does not allow technicalities to cause injustice.

Alternatively, the procedural error can be rectified by a direction.

18. Final hearing

This chapter covers the procedure of the final hearing.

First, the judge. Secondly, representation. Thirdly, the general rule that hearings are recorded, and in public. Fourthly, evidence is not usually on oath. Fifthly, cross-examination may be limited. Sixthly, the line between judicial intervention, and "entering the arena".

a. Judge

Generally, judicial functions are carried out by a district judge.

They may be carried out by a circuit judge (PD 27A at [1]). This requires her consent (PD 2B at [11.2(1)]). In practice, this is rare.

b. Representation

A lay, or professional, representative, may represent a party.

i. Lay

A party may be represented by a lay representative, provided that that party is present throughout the hearing (PD 27A at [3.2](2)).

On the basis of article 3 of the Lay Representatives (Right of Audience) Order 1999 (SI 1999/1225), the court's permission is required where a party wishes to be represented by a lay representative in three circumstances (PD 27A at [3.2(2) and (3)]).

First, her client does not attend the hearing. Secondly, at any stage after judgment. Thirdly, on any appeal brought against any decision made by a district judge.

ii. Corporate

Officers, or employees, may represent companies (PD 27A at [3.2(4)]).

iii. Unruly manner

Section 11 of the Courts and Legal Services Act 1990 prescribes that, where the court is of the opinion that a person, who would otherwise have a right of audience, is behaving in an *unruly manner* in any proceedings, the court may refuse to hear her.

If so, the court must specify the conduct that warranted refusal.

iv. Intentionally misled the court

Where the court has reason to believe that a person has *intentionally misled the court,* or otherwise demonstrates that she is *unsuitable to exercise a right of audience,* in the instant, or any other, proceedings, the court may order that person's *disqualification* from exercising any right of audience. Reasons must be given.

Appeal lies to the Court of Appeal. Any such order may be revoked, however, at any time, by any county court judge.

c. Public

In general, cases *must* be heard in public.

If there is any doubt as to whether or not it is a well-established, *common law* right, it is certainly a well-established, *statutory* right.

This follows from article 6 of the European Convention on Human Rights. A court is a public authority. It must act compatibly with Convention rights pursuant to section 6 of the Human Rights Act 1998.

d. Recording

Recording may be official, or unofficial.

i. Official

Hearings *will* be tape recorded (PD 27A at [5.1]).

A party may obtain a transcript by paying a fee to the transcriber.

In any event, "there is generally no right for either a party or a non-party to listen to the recording" (*Cape Intermediate Holdings Ltd v Dring* [2019] UKSC 38, [2020] AC 629 at [25]).

ii. Unofficial

Attention is drawn to section 9 of the Contempt of Court Act 1981, and *Practice Direction (Tape Recorders)* [1981] 1 WLR 1526, which relate to unofficial recordings (PD 27A at [5.2]).

1. Contempt of Court Act 1981

Section 9(1) of this Act provides that:

> ... it is a contempt of court—
>
> (a) to use in court, or bring into court for use, any tape recorder or other instrument for recording sound, except with the leave of the court;
>
> (b) to publish a recording of legal proceedings made by means of any such instrument, or any recording derived directly or indirectly from it, by playing it in the hearing of the public or any section of the public, or to dispose of it or any recording so derived, with a view to such publication;

(c) to use any such recording in contravention of any conditions of leave granted under paragraph (a).

2. Practice Direction (Tape Recorders) [1981] 1 WLR 1526

The PD provides guidance as to the *discretion* of the court to grant, withhold, or withdraw, leave to use tape recorders, or to impose *conditions* as to the use of the recording.

The discretion is unlimited.

The following three factors *may* be relevant.

First, any reasonable *need* for the recording. Whether a litigant, a person connected with the press, or broadcasting.

Secondly, the risk that the recording would be used *to brief witnesses* out of court, where a direction has been made to exclude one or more witnesses from court.

Thirdly, the possibility that proceedings will be *disturbed*, participants would be *distracted*, or otherwise *worried*.

Consideration should be given to whether or not *conditions* should be imposed. The *identity* of the person applying to use a tape recorder, and her role in the proceedings, may be relevant.

Tape recorders are *not* intended to replace official transcripts.

3. Consequences

The consequences can be serious, regardless of status.

a. Party or witness

In *Attorney General v Scarth* [2013] EWHC 194 (Admin), an 87-year-old man was sentenced to 28 days' imprisonment for each contempt of court, suspended for 12 months. In particular, making video or audio recordings, and publishing them on the internet.

b. Legal representative

In *Gubarev & Anor v Orbis Business Intelligence Ltd & Anor* [2020] EWHC 2167 (QB), [2020] 4 WLR 122, a trial was streamed outside the jurisdiction for three days without the court's permission.

The President of the Queen's Bench Division said that:

> "During this pandemic, there have been temporary changes ... Nonetheless, whether a court hearing is a remote hearing ... or a conventional face to face hearing, it must be conducted in a way that is as close as possible to the pre-pandemic norm."

Breach of express prohibitions in court orders, or prohibitions on broadcasting, "will be treated with the utmost seriousness." It may result in the papers being sent to the regulator (SRA / BSB), or the Attorney General, with a view to considering whether proceedings should be brought for contempt of court.

e. Evidence

The court need *not* take evidence on oath (CPR 27.8(4)).

i. In person

In practice, evidence is not on oath.

One reason is that cases involving a disputed allegation of dishonesty will not usually be suitable for, and therefore allocated to, the small claims track (PD 26 at [15(4)]).

ii. Remote

It is more common in remote, telephone and audio-visual, hearings, that a witness is required to give evidence on oath.

This may reflect the difficulty in maintaining the integrity of proceedings when a witness is giving evidence. As the President of the Queen's Bench Division said in *Orbis* (see above) at [51]:

> "In normal circumstances a judge can see and hear everything that is going on in court. … The judge can see whether someone is attempting to influence, coach or intimidate a witness whilst they are giving evidence. … That a judge can see and hear everything that happens in court enables the judge to maintain order, discipline and control over what is done in court, and thus to maintain the dignity and the integrity of the proceedings as a whole. …"

f. Examination-in-chief

When calling a witness to give evidence, ensure that they have an *unmarked* copy of any witness bundle, or *at least* their witness statement, in front of them.

Other documents, or notes, should *not* be in front of them.

It is usual to ask questions to the following effect.

First, their full name.

Secondly, their address (if they are giving evidence in a personal capacity), or their professional address (if they are giving evidence as an employee of a company). This is usually obvious from the first page of their witness statement.

Thirdly, whether they wish to amend anything in their statement.

Fourthly, (after any amendment(s)) whether everything in their statement is true and accurate.

Fifthly, whose signature is next to the statement of truth.

Open (as opposed to closed) questions should be asked. In other words, the question should not suggest the answer.

If you wish to ask any additional questions, it is good practice to relay the questions, and why you wish to ask them, to any other legal representative. The court will usually grant permission to ask an additional question or two if any other legal representatives do not object, or the questions self-evidently assist the court.

For example: "Who made the sketch plan attached to your witness statement." Followed by: "When?"

g. Cross-examination

Powers of case-management are set out before general advice.

i. Powers of case-management

The court may adopt *any* fair method of proceeding (CPR 27.8(1)).

This includes the following (PD 27A at [4.3]).

First, to ask questions of any witness before allowing any other person to do so. Secondly, to ask questions of all, or any of, the witnesses before allowing another to do so.

Thirdly, to refuse to allow cross-examination of any witness, until every witness has given evidence in chief. Fourthly, to limit cross-examination of a witness to a fixed time frame, subject or issue.

This does *not* allow the court to prevent *any* cross-examination.

In *Al Rawi & Ors v The Security Service & Ors* [2011] UKSC 34, [2012] 1 AC 531, Lord Dyson said that:

> "[10] There are certain features of a common law trial which are fundamental to our system of justice …
>
> [11] The open justice principle is not a mere procedural rule. It is a fundamental common law principle. …
>
> [13] Another aspect of the principle of natural justice is that the parties should be given the opportunity to call their own witnesses and to cross-examine the opposing witnesses. …"

In the unlikely event that the case is adjourned for lunch, or adjourned part-heard to another day, and cross-examination of a party has started but not finished, the legal representative for that party should not discuss that party's evidence with them.

In practice, the court is often content to sit into the luncheon adjournment, or after 4pm, so as to conclude a party's evidence.

If this is not possible, however, you can submit in open court that you will not discuss that party's evidence with them before they have finished giving evidence. The court will then often permit them to finish giving evidence before any adjournment.

ii. Putting your case

In *Griffiths v TUI (UK) Ltd* [2023] UKSC 48, [2023] 3 WLR 1204 at [70], Lord Hodge (with whom all other members of the Supreme Court hearing the appeal agreed) said (with emphasis added) that:

> "i) *The general rule in civil cases … is that a party is required to challenge by cross-examination the evidence of any witness of the opposing party on a material point which he or she wishes to submit to the court should not be accepted.* That rule extends to both witnesses as to fact and expert witnesses.
>
> …

vi) Cross-examination gives the witness the opportunity to explain or clarify his or her evidence. That opportunity is particularly important when the opposing party intends to accuse the witness of dishonesty, but there is no principled basis for confining the rule to cases of dishonesty.

vii) The rule should not be applied rigidly. It is not an inflexible rule and there is bound to be some relaxation of the rule … *Its application depends upon the circumstances of the case as the criterion is the overall fairness of the trial.* Thus, where it would be disproportionate to cross-examine at length or where … the trial judge has set a limit on the time for cross-examination, those circumstances would be relevant considerations in the court's decision on the application of the rule. …"

iii. General advice

There are ten general pieces of advice for cross-examination.

First, put *your best point / inconsistency first.* Otherwise, the witness may have built up credibility before you put it, thereby undermining the force of it.

Secondly, put your propositions as you go, and *put your case last.* Otherwise, the witness knows where you are going, will try and head you off, and the impact of putting your case will decrease.

Thirdly, do *not* ask a question unless you know why you are asking it, *and what you will do with the answer,* whatever it may be.

Fourthly, *the order is as important as the content* of the questions.

Fifthly, elicit supportive, *and* challenge unsupportive, evidence.

Sixthly, *use funnelling* by asking questions that get narrower, and narrower, until there is nowhere for the witness to go.

Seventhly, *block off all but one of the escape holes from the rabbit warren,* so that the witness must use the best hole for your case.

Eighthly, once you have got what you want, *move on.*

Ninthly, by asking a witness an open question, rather than hang themself, *they may hang you.*

Tenthly, *don't* ask a witness how someone else thinks / feels.

h. Re-examination

Don't. Unless, you know *why,* it can really *help,* and you are *quick.*

In any event, there are two rules.

First, it must be limited to issues that were *raised during cross-examination.* Secondly, the questions must be open (as opposed to closed), so that you do *not* lead your own witness.

i. Judicial intervention v entering the arena

There is a distinction between *judicial intervention*, which is sanctioned by the CPR, and "entering the arena", which is not.

Authority provides guidance as to when a party has a legitimate grievance, that the overriding objective has not been achieved, because the parties were not on an equal footing.

i. Judicial intervention

When contrasted to claims that have been allocated to another track, the procedure can appear much more *inquisitorial.* That is, as opposed to *adversarial.*

Judges should be cautious, however, not to enter the arena.

Especially when *both* parties have legal representation.

ii. Entering the arena

Serafin v Malkiewicz & Ors [2020] UKSC 23, [2020] 1 WLR 2455 is the leading authority on entering the arena, bias and unfairness.

1. Bias

There is a distinction between *bias,* and *unfairness.*

At paragraphs 38 and 39, Lord Wilson (with whom Lords Reed, Briggs, Kitchin and Lady Arden agreed) *assumed,* but did not decide, that bias means "a prejudice against one party or its case for reasons unconnected with the legal or factual merits of the case."

2. Unfairness

At paragraph 40, Lord Wilson said that the "leading authority on inquiry into the unfairness of a trial remains" *Jones v National Coal Board* [1957] 2 QB 55 (CA) at 65, in which Denning LJ (as he then was) said (with emphasis added) that:

> "… *interventions should be as infrequent as possible* when the witness is under cross-examination. It is only by cross-examination that a witness's evidence can be properly tested, and *it loses much of its effectiveness* in counsel's hands if the witness is given time to think out the answer to awkward questions; *the very gist of cross-examination lies in the unbroken sequence of question and answer.* Further than this, cross-examining counsel is at a *grave disadvantage* if he is prevented from following a preconceived line of inquiry which is, in his view, most likely to elicit admissions from the witness or qualifications of the evidence which he has given in chief. *Excessive judicial interruption inevitably weakens the effectiveness of cross-examination* in relation to both aspects that we have mentioned, for

> at one and the same time it gives a witness valuable time for thought before answering a difficult question, and diverts cross-examining counsel from the course which he had intended to pursue, and to which it is by no means easy sometimes to return."

3. Persons without a representative

At paragraph 46, Lord Wilson said that:

> "... Every judge will have experienced difficulty at trial in divining the line between helping the litigant in person to the extent necessary for the adequate articulation of his case, on the one hand, and becoming his advocate, on the other. ... Training and experience will generally have equipped the professional advocate to withstand a degree of judicial pressure and, undaunted, to continue within reason to put the case. The judge must not forget that the litigant in person is likely to have no such equipment and that, if the trial is to be fair, he must temper his conduct accordingly."

At paragraph 48, Lord Wilson concluded as follows:

> "... when one considers the barrage of hostility towards the claimant's case, and towards the claimant himself acting in person, fired by the judge in immoderate, ill-tempered and at times offensive language at many different points during the long hearing, one is driven, with profound regret, to [the] conclusion that he did not allow the claim to be properly presented; that therefore he could not fairly appraise it; and, that, in short, the trial was unfair. Instead of making allowance for the claimant's appearance in person, the judge harassed and intimidated him in ways which surely would never have occurred if the claimant had been represented."

For these reasons, a full retrial was ordered.

4. Practical guidance

The following should suffice.

First, keep your cool. If there is a sense on the transcript of proceedings that you are discourteous, argumentative, or otherwise dramatising, it will make any appeal more difficult.

Secondly, do *not* make an application for recusal, unless the unfairness is *absolutely* clear.

Thirdly, if it is clear, do *not* wait till the end of the hearing. Make the application promptly.

Fourthly, if you know of the reason for the *real*, or *potential* partiality, you may be held to have *waived* any right to raise it if you do not say something early on.

For example, in *Locabail (UK) Ltd v Bayfield Properties Ltd & Anor* [2000] QB 451 (CA) at [25], personal friendship, or animosity, between the judge and any member of the public involved in the case constitute "a real danger of bias".

Fifthly, if you identify any obvious unfairness, find a courteous, professional way to convey your concern.

Sixthly, your professional, ethical duty, requires you to put your client's interest first. Not your career. You protect the latter through keeping *calm*, strict adherence to professional *ethics*, and reasoned *judgement.*

Seventhly, speak to other members of chambers, who may know the judge. Seek *their* counsel.

19. Witness evidence

This includes witness statements and oral evidence.

It is usually an essential ingredient of a party's case.

To the extent that the evidence of a witness *chimes* with *agreed* or *known* facts, a judge is likely to follow it when giving judgment.

Where it is *in*compatible, however, the credibility of that witness will *diminish.* The ability to give evidence assisting the party who called her will, therefore, also *diminish.*

a. Contemporaneous

After a road traffic collision, a witness may complete a *questionnaire.* Often, on the same day, or shortly thereafter.

This will likely state the location, registration number of the relevant vehicles, and mechanism of collision.

There may also be a *sketch plan* indicating the following.

First, the lane that a vehicle was in. Secondly, whether the claimant's vehicle was in front of, or behind, the defendant's vehicle. Thirdly, the part of the respective vehicles where the impact occurred. Fourthly, who was at fault. Fifthly, the reason why.

i. Weight

Is it signed and dated?

Is it contemporaneous to the collision?

If so, it is likely to pre-date a witness statement by many days, months, or even *years*. If it is consistent with a witness' statement or oral evidence, this can be particularly persuasive.

Weight usually increases where the author of the questionnaire is not a party, but an *independent* witness. She would therefore not have known either party.

ii. Cross-examination

Where *in*consistent with a witness statement, or oral evidence, it is likely to be *good evidence* on which to cross-examine.

A concession in cross-examination, that there is no good reason why a witness has changed her account, can undermine that witness as a reliable historian of events. The later account may be in the form of a witness statement, or answers in cross-examination.

In *Onassis v Vergottis* [1968] 2 Lloyd's Rep 403 (HL) at 431, Lord Pearce famously said that: "With every day that passes memory becomes fainter and the imagination becomes more active".

iii. Filed & served

Has it been filed, and served?

If in doubt, speak to your professional client. If it has not been filed, and served, in accordance with the directions for the final hearing, the judge may refuse to admit it.

If you provide copies to the court and any other party, they may agree to it being admitted into evidence.

Where the court or another party does not agree, however, an oral application can be made to the judge, requesting permission, where it is in accordance with the overriding objective.

b. Statements

A "witness statement" is a written statement of a witness. It has a signed statement of truth by that witness. It contains the evidence that that witness would be allowed to give orally.

At a final hearing, where a witness is called to give oral evidence, her witness statement will usually stand as her evidence in chief.

The witness will usually be cross-examined.

Answers in examination-in-chief, cross-examination, and any re-examination, constitute a witness' oral evidence.

Written statement and oral evidence is the "evidence" of a witness.

i. Formalities

The CPR prescribing the form of witness statements is expressly disapplied (CPRs 27.2(1)(c) and 32.8).

They should, however, aspire to follow the same formalities.

ii. Form

The notice of allocation often prescribes form.

First, start with the name of the case and claim number. Secondly, state the full name and address of the witness. Thirdly, set out the witness' evidence clearly in numbered paragraphs, on numbered pages. Fourthly, end with a statement of truth. Fifthly, be signed by the witness, and dated.

Additionally, it should have a header with the name of the court that the proceedings will be heard in, be in a legible font, and the text should be sized so that it can be read easily.

iii. Statement of truth

Witness statements *must* be verified by a statement of truth.

The statement of truth in a witness statement *must* be signed by the maker of that statement (CPR 22.1(6)(b)). That is, *not* by a legal representative, or anyone else.

The statement of truth *must* be in the witness' own language (PD 22 at [2.6]).

There will usually be two reasons that witness statements need to be verified with a statement of truth.

First, the *rule* prescribing that witness statements *must* be verified by a statement of truth, the PD prescribing the *form* that it must be in, and the CPR prescribing the *consequences* of default.

CPRs 27.2(2) and 22.1(1)(b) prescribe that witness statements *must* be verified by a statement of truth.

PD 22 at [2.2] prescribes that it should be in the language of the witness statement, and as follows (PD 22 at [2.2]):

> I believe that the facts stated in this witness statement are true. I understand that proceedings for contempt of court may be brought against anyone who makes, or causes to be made, a false statement in a document verified by a statement of truth without an honest belief in its truth.

CPR 22.3 prescribes the consequence of default is that 'the court may direct that it shall not be admissible as evidence'.

Secondly, a *court order* prescribing that witness statements *must* be verified by a statement of truth, the *form* that it must be in, and the *consequences* of default.

This is the notice of allocation, often including a direction that:

> Witness statements must:
>
> ...
>
> d) End with this paragraph: 'I believe that the facts stated in this witness statement are true. I understand that proceedings for contempt of court may be brought against anyone who makes, or causes to be made, a false statement in a document verified by a statement of truth without an honest belief in its truth.'
>
> ...
>
> The court may decide not to take into account a document or the evidence of a witness if these directions have not been complied with.

iv. Inability to read or sign

Where a statement of case or witness statement containing a statement of truth is to be signed by a person who is *un*able to read or sign it, *other than by reason of language alone,* there are three requirements (CPR 22.1(9)).

First, it *must* contain a *certificate* made by an *authorised person.*

That is, someone who is able to administer oaths, and take affidavits. She need *not* be independent of the parties, or their representatives.

Secondly, the authorised person *must* certify the following.

The document has been read to the person approving it. That person appeared to understand it, and approved its contents as accurate. The declaration of truth has been read to that person. That person appeared to understand the declaration, and the consequences of making a false declaration. That person signed, or made their mark, in the presence of the authorised person.

The form of the certificate is prescribed (PD 22 at [2.4]):

> I certify that I [name and address of authorised person] have read over the contents of this document and the declaration of truth to the person approving the document [if there are exhibits, add 'and explained the nature and effect of the exhibits referred to in it'] who appeared to understand (a) the document and approved its content as accurate and (b) the declaration of truth and the consequences of making a false declaration, and made their mark in my presence

Failure to follow these requirements will mean that the document is not verified by a statement of truth.

v. Contemporaneous

When was the statement dated?

In the context of a road traffic collision, for example, it may have been signed months, or, in many cases, *years* after the collision.

Drawing the court's attention to how *long* after the collision can *reduce* the *weight* that the court places on it.

The number of days between the date of the collision, and the date that the statement was signed, can be precisely calculated. Where the number is high, a submission may be made that little weight should be attached to the statement.

Alternatively, the statement may be dated *shortly* after the collision. In oral evidence, the witness may contradict a key fact that is confirmed to be true within her statement. If so, her recollection is likely to have been *greater* when her statement was signed, compared to the *later* date that oral evidence is given.

Where *later,* oral evidence, is inconsistent with *earlier,* written evidence, the *latter* will likely be given more weight.

vi. Detail

Witness statements should be *detailed.*

For example, in a claim for repairs and credit hire following a road traffic collision, a few paragraphs in the claimant's statement are unlikely to convey the necessary detail.

During cross-examination, at least one "important" detail will often emerge that has been omitted from a witness statement. This is one purpose of cross-examination. To elicit evidence that *assists* one party's case, and *undermines* that of another.

Quality, but also *quantity,* is important.

If a *single* important fact has been omitted, it may *severely* undermine a witness' credibility. Where *several,* less important, facts, are left out of a statement, however, this may be *understandable.* It is therefore less likely to substantially undermine credibility.

In a road traffic collision, the location, and the mechanism of the collision, should both be set out. Clearly. In detail.

In a claim for credit hire, the need to hire should be set out in reasonable detail. 'Social, domestic and pleasure' is insufficient. This is legal jargon. People do not usually use this phrase in everyday life. They are likely to be the words of a legal representative.

'I needed a vehicle to drop off my two young children to school in the morning, and to take my eldest child to judo on Tuesday and Thursday evenings' is approaching the particularity required.

vii. Hearsay notice

If a witness is unable to attend a hearing, there is *no* need for a hearsay notice. Nevertheless, one is often provided by a party who has legal representation. This is because it is necessary for cases allocated to another track.

It is also good practice, and courteous, promptly to inform another party of the reason that a witness will not attend. Otherwise, there is a legitimate expectation that a witness, who *has* written a statement, *will* attend to give oral evidence.

Without the benefit of cross-examination, the court may give that witness' evidence *little* weight. It may even be given *no* weight.

For example, there is a claim after a road traffic collision. Liability is in dispute. It is unlikely that a claimant whose witness failed to attend will be able to discharge the burden of proving that the defendant's driving fell below a reasonable standard.

Likewise, a defendant whose witness did not attend will likely be found liable where a claimant gives oral evidence that the defendant's driving caused a collision.

viii. Non-attendance

The *strict* rules of evidence do *not* apply.

Nevertheless, the Civil Evidence Act 1995 is a useful resource.

Section 4 prescribes that, when attributing weight to hearsay evidence, the court 'shall have regard to any circumstances from which any inference can reasonably be drawn as to the reliability or otherwise of the evidence'.

1. Factors

Hearsay evidence does not necessarily attract *any* weight.

The following *non*-exhaustive considerations are relevant.

First, whether it would have been reasonable, and practicable, for the party by whom the evidence was adduced to have produced the maker of the original statement as a witness. Secondly, whether the original statement was made contemporaneously with the occurrence, or existence, of the matters stated. Thirdly, whether the evidence involves multiple hearsay.

Fourthly, whether any person involved had any motive to conceal, or to misrepresent matters. Fifthly, whether the original statement was an edited account, made in collaboration with another person, or for a particular purpose. Sixthly, whether the circumstances in which the evidence is adduced as hearsay are such as to suggest an attempt to prevent proper evaluation of its weight.

2. Practice

In practice, the fourth and sixth are likely to be decisive.

Even if there was not a *deliberate attempt* to prevent proper evaluation of the weight of a witness' evidence, if that witness does not undergo cross-examination, the *practical effect* is that a proper evaluation has, in fact, been prevented.

The first consideration is often answered by promptly informing the parties and the court of the good reason for non-attendance.

If a witness does not attend court for cross-examination, two submissions can be made.

First, it should not be admitted into evidence, because the party who you represent is not on an *equal footing* because she cannot *put her case* to that witness in cross-examination.

Secondly, even if it is admitted into evidence, it should be given little, if *any* weight.

In practice, the court will often allow the statement into evidence, but give it little, if any, weight, depending on the circumstances.

If the claimant / defendant has written a witness statement, but does not attend, it is also worth checking to see who signed the statement of truth in support of their statement(s) of case.

If it was a legal representative, the court will likely place little, if any, weight on the statement(s) of case. For example, in a claim following a road traffic collision, if liability is in dispute, this will likely persuade the court to give judgment against that party.

c. Oral

A party wishing to rely on a witness in relation to an issue of fact to be decided at a final hearing *must* file and serve a witness statement, written by that witness, and verified by a statement of truth.

If a party has filed and served a witness statement, and she wishes to rely on that statement at a final hearing, she should call that witness to give oral evidence.

Where a party knows that a witness is unable to attend, notice should be given to the other party, and the court, of the good reason that that witness is unable to attend. It should be *prompt.*

Where a party is unable to attend a final hearing, she should give written notice, in accordance with CPR 27.9. If a party fails to do so, the court may strike out the claim, defence, or counterclaim.

If it appears as though a witness for the other party has not attended, and that party is legally represented, politely enquire whether that witness will attend the hearing. Dishonestly stating that a witness has attended, when an advocate knows that they have not, or knows that they will not attend, is unethical.

If you know that a witness has not attended, this will strengthen your negotiating position in relation to settlement.

i. Application to decide in absence

Where three conditions are met, if a party does not attend a hearing, the court *must* take into account that party's statement of case, and any other documents that she has filed and served, when the claim is decided (CPR 27.9(1)).

First, written notice that the party will not attend has been given to the court, and to the other party, at least seven days before the final hearing.

Secondly, at least seven days before the final hearing, any other documents which she has filed with the court are served on the other party.

Thirdly, in the written notice, a request is made that the court decides the claim in her absence, and compliance with the first and second conditions are confirmed.

Where these conditions are satisfied, there is "written notice".

The judge will then provide *written* reasons for her judgment.

A copy *will* be sent to each party (PD 27A at [5.4]).

ii. Claimant

If a claimant does not attend the final hearing, and does not give written notice, the court *may* strike out the claim.

The claimant must then apply for the order striking out the claim to be set aside, so that the claim can be heard (CPR 27.11).

iii. Defendant

The court may decide the claim on the basis of the claimant's evidence alone in the following circumstances (CPR 27.9(3)).

First, the *defendant* does not attend the final hearing, or give written notice. Secondly, the *claimant* attends, or gives written notice.

Where the defence has been struck out, the defendant *must* apply for the order striking out the defence to be *set aside,* so that the claim can be heard (CPR 27.11).

iv. Claimant & defendant

If *neither* party attends, *or* gives written notice, the court *may* strike out the claim, defence, and counterclaim (CPR 27.9(4)).

20. Independent & objective evidence

Directions in a claim following a road traffic collision usually order that documents and information sent to the court, and to each party, should, where possible, include plans, maps, photographs of the scene, and photographs of the damage.

If possible, they should be agreed.

A police accident report is also likely to assist the court.

In principle, *original* documents must be available at the hearing.

In practice, copies suffice – unless they are illegible.

a. Witnesses

In disputes arising out of a road traffic collision, an *independent* witness is likely to tip the balance.

She must usually write a witness statement, attend court to give oral evidence, and thereby undergo cross-examination.

Either party may call an independent witness.

What matters is that she is *not* previously known to either party, *expresses an opinion as to fault,* and provides *cogent* reasons.

b. Photographs

For example, photographs were taken immediately after a road traffic collision. They show that the vehicles are touching. The defendant's vehicle is in the claimant's lane.

This can be persuasive evidence that the defendant veered into the claimant's lane.

Ideally, photographs should be exhibited to a witness statement, identifying *when* they were taken, by *whom*, and *what* they show.

As the formal rules of evidence do not apply, however, a witness may confirm the same in oral evidence.

i. Clear

Photographs should be in *colour.*

Black and white photographs are often of poor quality. This is especially the case where they have been copied.

It may be that the electronic version is in colour. The printer was set to black and white, however, when printed.

In any event, enquire with your professional client whether colour photographs exist. If so, they can be promptly filed, served, and relied on at the hearing.

ii. Location

In a claim following a road traffic collision, if there are no colour photographs of the location of the collision, consider Google Maps.

Pictures can usually be found.

If the party who you represent states that the pictures show the location of the collision, speak to the other side. The parties may agree that the pictures show the location of the collision.

If so, the other party will usually be grateful to accept a colour copy. The court is also likely to be grateful.

If the other side does not agree that these pictures show the location of the collision, however, you will need to ask permission from the court to rely on them.

This is likely to be granted. Evidence of the *alleged* location of the collision is likely to assist the court with the road layout.

iii. Road layout

The number of lanes on a road, whether there were traffic lights, signs, and road markings, should all be apparent.

There may also be an indication of the speed limit.

For example, streetlights generally indicate 30 miles per hour, and 20 miles per hour in Wales (rule 124 of *The Highway Code*).

iv. Damage

Where liability is in dispute following a road traffic collision, colour photographs may show the extent of any damage.

For example, whether the damage to the claimant's vehicle is a scratch, perhaps showing that the vehicles were moving at the point of impact. Or a large dent, perhaps showing that the collision could not properly be described as "low velocity".

It may be possible to deduce the direction of impact from photographs of the damaged vehicles. This may chime with an engineer's report depicting the direction of impact.

c. Sketch plans

They may be of central importance in the following circumstances.

First, they are contemporaneous. Secondly, they are detailed. Thirdly, they are consistent with a party's statement of case.

Fourthly, they are consistent with known, or agreed, facts. Fifthly, they are consistent with independent, or objective, evidence. Sixthly, they are consistent with a party's written and oral evidence.

Where there is a material *in*consistency with a statement of case, known or agreed facts, independent or objective evidence, or a party's evidence, however, this can be put in cross-examination.

Demonstrating the *extent* of inconsistency often correlates with the *weight* that is given to the sketch plan.

Either way, it will usually *either* assist, or undermine, a case.

Sketch plans often assist with the following.

First, the direction along the road that the relevant vehicles were travelling. Secondly, the lane that a vehicle was in. Thirdly, the location of the collision. Fourthly, the mechanism of collision. Fifthly, the point of impact.

Ideally, sketch plans should be exhibited to a witness statement.

They should identify *when* they were taken, by *whom*, and *what* they show. As the formal rules of evidence do not apply, however, a witness can usually give these details in oral evidence.

d. Engineers' reports

The court usually needs an engineer's report in claims following a road traffic collision (PD 27A at Appendix A).

The report should also contain a statement identifying *who* commissioned it, that the engineer understands her *overriding duty to the court,* and that she has in fact *complied* with that duty.

An engineer's report usually contains the following evidence.

i. Collision

If the *date* of the collision is inconsistent to that pleaded in a statement of case, the written or oral evidence of a witness, it is either an error, or the report relates to damage that is unrelated to the index incident. Either way, this is an important inconsistency in a party's case, or evidence. It requires an explanation.

ii. Impact

If air bags were fitted, and in fact deployed, this suggests that the impact was considerable.

In a claim for personal injury, it makes it more likely that an occupant of that vehicle suffered injury; and vice versa.

iii. Damage

On the location of any damage, the report may evidence 'moderate accidental damage to the right-hand side'.

If this is *in*compatible with the pleadings, or the written or oral evidence of a witness, it is either an *error,* or the report relates to damage that is *un*related to the index collision.

Either way, this is an important inconsistency in a party's case or evidence, requiring an explanation from that party.

The report is likely to indicate the results of a vehicle history check. Is there a record of any adverse history? For example, isolated dents and scratches, and the effect on the pre-accident value.

iv. Value

What is the pre-accident value?

It is likely to be based upon the following.

First, when the vehicle was first registered. Secondly, the adjusted retail value for the type and age of the vehicle. Thirdly, trade value.

What is the cost of repair? This should include the time involved in conducting repairs using Glass' Repair Estimate, and the reasonable labour charge. The rate per hour should be stated.

Where the damage is extensive, these are more likely to be higher.

The collision is more likely to have been significant.

Any applicable VAT should be set out.

The repair schedule will usually include the following.

First, new parts. Secondly, parts that only require repainting. Thirdly, specialist and sundry charges, such as corrosion protection materials. Fourthly, parts that require removal, and refitting.

v. Write-off

Does the value mean that it is uneconomical to repair?

If so, what is the salvage value? This is the value of parts that can be removed, and sold, where the cost of repair exceeds the pre-accident value. So as to mitigate their loss, claimants are expected to offset this sum when claiming for repairs.

vi. Roadworthy

Is the vehicle roadworthy?

A typical sentence may read: 'In our opinion, this vehicle was not roadworthy at the time of our inspection as a result of the damage sustained due to suspension damage'.

In this circumstance, if towing and storage charges for a reasonable period are claimed, they are likely to be agreed, or otherwise allowed.

Are temporary repairs practical to make the vehicle roadworthy?

If so, it undermines the need for a hire vehicle. If temporary repairs are impractical, it supports the need to hire.

vii. Pictures

Pictures of the vehicle are likely to be attached.

The registration should match the vehicle registration set out in the report. Many pictures will be irrelevant. Some will show the relevant damage. In any event, they should be in colour.

e. The Highway Code

The Highway Code is often essential where liability is in dispute, at a final hearing, following a road traffic collision.

It is the starting point for the standard of care of a reasonable driver. Section 38(7) of the Road Traffic Act 1988 provides that:

> A failure on the part of a person to observe a provision of the Highway Code … may in any proceedings … be relied upon by any party to the proceedings as tending to establish or negative any liability …

It can be *highly* persuasive. It is *not* determinative. Whether or not a breach is evidence of negligence depends on the circumstances.

In *Goad v Butcher & Anor* [2011] EWCA Civ 158 at [9], Moore-Bick LJ (with whom Mummery LJ agreed) said that:

> "One can well understand the temptation in a case of this kind to place some emphasis on a breach of the Highway Code when it can be so clearly established, but in my view it was little more than an unfortunate red herring. A failure to observe the Code may be evidence of negligence, but whether it is will depend very much on the circumstances in which the act in question was committed and who is the claimant. ..."

At paragraph 20, Jackson LJ dissented in these terms:

> "A breach of the Highway Code does not give rise to a presumption of negligence ... It is, however, a relevant circumstance, which the court should take into account when determining whether the driver was negligent: see *Powell v Phillips* [1972] 3 All ER 864."

In *Powell v Phillips* [1972] 3 All ER 864 (CA) at [868D], Stephenson LJ (with whom Davies and Buckley LJJ agreed) said that:

> "It is, however, clear that a breach [of *The Highway Code*] creates no presumption of negligence calling for an explanation, still less a presumption of negligence making a real contribution to causing an accident or injury. The breach is just one of the circumstances on which one party is entitled to rely in establishing the negligence of the other and its contribution to causing the accident or injury."

f. Judicial College Guidelines

In claims for personal injury, the *Judicial College Guidelines for the Assessment of General Damages in Personal Injury Cases* (17th edn, OUP, 2024) is essential.

It achieves the following.

First, a clear and logical framework for the assessment of general damages in personal injury cases. Secondly, takes into account inflation since the previous edition. Thirdly, it reflects the decisions of the higher courts on quantum.

Chapter 14, 'Minor Injuries' is likely to be a relevant chapter.

21. Submissions

It is unusual to give *opening* submissions.

There are frequently *preliminary* submissions.

In any event, *closing* submissions are often the only opportunity for a party to invite the court to find in accordance with her case.

a. Preliminary

Preliminary submissions are made before the evidence is heard.

In practice, there are three common examples.

All relate either to identifying the issues at an early stage, or otherwise deciding promptly which issues need a final hearing, and disposing summarily of others.

First, an application for early termination. For example, to strike out a statement of case on the basis that it is an abuse of process.

Secondly, an application for relief from sanctions following failure to comply with an unless order. For example, following failure to file and serve evidence of impecuniosity in a claim for credit hire, in accordance with a direction in the notice of allocation.

Thirdly, an application for an adjournment. For example, a key witness has indicated on the morning of a final hearing that she will not attend. The court needs to determine this application before hearing the evidence, and giving judgment on the claim.

b. Opening

There is usually *no* need for opening submissions. This is because there are not often complicated issues of fact, law or evidence.

i. Issues

In practice, if the parties are represented, the court will invite the advocates to outline the issues.

Claimants state whether liability, quantum, or both, are in dispute.

In a credit hire claim, the defendant usually outlines the issues related to this head of loss. They often include the following.

First, need to hire. Secondly, enforceability. Thirdly, need to hire a vehicle of the type hired. Fourthly, period of hire. Fifthly, impecuniosity. Sixthly, rate of hire. Seventhly, additional extras, such as delivery and collection.

ii. Agreement

If quantum is agreed subject to liability, this should be flagged.

If any head of loss is agreed, this should also be flagged. A head of loss, and the amount for that head of loss, may be agreed in a statement of case, later correspondence, or on the day of the hearing.

iii. Payment

If an interim, or final, payment has been made, it should be flagged.

c. Closing

The court may adopt any fair method of proceeding (CPR 27.8(1)).

Submissions may not be invited from a party at the conclusion of a hearing. This often indicates that the *other* party has not yet persuaded the court of her case. It would *not* normally be just to dismiss a party's case with*out* hearing submissions from her.

Submissions should be *clear, concise, and consistent* with the statement(s) of case, and evidence, of the party who you represent.

i. Order

The claimant usually has the last word. It is *her* case.

Even when there is a counterclaim.

Where the burden of proof is on the defendant, the court still usually allows the claimant to have the last word.

For example, in a claim for credit hire, where the defendant has the burden of proving that there is a difference in hire rates.

In this case, once you have made submissions, you can invite the judge to hear any reply to points raised by the claimant that you have not yet addressed. Although the court is not obliged, in practice, if you ask for a right to reply, it is often granted.

The *defendant* is often asked to give closing submissions first.

If so, the *claimant* may benefit from the following.

First, a careful note of the defendant's submissions can be taken, and responses to those submissions can be incorporated into the claimant's submissions. Secondly, there is not usually an opportunity for the defendant to reply to the claimant's submissions.

ii. General advice

There are ten pieces of general advice for closing submissions.

First, the *first* minute is the most important. Use it to best effect.

Secondly, formulate the issues on which the court must make findings in the most attractive way for the party who you represent.

Thirdly, be upfront about the good *and* bad points for both cases. What is a fair summary of the case against you? Why is it that, contrary to first impressions, it is not insurmountable?

Fourthly, rely on contemporary, documentary, and / or independent evidence, *before* written and oral evidence.

Fifthly, if you take the court to a document, *wait* for the judge to turn to it, *then* make your submission on it.

Sixthly, put your proposition first, then the evidence in support.

Seventhly, why are the *in*consistencies in *your* witness' evidence in fact evidence of their *credibility,* whereas, the *in*consistencies of the *other* party's witnesses mean that they are *un*reliable?

Eighthly, be a *willow,* not an oak, and *go with the judicial wind.* Keep an eye on the judge. Take judicial steers. Time invested in understanding judicial interventions is seldom wasted. If you don't understand the question, say so. Address (don't avoid) it.

Ninthly, allegations of *bad faith* are a *last resort.* They may blow up in your face. They are also unattractive. Look for another way. The court is *much* more likely to find two honest witnesses with differing, but honest, recollections, to bath faith.

Tenthly, if there is a dispute as to the law, use a binding / persuasive authority; if the law is well-settled, state it and move on.

iii. Approach to fact-finding

To use Stewart's J words in *Kimathi & Ors v The Foreign & Commonwealth Office* [2018] EWHC 2066 (QB) ("*Kimathi*") at [95], there are three judgments that have "helpfully crystallised and advanced learning in respect of the approach to evidence."

First, *Gestmin SGPS SA v Credit Suisse (UK) Ltd & Anor* [2013] EWHC 3560 (Comm), [2020] 1 CLC 428.

Secondly, *Lachaux v Lachaux* [2017] EWHC 385 (Fam), [2017] 4 WLR 57.

Thirdly, *Carmarthenshire County Council v Y* [2017] EWFC 36, [2017] 4 WLR 136.

Stewart J summarised the key principles in *Kimathi* at [96]:

"i) *Gestmin:*

- We believe memories to be more faithful than they are. Two common errors are to suppose (1) that the stronger and more vivid the recollection, the more likely it is to be accurate; (2) the more confident another person is in their recollection, the more likely it is to be accurate.
- Memories are fluid and malleable, being constantly rewritten whenever they are retrieved. This is even true of 'flash bulb' memories (a misleading term), i.e. memories of experiencing or learning of a particularly shocking or traumatic event.
- Events can come to be recalled as memories which did not happen at all or which happened to somebody else.
- The process of civil litigation itself subjects the memories of witnesses to powerful biases.
- Considerable interference with memory is introduced in civil litigation by the procedure of preparing for trial. Statements are often taken a long time after relevant events and drafted by a lawyer who is conscious of the significance for the issues in the case of what the witness does or does not say.

- The best approach from a judge is to base factual findings on inferences drawn from documentary evidence and known or probable facts. 'This does not mean that oral testimony serves no useful purpose... But its value lies largely... in the opportunity which cross-examination affords to subject the documentary record to critical scrutiny and to gauge the personality, motivations and working practices of a witness, rather than in testimony of what the witness recalls of particular conversations and events. Above all, it is important to avoid the fallacy of supposing that, because a witness has confidence in his or her recollection and is honest, evidence based on that recollection provides any reliable guide to the truth'.

ii) *Lachaux:*

- Mostyn J cited extensively from *Gestmin* and referred to two passages in earlier authorities. I extract from those citations, and from Mostyn J's judgment, the following:

- 'Witnesses, especially those who are emotional, who think they are morally in the right, tend very easily and unconsciously to conjure up a legal right that did not exist. It is a truism, often used in accident cases, that with every day that passes the memory becomes fainter and the imagination becomes more active. For that reason, a witness, however honest, rarely persuades a judge that his present recollection is preferable to that which was taken down in writing immediately after the incident occurred. Therefore, contemporary documents are always of the utmost importance ...'

- '... I have found it essential in cases of fraud, when considering the credibility of witnesses, always to test their veracity by reference to the objective fact proved independently of their testimony, in particular by reference to the documents in the case, and also to pay particular regard to their motives and to the overall probabilities ...'

- Mostyn J said of the latter quotation, 'these wise words are surely of general application and are not confined to fraud cases... it is certainly often difficult to tell whether a witness is telling the truth and I agree with the view of Bingham J that the demeanour of a witness is not a reliable pointer to his or her honesty.'

iii) *Carmarthenshire County Council:*

- The general rule is that oral evidence given under cross-examination is the gold standard because it reflects the long-established common law consensus that the best way of assessing the reliability of evidence is by confronting the witness.
- However, oral evidence under cross-examination is far from the be all and end all of forensic proof. Referring to paragraph 22 of *Gestmin*, Mostyn J said:

  > '...this approach applies equally to all fact-finding exercises, especially where the facts in issue are in the distant past. This approach does not dilute the importance that the law places on cross-examination as a vital component of due process, but it does place it in its correct context.'"

iv. Credibility

In *Kimathi* at [98], Stewart J endorsed the late Lord Bingham's approach to witness credibility. There are "three main tests which in general give a useful pointer as to where the truth lies, although their relative importance will vary from case to case".

First, consistency with agreed facts.

Secondly, internal consistency.

Thirdly, consistency with what has previously been asserted.

1. Agreed facts

Agreed facts provide an *anchor* from which the court can build a picture as to what happened.

A witness giving evidence that is disputed, but consistent with *agreed* or *known* facts, will likely be given *significant* weight.

Where her account is *in*consistent, however, it is *un*likely to be given much weight. Her credibility is therefore likely to *diminish.*

The following submissions can be made.

First, to what extent a party's evidence is *consistent* with agreed, and known, facts. Secondly, how *near* to the safe, judicial ground of agreed, and known, facts, that party's case is. Thirdly, how *far* it is from this safe ground to the other party's case.

2. Internal inconsistency

Why is a case inconsistent with its statement of case and evidence?

For example, a party's statement of case pleads X. That party's written and oral evidence confirms the truth of Y. X and Y are inconsistent. That party's case appears to be internally inconsistent.

If this party is the claimant, who has the burden of proving that what is pleaded in her statement of case is more likely than not, the court may cite this submission as a reason to dismiss the claim.

For example, the particulars of claim plead that the mechanism of collision was a rear-end shunt. The claimant's statement confirms that the impact was to the left, passenger-side of her vehicle.

The objective evidence supports the claimant's statement. An engineer's report confirms that the damage to the claimant's vehicle is to the left, passenger-side. Supporting photographs are attached. The claimant's answers in cross-examination evidence that the damage was to the left, passenger-side of her vehicle.

The pleaded mechanism of collision is incompatible with the claimant's written and oral evidence, and the objective evidence.

The claimant's case is internally *in*consistent.

As the claimant has the burden of proving, on a balance of probabilities, that the collision occurred in accordance with her statement of case, if she has failed to do so, her case will be dismissed.

3. Consistent previous statements

In *Painter v Hutchison & Anor* [2007] EWHC 758 (Ch) at [3], Lewison J (as he then was) discussed unsatisfactory witness evidence.

He also set out eight indicators.

Where they *apply*, they may indicate that a witness has been *in*consistent. Where they do *not* apply, they may indicate that a witness has been *consistent*.

In either case, the following can be used in closing submissions as a powerful pointer to (in)consistency.

First, evasive and argumentative answers. Secondly, tangential speeches, avoiding the question. Thirdly, blaming legal advisers for documentation, such as statements of case, and witness statements. Fourthly, self-contradiction. Fifthly, internal inconsistency. Sixthly, shifting case. Seventhly, introducing new evidence.

HHJ Richard Williams repeated them in: *Rancom Security Ltd v Ms Helen Girling & Two Ors* [2023] EWHC 1115 (Ch) at [33]; and *Ashok Singh v Parminder Singh Jhutti* [2021] EWHC 2272 (Ch) at [61].

If none of the indicators apply to your witness, it may be helpful to *show* it. Likewise, if one or more of these indicators apply to the other party's witness, it may also be worth *demonstrating*.

Show the contradiction between *earlier* and *later* oral evidence.

This is usually more persuasive than merely stating the fact that there has been a contradiction. This is because the court is able to come to the same conclusion of its own accord.

An accurate note of the hearing is invaluable. This will enable you to quote the witness. Paraphrasing invites dispute.

You are also able to *show* that the witness said "*X*" at the beginning of cross-examination. Then, she said "*Y*" at the close of it.

X and Y are incompatible.

Therefore, she changed her position in oral evidence.

Y is in accordance with your client's case.

The words should chime with the court's note for full impact.

This should give the court confidence to place *little* weight on the evidence of the witness who has been *in*consistent.

v. Inherent unlikelihood

Even if a party's case is consistent with agreed or known facts, and internally consistent, it may be *unlikely*.

What is pleaded in a statement of case? What is stated in a witness statement? What is asserted in oral evidence?

Is it more likely than not? If not, then it is *inherently unlikely*.

This is often the least persuasive submission, however, so prioritise your time on agreed and known facts, internal consistency, and consistent previous statements. If time permits, go on to demonstrate the inherent unlikelihood of the other party's case.

vi. Expert evidence

Without independent, expert, evidence, the court will be slow to find that works are defective. Accordingly, if there is no such evidence, this submission can be particularly persuasive.

There are defects, however, that are so blatant, that expert evidence is not necessary. For example, where it is alleged that the work has not been done at all. Photographic evidence will suffice.

Although this may be the case for liability, when it comes to assessing the amount of damages in respect of quantum, the lack of expert evidence is also relevant. Without it, or any quote(s) to remedy the work, there may be no evidence as to what labour, materials and costs are needed for cure.

If the cost of (some of) the defective items are set out in the quote for the works by the defendant that was accepted by the claimant, then, that can be a starting point for submissions on quantum.

If there is expert evidence, think about the *propositions* on which the *conclusion* rests like *bricks* in a wall supporting a *roof*.

Take a brick *out*. Or, put another brick *in*. Does the roof fall *down?*

Check whether the expert has been given, and in fact considered, the key documents. If not, does it change the conclusion?

vii. Interest

Work out any interest claimed before the hearing.

Type 'days between dates' calculator into an internet search engine. Put the start date and end date into the calculator. Do not include the day of the hearing in the calculation.

For example, £210.01 interest is claimed up to the date of the particulars of claim. Thereafter, interest is claimed at a daily rate of £1.82.

From the date of the particulars of claim, 14 April 2024, to the date of (but not including) the hearing, 1 September 2024, there are 140 days. £1.82 x 140 = £254.80.

£210.01 plus £254.80 is £464.81.

So, the total sum of interest claimed is £464.81.

Interest may also be claimed on general damages in respect of personal injuries. For example, £1,500 in damages are awarded in respect of personal injury.

To calculate interest, there are five steps.

First, divide the award of general damages by 365 (the number of days in a year). Secondly, divide it by 100 (to get a percentage). Thirdly, multiply it by the number of days between the date of service of the claim form to the date of (but not including) the hearing. Fourthly, multiply it by two percent.

For example, £1,500 / 365 / 100 x 136 x 2 = £11.18 interest.

viii. Costs

Work out fixed costs likely to be claimed before the hearing.

For example: £901 total (£455 issue fee; £100 legal reps costs; and £346 hearing fee).

You can find the issue fee on the claim form. You can usually also find the legal representative's fee on the claim form. The hearing fee can usually be found on the notice of allocation.

If *substantial* costs are claimed, pursuant to a contractual right, or a party has behaved unreasonably, there are two main issues that can be taken to challenge a statement of costs.

First, the costs are not *reasonable in amount.*

As part of your preparation, set out the rate claimed in the statement of costs, and the relevant rate in the Guidelines. If the former is greater than the latter, then you can submit that the amount claimed is not reasonable in amount.

Secondly, the costs are not *reasonably incurred.*

Again, as part of your preparation, set out: the total number of hours for attendances; the total hours of work done on documents in the schedule; and, if there is one, counsel's fee.

It is rare that a Grade A fee is reasonably incurred.

If any costs appear to be not reasonably incurred, then you can submit that the amount claimed is not reasonable in amount.

22. Orders & judgment

An "order" may be made without a judgment.

A "judgment" is usually followed by an order.

Confusingly, "judgment" and "order" are used in the CPRs interchangeably. At other times, they are used in conjunction.

a. Orders

Judgments and orders are usually drafted by the court.

The parties can draw up draft orders, however, including those that are attached to applications, proposed consent orders before judgment, and draft minutes of order following judgment.

i. Carriage

The court usually draws up an order after disposing of a claim, or deciding an application.

A party may also be ordered to do so (CPR 40.3(1)(a)).

If so, the party bringing the claim, or making the application, will have "carriage" of the order. If only one of the parties is represented, however, that party will be directed to draw up the order.

1. Deadline

In principle, where an order is drawn up by a party, it *must* be filed no later than seven days after the date on which the court so ordered (CPR 40.3(3)(a)). In practice, orders should be drawn up on the day. In any event, no later than 24 hours after the hearing.

Usually, the judge will give a deadline by which it must be filed.

2. Email addresses

If requested to draw up the order, ensure that you don't leave the hearing without the relevant email address. Usually, the judge will provide her judicial email address.

If your hearing is in person, you can ask the usher for the relevant email address. Stating that you have been directed to draft the order by the court following a hearing often allays any concerns.

Remote hearings are usually also public. For this reason, the judge may not wish to state her email address in open court. If so, you can give *your* email address, so that she can *reply* to it, and you will then have *her* email address.

Do not leave the hearing before confirming the email address for any other legal representative, so that you can agree a minute of order with them.

If you are a legal representative with carriage, and the other side does not have legal representation, it is more common to draft an order, and send it to the judge for her approval, without the need to agree it with a person without a representative.

Similarly, if the other side does not attend a hearing, as they will not know the terms of the order that you have been directed to draft, it is usually unnecessary to copy them in to an email filing the draft minute of order with the court.

In any event, it is a good idea to confirm this during the hearing.

3. Form

A minute of order should have a header.

This should be substantially the same as a statement of case, however, 'ORDER' will appear within the tramlines.

In the first instance, use a court order, or the notice of hearing / trial to confirm the names of the parties and claim number. Check that against the statements of case.

4. Content

After the header will be the date, and name of the court, followed by the status and name of the judge.

If the hearing was remote, that will also be reflected.

For example: 'On 1 September 2024, in the County Court at Central London before Deputy District Judge Adam by way of a remote hearing via CVP'.

Next, a recital will confirm who attended. For example: '**UPON** hearing from Counsel for the Claimant, and the Defendant not attending, nor being represented'.

The first word of a recital is in capital letters, and emboldened. The first recital starts: '**UPON**'. Subsequent recitals start: '**AND UPON**'.

Solicitor, and solicitors' agents, are usually named using their title and surname.

A person without a representative is referred to as "in person".

For example: '**UPON** hearing from the Claimant's Solicitor, Mr Boden, and the Defendant in person'.

Any further recitals are preceded by the words '**AND UPON**'.

The operative (binding) part follows in numbered paragraphs.

If the court has heard an application, and disposed of it, then it should be reflected in the operative part of the order.

For example: 'Claimant's oral application for relief from sanctions in respect of failure to serve wage slips granted'.

If judgment is given, that should be reflected, together with any interest awarded. For example: 'Judgment for the Claimant in the sum of £4,800, and £200 interest, £5,000 total.'

Any order as to costs should be reflected. For example: 'Defendant to pay the Claimant's fixed costs in the sum of £910.00'.

If costs have been awarded on the basis that a party has behaved unreasonably, that should be reflected. For example: 'Claimant to pay the Defendant's costs, pursuant to CPR 27.14(2)(g), summarily assessed in the sum of £420'.

If no order as to costs was made, that should be reflected, however, an order that does not mention costs usually means no order as to costs (CPR 44.10; and PD 44 at [4.2]).

If a witness' loss of earning and / or travel expenses are awarded, that should be set out, either separately, or together with the order as to costs. For example: 'Defendant to pay the Claimant's fixed costs of £910, and witness expenses of £20, £930 total.'

If a final / an interim payment has been made, either the judgment sum can be reduced accordingly, or an order can be made to the following effect: 'Credit to be given for any sums already paid'.

If a party has applied for permission to appeal, the order should reflect whether or not permission was granted. For example: 'Defendant refused permission to appeal in respect of liability'.

After the operative part of the order, the draft should be dated. In practice, this is emboldened as follows: '**Dated this 1st day of September 2024.**'

Ideally, the whole draft minute of order should fit on a single page.

5. Agreement

When you send a draft minute of order to another legal representative for agreement, the name of the file should include the words 'Draft minute of order', the case number, the names of the parties, the name of the court, and the date of the hearing.

For example: 'Draft minute of order_K48ZY612_Mr Jones v Mrs Jacob_County Court at Birmingham_1 September 2024'.

For legal representatives, it is usual to address the email using only the first name of the legal representative for the other side.

Confirm that the above is attached for their agreement, and, if it can be agreed, that you will copy them into your email filing the agreed minute of order.

Sign off with your status. For example: 'Counsel for the Defendant'.

6. Failure to agree

In the unusual event that a draft minute of order cannot be agreed, send an email to the other legal representative, confirming what you propose to send in the body of the email to the Judge. This should be a neutral summary if not the exact words used by the other person as to why the minute of order cannot be agreed.

Once the other party has confirmed their agreement to that wording, via return email, a separate email can be sent to the court, copying in the other legal representative, and attaching both draft minutes of order, or one draft minute of order with the area(s) of disagreement set out in the body of the email.

In the even more unusual event that the other legal representative does not respond, send follow up emails, a reasonable period of time apart.

In them, request a response, and write that, unless you hear from them before a certain time and date (the deadline that the court directed for the draft should be filed), you will forward the email to the judge, confirming that, further to the below, it has not been possible to agree a minute of order, and leave the draft minute of order for the consideration of the judge.

7. Filing

When you send an agreed minute of order to the court, copy and paste the name of the file into the subject line.

In the body of the email, start with 'Dear Judge'. Then, confirm that the legal representative for the claimant / defendant is copied in to the email, their identity and capacity (CPR 39.8(4)).

It is usual practice to write words to the following effect: 'Please find the above attached for your consideration.'

End with 'Kind regards', followed by your full name, and capacity.

ii. Consent

Where the parties have settled a claim, or an application has been agreed, before the court has given a decision on the same, the parties should draw up a "consent" order.

For a party without a representative, judicial approval is *always* necessary (CPR 40.6(2)(b) and (5)).

There are three requirements (CPR 40.6(7); and PD 40B at [3.4]).

First, it must be drawn up in the terms that have been agreed. Secondly, it must be expressed as being "By Consent". Thirdly, it must be signed by the legal representatives acting for the parties. If a party is not represented, it must be signed by that party.

iii. Tomlin

Parties who have settled their dispute may wish to set out the terms that have been agreed, otherwise than in an order itself.

As court orders are public documents, a "Tomlin" order is useful.

It enables the parties to keep the terms of their agreement *confidential.* It also stays all further proceedings on the agreed terms.

There are two main ways to record these terms.

First, in a schedule following the order. Secondly, in a settlement agreement, attached to the order.

In any event, the parties may apply to the court for enforcement.

The Tomlin order itself should provide for costs. Not the schedule, or the settlement agreement.

In practice, one of the following is often used.

First, payment and assessment of costs. Secondly, no order.

There are three benefits to including the agreement for payment, and assessment, of costs, in the Tomlin order itself.

First, there is a judgment for costs. Secondly, interest will accrue. Thirdly, the right to a detailed assessment.

The court is reluctant to go behind what the parties have agreed.

iv. Unless

An "unless" order *usually* specifies three details.

First, what act must be done. Secondly, the time within which that act must be performed. Thirdly, the consequence of default.

It *must* specify the *time* within which the act must be performed.

The following, suitably adapted, wording *must* be used where possible (PD 40B at [8.2(1)]):

> Unless the [claimant / defendant] [files with the court and serves on the other party] [an amended, fully particularised particulars of claim / defence / counterclaim] by 4.00pm on [Friday, 20 September 2024] his [claim / defence / counterclaim] will be struck out and judgment entered for the [defendant / claimant].

The key point is that a *fixed* date is given. It does not depend on an *event.* If the event does *not* take place, uncertainty does *not* arise.

b. Judgment

In general, "judgment" is a final, reasoned decision of the court. It determines whether a claim is allowed, or dismissed.

Judgment takes effect when it is made, declared, or announced.

i. Default

"Default judgment" is the determination of a claim following failure to file an acknowledgment of service, defence, or defence to counterclaim, within the relevant time limit.

ii. After final hearing

Judgment *may* be given after the date of a final hearing.

1. Ex tempore

Judgment is usually given orally. Often, immediately after the hearing. This is known as an "ex tempore" judgment.

Take a note, along with the time that it started, for six reasons.

First, you may be directed to draw up a draft minute of order.

Secondly, to identify grounds of appeal.

Thirdly, to advise on prospects of appeal.

Fourthly, so that both your professional client, and your lay client, are able to reflect on the reasoning of the judgment.

Fifthly, transcripts are unnecessary to appeal.

Sixthly, if a transcript is necessary, the time that the oral judgment started will assist the transcription service.

2. Reserved

Occasionally, judgment will be "reserved".

This may be the case where there is an *exceptionally* large amount of evidence, *authority* that the court wishes to consider in her own time, or where there is *insufficient time* to give an oral judgment.

Reserved judgments may be given at a later hearing, or in writing.

Written judgments are *un*usual.

If an oral judgment will be given at a later hearing, and you ask for that hearing to be listed *remotely* (as opposed to attended in court) with a time estimate of 30 minutes, it will likely be granted.

iii. Slip rule

Once judgment has been entered, the decision cannot be reconsidered. The sole exception is to correct an accidental slip, or omission, under the "slip rule" (CPR 40.12(1)).

A party may apply for an error in a judgment, or an order, to be corrected (PD 40B at [4.1]). It may be without notice.

The application notice should achieve the following.

First, describe the error. Secondly, state the required correction.

This may be by means of an informal document, such as a letter.

In any event, applications may be considered without a hearing in three circumstances.

First, the application so requests. Secondly, with the consent of the parties. Thirdly, where the court does not consider that a hearing would be appropriate.

If the slip is *obvious*, the court may deal with the application without notice, or direct that notice is served on the other party.

If the application is opposed, it should, if practicable, be listed for a hearing before the judge who gave judgment, or made the order.

The court has an inherent power to vary its orders, so as to make the *meaning*, and the *intention,* of the court clear (PD 40B at [4.5]).

iv. Reasons

The court *must* give reasons for its decision (CPR 27.8(6)).

1. Duty

The court owes a *general duty* to give reasons.

In *Flannery & Anor v Halifax Estate Agencies Ltd* [2000] 1 WLR 377 (CA) at 381G-382C, Henry LJ handed down judgment on behalf of Laws LJJ and Hidden J (with emboldened emphasis added):

"(1) The duty is a function of due process, and therefore of justice. Its rationale has two principal aspects. The first is that *fairness surely requires that the parties especially the losing party should be left in no doubt why they have won or lost.* This is especially so since without reasons the losing party will not know … whether the court has misdirected itself, and thus whether he may have an available appeal on the substance of the case. The second is that **a requirement to give reasons concentrates the mind; if it is fulfilled, the resulting decision is much more likely to be soundly based on the evidence than if it is not.**

(2) The first of these aspects implies that want of reasons may be a good self-standing ground of appeal. Where because no reasons are given it is impossible to tell whether the judge has gone wrong on the law or the facts, the losing party would be altogether deprived of his chance of an appeal unless the court entertains an appeal based on the lack of reasons itself.

(3) The extent of the duty, or rather the reach of what is required to fulfil it, depends on the subject matter. Where there is a straightforward factual dispute whose resolution depends simply on which witness is telling the truth about events which he claims to recall, **it is likely to be enough for the judge (having, no doubt, summarised the evidence) to indicate simply that he believes X rather than Y; indeed there may be nothing else to say.** But where the dispute involves something in the nature of an intellectual exchange, with reasons and analysis advanced on either side, the judge must enter into the issues canvassed before him and explain why he prefers one case over the other. This is likely to apply particularly in litigation whereas here there is disputed expert evidence; but it is not necessarily limited to such cases.

(4) This is not to suggest that there is one rule for cases concerning the witnesses truthfulness or recall of events, and

> another for cases where the issue depends on reasoning or analysis (with experts or otherwise). The rule is the same: the judge must explain *why* he has reached his decision. The question is always, what is required of the judge to do so; and that will differ from case to case. **Transparency should be the watchword.**"

This was recently quoted by Jacobs J in *Merlin Entertainment Plc v Emilia Idziak* [2023] EWHC 1597 (KB) at [71].

Without *reasons,* a judgment is not *transparent.*

The appeal court cannot determine whether or not the judge had adequate *reasons* for the *conclusions.*

Reasons may be as brief, and simple, as the nature of the case allows. They will usually be given at the end of a hearing. The court may give them at another hearing, or in writing (PD 27A at [5.3]).

2. Note

A judge will prepare a note of the reasons for judgment, which will then be sent to each party, in two situations (PD 27A at [5.4]).

First, the case was decided without a hearing. Secondly, a party did not attend a hearing, but gave written notice (CPR 27.9(1)).

3. Failure

Where permission to appeal due to lack of reasons is made out immediately after judgment, *English v Emery Reimbold & Strick Ltd* [2002] EWCA Civ 605, [2002] 3 All ER 385 at [25] prescribes the proper procedure (with emphasis added):

> "… the Judge should consider whether his judgment is defective for lack of reasons, adjourning for that purpose should he find this necessary. If he concludes that it is, *he should set out to remedy the*

> *defect by the provision of additional reasons refusing permission to appeal on the basis that he has adopted that course.* If he concludes that he has given adequate reasons, he will no doubt refuse permission to appeal. If an application for permission to appeal on the ground of lack of reasons is made to the appellate court and it appears to the appellate court that the application is well founded, it should consider adjourning the application and remitting the case to the trial Judge with an invitation to provide additional reasons for his decision or, where appropriate, his reasons for a specific finding or findings. Where the appellate court is in doubt as to whether the reasons are adequate, it may be appropriate to direct that the application be adjourned to an oral hearing, on notice to the respondent."

v. Reconsideration

An application for permission to appeal may be well-founded where there are any of the following failures.

First, to *identify the elements* of the claim or defence. Secondly, to *analyse contemporary documents*. Thirdly, to *deal with the thrust of expert evidence*. Fourthly, to take a *balanced approach* to assessing the credibility of witnesses of fact.

In *Simetra Global Assets Ltd & Anor v Ikon Finance Ltd & Ors* [2019] EWCA Civ 1413, [2019] 4 WLR 112 at [46], Males LJ (with whom Peter Jackson and McCombe LJJ agreed) gave the following guidance (with emphasis added):

> "First, succinctness is as desirable in a judgment as it is in counsel's submissions, but *short judgments must be careful judgments*. Second, it is not necessary to deal expressly with every point, but *a judge must say enough to show that care has been taken and that the evidence as a whole has been properly considered.* Which points need to be dealt with and which can be omitted itself requires an exercise of judgment. Third, the best way to demonstrate the exercise of the necessary care is to make use of 'the building blocks of the reasoned judicial process' by *identifying the issues which need to be decided,*

> *marshalling* (however briefly and without needing to recite every point) *the evidence which bears on those issues, and giving reasons why the principally relevant evidence is either accepted or rejected as unreliable.* Fourth, and in particular, fairness requires that *a judge should deal with apparently compelling evidence,* where it exists, *which is contrary to the conclusion which he proposes to reach and explain why he does not accept it.*"

In the next paragraph, Males LJ said that failure to follow this guidance does not *necessarily* mean that a judgment is *in*adequately reasoned. Nevertheless, "the judgment will need to be particularly cogent if it is to satisfy the demands of justice."

This is because of the risk that an appellate court will conclude that the judge has plainly failed to take the evidence into account.

vi. Appeals

Section 80 of the County Courts Act 1984 applies (PD 27A at [5.5]).

1. Note

A party may request a judge to note the following.

First, any question of law raised at the hearing. Secondly, the facts in evidence in relation to any such question. Thirdly, her decision on any such question, and of her determination of the proceedings.

2. Signed copy

The judge must provide a signed copy of this note where the following two conditions are satisfied.

First, a party has made an application. Secondly, the relevant fee has been paid. It is *irrelevant* whether a notice of appeal has been served. This note must be used at the hearing of the appeal.

c. Time limits for compliance

The general rule is that the time limit for complying with a judgment, or an order, is within 14 days (CPR 40.11).

The court may order otherwise. In August, over the summer holidays, for example, requests for 21 days are usually successful.

The date must be expressed as a *calendar* date. It must also include the *time of day* by which the act must be done (CPR 2.9(1)).

23. Costs, disbursements & witness expenses

The general rule is that *no* order will be made for *substantial* costs.

The exception is where the court finds that a party has *behaved unreasonably.*

Usually, recoverable costs and disbursements from a defendant after a successful claim can be determined in advance of issue.

a. General discretion

As night follows day, costs do *not* always follow the event.

If the court decides to make an order about costs, the *general* rule is that the unsuccessful party will be ordered to pay the costs of the successful party.

The court *may* make a different order (CPRs 27.2(2) and 44.2(2)).

The court has a *general* discretion. This can be broken down into three, *particular* discretions (CPR 44.2(1)).

First, *whether* costs are payable by one party to another. Secondly, the *amount.* Thirdly, *when* they are to be paid.

i. Payable

The rule in CPR 27.14(2) does *not* fetter this general discretion:

> The court may not order a party to pay to another party in respect of that other party's costs, fees and expenses, including those relating to an appeal, except ...

It does *not* prescribe that the court *will* make an order.

A defendant who has been unsuccessful after a final hearing *may* still argue that the court should not make an order for (the full amount of) fixed costs.

To do so, the court should be invited to have regard to all the circumstances. In particular, the following (CPR 44.2(4)).

First, the *conduct* of the parties.

Secondly, whether a party has succeeded on *part* of its case, even if that party has not been wholly successful.

Thirdly, any admissible *offer* to settle made by a party, which is drawn to the court's attention.

1. Conduct

Conduct includes the following (CPR 44.2(5)).

First, conduct *before*, as well as *during*, proceedings. In particular, the *extent* to which the parties followed the Practice Direction – Pre-Action Conduct, or any relevant pre-action protocol.

Secondly, whether it was reasonable for a party to *raise*, *pursue*, or *contest*, a particular allegation, or issue.

Thirdly, the *manner* in which a party has pursued, or defended, its case, a particular allegation, or issue.

Fourthly, whether a claimant who has succeeded, in whole or in part, *exaggerated* the claim.

In the *alternative* to the submission that a party has behaved unreasonably, the *same* factors can be used to argue that the conduct is such that: there should be *no order* as to costs; or, that *not all* of the claimable costs should be awarded.

2. Limited success

For example, there is a claim for £8,000 in respect of three heads of loss. The court dismisses two heads of loss. One is allowed in the sum of £3,000. There has been "limited success".

In principle, there is an argument that there should be no order as to costs. The reason is that there has been *such* limited success.

In practice, the court is likely to make an order as to costs in favour of the claimant. The real question is the *amount.*

3. Offers

Rejection is *not* a necessary or sufficient condition (CPR 27.14(3)):

> A party's rejection of an offer in settlement will not of itself constitute unreasonable behaviour under paragraph 2(g) but the court may take it into consideration when it is applying the unreasonableness test.

It *may* found a submission that there should be *no order* for costs.

Relevant circumstances of any offer include the following.

First, whether it was *before* the *issue* fee was paid.

Secondly, whether it was made *before* the deadline by which the *hearing* fee must have been paid.

Thirdly, whether it was for *more* than the *judgment* sum.

If an offer for *more* than the judgment sum was made *after* the issue fee was paid, it is difficult to resist an order to pay the issue fee. The offer did not mean that the issue fee was unnecessary. It was not possible to accept the offer, and avoid paying the issue fee.

Where the offer was made *before* the issue fee was payable, however, the submission is that, *if* the offer was accepted, the issue fee would *not* have been incurred. The issue fee was *un*necessary.

So was the defence, the notice of allocation containing court directions, witness evidence, and the hearing, including oral evidence, submissions, and judgment.

ii. Amount

If costs *are* payable, that is *not* the end of the matter.

The court still has a discretion as to the *amount* of those costs.

1. Issue fee

If there has been *limited* success, the submission is that the amount of the issue fee should be *proportionate* (or, at least, not *dis*proportionate) to any judgment sum.

This submission has even greater force where there is an offer.

For example, the *claimed* sum is £9,000. The *judgment* sum is £3,000. The issue fee for the former is £455. The issue fee for the latter is £115. About *four times less.*

The submission is that the *proportionate* fee is £115.

This deals with the issue fee in accordance with the overriding objective. In other words, dealing with the issue of costs *justly*, and in a way that is *proportionate* to the *amount of money* involved.

2. Hearing fee

The *same* arguments apply in relation to the *hearing* fee.

For example, the *claimed* sum is £9,000. The *judgment* sum is £3,000. The hearing fee for the former is £346. The hearing fee for the latter is £181. About *half.*

3. Legal representative's costs

The *same* arguments apply for the *legal representative's* costs.

For example, the *claimed* sum is £9,000. The *judgment* sum is £3,000. Where the claim form is served by the court, the legal representative's costs for the former is £100. The legal representative's costs for the latter is £80. *One-fifth* less.

iii. When

The court has a discretion as to *when* costs are to be paid by.

The *general* rule is that, unless the court orders otherwise, the time limit for payment of costs is within 14 days (CPR 40.11).

When requested, during late December, for example, when solicitors and insurers may be on holiday, the court routinely makes orders that costs are payable within 21 days.

b. Fees

Issue, hearing, and application, fees, are payable by the party who starts a claim, requires a final hearing, or makes an application.

They are also claimable (CPR 27.14(2)(c)).

They are prescribed in the Civil Proceedings Order 2008 (SI 2008/1053), Schedule 1, paragraph 1 at [1.1], [2.1], and [2.3]-[2.5]. They are also in Form EX50A (1 May 2024).

A party is entitled to apply for help with fees where they have *limited means,* or they are on a *low income.*

i. Issue

To start a claim, a claim form, or counterclaim, must be "issued".

This can either be done *online,* or by using hard, *paper* copies.

If you do not know the exact amount that you are claiming, it can*not* be issued online.

The issue fee is based on the "amount claimed" including interest.

The issue / court fee can be found in the bottom, right-hand corner of the first page of a paper claim form (Form N1).

See appendix F for issue fees.

The amount claimed in the claim form does *not* limit the jurisdiction of the court. More than the amount claimed may be awarded if the court finds that the claimant is entitled to it (CPR 16.3(7)).

ii. Hearing

On the court fixing a final hearing, an *unless* order will be made to pay a *hearing* fee. This will be in the *notice of allocation.*

The hearing fee is often called the "trial" fee.

This is because, in proceedings allocated to another track, the hearing at which evidence is heard, judgment is given, and the proceedings are disposed of, is called a "trial".

See appendix G for hearing fees.

If the case is settled before a hearing fee is payable, it does not need to be paid. If the hearing fee is paid, and the case is then settled, it will not be returned.

iii. Application

In practice, there are three common types of application.

1. On notice

This means the other side has been notified of the application.

Where no other fee is specified, it is £303.

To set aside judgment, the fee is also £303.

2. Consent

Where an application is made by consent, and no other fee is specified, the fee is £119. For example, to vacate, or adjourn, a hearing.

There is *no* fee for an application by consent to adjourn, if it is received by the court, at least 14 days before the date of the hearing.

3. Permission to appeal

On filing an appellant's, or respondent's, notice, the fee is £142.

iv. Remission

A party can apply for help with fees.

c. Legal representatives

Claimants may recover the costs that are attributable to issuing the claim (CPR 27.14(2)).

These are "fixed commencement costs".

They are concerned with amounts that are allowable in respect of *legal representatives'* charges.

i. Specified sum

Fixed commencement costs are prescribed in CPR 45.17 and Table 2 of PD 45.

See appendix H.

ii. Unspecified sum

Fixed costs will be calculated by reference to the judgment sum awarded after a final hearing. See appendix H.

iii. Counterclaim

There are no fixed costs.

iv. Injunction / specific performance

A party may be ordered to pay a sum not exceeding £260 for legal advice and assistance (CPR 27.14(2)(b); and PD 27A at [7.2]).

d. Party or witness expenses

The court may award the following.

First, loss of earnings, or loss of leave. Secondly, travel expenses.

These can usually be agreed, subject to liability.

i. Loss of earnings or leave

The court may award *not more than* £95, per person, per day.

There are two grounds (CPR 27.14(2)(e); and PD 27A at [7.3(1)]).

First, due to attending a hearing.

Secondly, due to staying away from home for the same purpose.

1. Employed

When the final hearing is both listed, and disposed of, in a morning, or an afternoon, half a day's loss of earnings can be calculated.

First, ask what the witness' salary is *after* tax. Secondly, divide that by the number of working days in a year. About 250. Thirdly, divide that by two.

For example: £30,000 / 250 = £120. £120 / 2 = £60.

When on a floating list, however, and the matter goes into the afternoon, the daily rate will be appropriate. The court is also able to compensate a witness who has taken leave to attend a hearing.

In the above example, the witness earns more per day than the allowable amount of £95. Accordingly, the maximum that she can be awarded in respect of her loss of earnings is £95.

2. Self-employed

Was there a requirement to work during the hearing?

Was an opportunity to work lost? If so, it is claimable.

Take the following examples.

First, a beautician who lost an appointment.

Secondly, a driver with set hours.

Where the driver is able to work at any time, however, she may not have lost earnings *due to attending a hearing.* This is because there was no *requirement* to work at the time.

3. Other

For example, the cost of a carer to look after an elderly dependent.

ii. Travel expenses

These must be *reasonably incurred* for the *purpose of attending a hearing.* This includes the following (CPR 27.14(2)(d)).

First, travelling to, and from, a hearing.

Secondly, staying away from home.

Take the following examples.

First, use of a private car. Secondly, parking.

For an in-person hearing, a witness may travel from her home address to court. The postcode of her address will usually be in her statement. The mileage to and from court can be easily calculated.

Search online for directions from that postcode to court.

If the witness is going to drive home, the mileage is doubled. In practice, it is multiplied by 0.45 to work out the amount in pounds. This is the expense of private car use. This includes fuel, a share of wear and tear, expendables, and tax.

There are two key arguments.

First, the amount claimed is not *reasonable*. Secondly, the expenses were not *solely* for the purpose of attending a hearing.

1. Reasonable

Where travel expenses appear to be unusually high, a suspiciously round figure, or both, a party can request to see evidence.

In any event, cross-examination may be fruitful.

For example, a successful claimant claims the cost of staying the night in a Central London hotel. Her evidence is that this is for the purpose of attending a final hearing in the County Court at Central London. She *lives* in Central London. This may *not* be reasonable.

2. Purpose

For example, a witness drove her car to court. She picked up something from her place of work on the journey. From her home address, court is South. Her office is North. The route was *in*direct.

Her journey North was *not* for the purpose of attending a hearing. It was for an *un*related purpose. That part cannot be awarded.

e. Expert

No more than £750 may be awarded (CPR 27.14(2)(f); and PD 27A at [7.3(2)]).

f. Lay representative

CPR 27.14 applies to lay representatives' fees (CPR 27.14(4)).

g. Personal injury

Stage 1 fixed costs, and where relevant Stage 2 fixed costs, under CPR 45.29 and Tables 10 and 11 of PD 45, may be claimed on the following four conditions.

First, the claim was within the scope of the Pre-Action Protocol for Low Value Personal Injury Claims in Road Traffic Accidents, or the Pre-Action Protocol for Low Value Personal Injury (Employers' Liability and Public Liability) Claims.

Secondly, the claimant reasonably believed that the claim was valued at more than the small claims track limit, in accordance with the relevant protocol.

Thirdly, the defendant admitted liability within the protocol process. Fourthly, the defendant has not already paid these costs.

h. Appeal

CPR 27.14 applies to the costs of an appeal.

This is clear from the wording of CPR 27.14 – 'including those relating to an appeal' – and case law (*Akhtar v Boland* [2014] EWCA Civ 943, [2014] CP Rep 41 at [7]).

If the cost of a transcript has been reasonably incurred, the cost of it may be claimed (CPR 27.14(2)(i)).

More often than not, a transcript will at least *assist* with, if not be *reasonably necessary* to, the just disposal of an appeal.

The fee of £142 for an appellant's, or respondent's, notice, may also be claimed (CPR 27.14(2)(c)).

i. Re-allocation

There are separate rules when a claim has been re-allocated.

i. After leaving the small claims track

CPR 27.14 does *not* apply *after* re-allocation.

The rules that apply to the *new* track are applicable, as if the claim had been allocated to the new track at the outset (CPR 27.15(1)).

ii. From the multi-track

Where a claim is re-allocated from the multi-track to the small claims track, CPR 27.14 applies to the period before, as well as after, re-allocation (CPR 27.15(2)).

The exception is where a court order directed, or a CPR or PD prescribes, otherwise.

j. Discontinuance

Generally, a party who discontinues a claim / counterclaim is *not* liable for the costs of the other party (CPRs 27.2(2) and 38.6(3)).

k. Terms & effects

"Costs" means that the party in whose favour the order for costs is made is entitled to her costs in respect of the part of proceedings to which the order relates, whatever other costs orders are made (PD 44 at [4.2]).

"Costs reserved" means that the decision about costs is deferred to a later occasion, but, if no later order is made, the costs will be in the case.

"Claimant's / Defendant's costs in the application" means that, if the party in whose favour the costs order is made is awarded costs at the end of the proceedings, she is entitled to her costs of the application to which the order relates.

"No order as to costs" means that each party is to bear her own costs of the part of the proceedings to which the order relates, whatever costs order the court makes at the end of the proceedings.

Where an order does not mention costs, in general, this means that no party is entitled to costs in respect of the part of proceedings to which that order relates (CPR 44.10(1)).

24. Unreasonable behaviour

Substantial (as opposed to fixed) costs may be recovered.

a. Further costs

CPR 27.14(2)(g) provides (with emphasis added) that:

> The court may not order a party to pay a sum to another party … except *such further costs* as the court may assess by the summary procedure and order to be paid by a party who has *behaved unreasonably*

This requires a finding that a party has 'behaved unreasonably'.

The court may then find that 'further costs' are payable.

b. Definition

There is no definition in a CPR or PD of "behaved unreasonably".

So, we look to authority for guidance.

There are three, recent authorities.

i. *Dammermann*

In *Dammermann v Lanyon Bowdler LLP* [2017] EWCA Civ 269, [2017] 2 Costs LR 393 ("*Dammermann*"), Longmore LJ and McFarlane LJ (as he then was) gave the following guidance (with emphasis added):

> "[30] … We doubt if we can usefully give general guidance in relation to the circumstances in which it will be appropri-

ate for a court to decide whether a party 'has behaved unreasonably' since *all such cases must be highly fact-sensitive.* In the somewhat different context of the jurisdiction to order a party's legal (or other) representative to meet what are called 'wasted costs' (defined as costs incurred 'as a result of any improper, unreasonable or negligent act or omission' of such representative), the court speaking through Sir Thomas Bingham MR said:

> 'conduct cannot be described as unreasonable simply because it leads in the event to an unsuccessful result or because other more cautious legal representatives would have acted differently. *The acid test is whether the conduct permits of a reasonable explanation.* If so, the course adopted may be regarded as optimistic and as reflecting in a practitioner's judgment, but it is not unreasonable.'

See *Ridehalgh v Horsefield* [1994] Ch 205, 232F.

[31] While we would not wish to incorporate all the learning about wasted costs orders into decisions under CPR Part 27.14(2)(g), we think that *the above dictum should give sufficient guidance on the word 'unreasonably'* to district judges and circuit judges dealing with cases allocated to the Small Claims Track. *Ridehalgh* was, of course, dealing with acts or omissions of legal representatives but *the meaning of 'unreasonably' cannot be different when applied to litigants in person in small claims cases. Litigants in person should not be in a better position than legal representatives but neither should they be in any worse position than such representatives.*

[32] The only other thing we can usefully add is that *it would be unfortunate if litigants were too easily deterred from using the Small Claims Track* by the risk of being held to have behaved unreasonably and thus rendering themselves liable for costs. ..."

This can be summarised into three, key points.

First, cases are fact-sensitive. Secondly, the test is *whether the conduct permits of a reasonable explanation*. Thirdly, the meaning of "unreasonably" is not dependent on legal representation.

ii. *Gempride*

In *Gempride Ltd v Bamrah & Anor* [2018] EWCA Civ 1367, [2019] 1 WLR 1545 at [26], Hickinbottom LJ (with whom Davis LJ agreed) provided further guidance, albeit in the context of wasted costs.

First, mistake, error of judgment, or negligence, without more, will be *in*sufficient to amount to unreasonable conduct.

Secondly, although the conduct of the relevant legal representative *must* amount to a breach of duty owed by that representative to the court, the conduct does *not* have to be in breach of any formal professional rule, or amount to dishonesty.

Thirdly, the burden of proof lies on the *applicant*.

Fourthly, even where the threshold criteria are satisfied, the court *still* has a discretion whether to make an order.

Fifthly, if the court finds "unreasonable behaviour", the sanction must be proportionate to the misconduct in all the circumstances.

iii. *Lastminute.com*

In *Lastminute.com v Tatiana Moskalevitch* [2019] EWHC 1091 (QB), there were two issues.

First, costs of the final hearing. Secondly, costs on appeal.

The submission on the first was that, once the statement accompanying the defence had gone in, the claimant ought to have recognised that the claim could not succeed. It should have been discontinued. Therefore, costs after that date were recoverable.

At paragraph 26, Yip J disposed of the first issue in these terms:

> "I do not accept that that comes close to unreasonable behaviour. If that were the position, then essentially every defended action where a full defence is put forward, and where the claimant then proceeds, would give rise to a costs order, and that would wholly defeat the usual principle that costs on the small claims track are not recoverable. …"

On the second, the "usual rule" is that an unsuccessful respondent pays the court fees, and costs of reasonably obtaining a transcript.

Yip J took an "unusual course", however, for these reasons.

First, the court has a discretion whether to follow the usual rule. Secondly, unusual circumstances. Thirdly, the erroneous order was made on the court's own initiative. The unsuccessful respondent was not responsible. Fourthly, the court had to do justice between the parties. Neither party was to blame.

Fifthly, the successful appellant could have raised the issue of whether the respondent wished to defend the appeal, and explain that costs of appealing would be incurred. The appellant had legal representation. Resolution could have been sought outside of court, but this failure did not amount to behaving unreasonably.

c. Relevant circumstances

The court *will* have regard to all the circumstances.

In particular, this includes the following (CPR 44.2(4)).

First, the conduct of *all* parties. Secondly, whether a party has succeeded on *part* of its case, even if that party has not been wholly successful.

Thirdly, any admissible offer to settle, which is drawn to the court's attention.

Conduct of the parties includes the following (CPR 44.2(5)).

First, conduct *before*, as well as *during*, proceedings. In particular, the extent to which the parties have followed the Practice Direction – Pre-Action Conduct ("the Practice Direction"), or any relevant pre-action protocol (see appendix E).

Secondly, whether it was reasonable for a party to *raise*, *pursue*, or *contest*, a particular allegation, or issue.

Thirdly, the *manner* in which a party has pursued, or defended, a particular allegation, or issue.

Fourthly, whether a claimant who has succeeded, in whole or in part, *exaggerated* her claim.

i. Pre-Action Protocols & Practice Direction

Pre-Action Protocols and the Practice Direction explain the conduct, and the steps, that the court would normally expect parties to take, before commencing proceedings.

1. Non-compliance

Non-compliance in *substance* will be taken into account. Not *minor*, or *technical*, infringements (Practice Direction at [13]).

There may be non-compliance in the following circumstances.

First, failure to provide sufficient information to enable the objectives of pre-action conduct to be achieved. Secondly, unreasonably refusing a form of alternative dispute resolution.

For example, on numerous occasions before proceedings are commenced, the defendant requested a key document. This may be an invoice evidencing the sum claimed.

This evidence would have enabled the defendant to understand the strength of any potential claim. A decision could then have been made as to how to proceed. A genuine attempt to settle may have been made without the need for, and cost of, proceedings.

Unreasonable failure to provide this invoice may amount to a failure to comply. Sufficient information had not been provided to enable the objectives of pre-action conduct to be achieved.

This will likely amount to a failure to take reasonable and proportionate steps before commencing proceedings.

2. Evidence

Ahead of the hearing, a *professional* client may settle a *very* short witness statement setting out substantial non-compliance. Where appropriate, relevant correspondence should be exhibited.

There is *no* requirement to file a witness statement for the purpose of costs *before* a hearing. The statement may attach an offer, for example, which may *not* be seen by the judge until *after* she has given judgment, and the issue of costs is being decided.

The witness statement can still be served on the other party.

Service shows transparency. It also provides the other party with an opportunity to respond. Ambush cannot then be asserted.

Having had the benefit of notice, where no persuasive response is forthcoming, this will only strengthen your position.

In any event, any correspondence that you are relying on *must* be available to all court actors when making an application for costs on the basis that a party has behaved unreasonably.

In practice, you should have sufficient copies for all court actors.

iii. Issues raised, pursued or contested

Unreasonably raising, pursuing, or contesting, issues, show a party's failure to help the court to further the overriding objective.

The case will not have been dealt with justly, and at proportionate cost, so far as practicable. This includes the following (CPR 1.1(2)).

First, saving expense. Secondly, ensuring that it is dealt with both expeditiously, and fairly. Thirdly, allotting to it an appropriate share of the court's resources, while taking into account the need to allot resources to other cases.

1. Abuse of process

A statement of case that is struck out as an abuse of process *should* attract a finding that a party has behaved unreasonably.

Abuse reflects a *grievous* breach of the duty to help the court to further the overriding objective. This includes ensuring that a case is dealt with both expeditiously, and fairly.

Breach of a CPR, PD, or court order, is unnecessary.

2. Summary judgment

A claim or defence which is summarily judged to have no real prospect of success *may* attract a finding that a party has behaved unreasonably. The statement of case was *un*arguable.

The court is likely to require something more, however, before making a finding that a party has behaved unreasonably.

In *Dammermann* at paragraph 32, Longmore LJ and McFarlane LJ (as he then was) said that "it would be unfortunate if litigants were too easily deterred from using the Small Claims Track by the risk of being held to have behaved unreasonably and thus rendering themselves liable for costs".

There is a *qualitative* difference between an *abusive* statement of case, and one that merely has *no prospects of success.*

Where the party with the offending statement of case had legal representation, this may constitute a material circumstance.

a. Represented

Where there has been a failure to comply with a CPR or PD, in general, it is not a good reason that that failure may be solely attributable to a legal representative.

b. Unrepresented

Permission is more likely to be granted to amend a statement of case. This must bring with it a reasonable prospect of success.

In any event, the court is likely to hesitate before finding that an *un*represented party, drafting her *own* statement of case, has behaved unreasonably because there is no real prospect of success.

3. Manner in which a case is pursued

There are two scenarios in which the *manner* that a party has conducted her case may amount to behaving unreasonably.

First, where there are *additional factors* surrounding failure to accept a reasonable, and timely, offer to settle, in light of the amount awarded following judgment.

Secondly, *non-attendance* of a party, or a key witness, where there has been no written notice, and no good reason for absence.

a. Offers

Rejecting an offer is *not* sufficient (CPR 27.14(3)):

> A party's rejection of an offer in settlement will not of itself constitute unreasonable behaviour under paragraph (2)(g) but the court may take it into consideration when it is applying the unreasonableness test

Relevant circumstances around an offer include the following.

First, who made it? Claimant, or defendant?

Secondly, when was it made? Pre-action, early on in proceedings, or on the day of the final hearing?

Thirdly, was it for more, or less, than the judgment sum?

The mere fact that an offer was rejected is *not* sufficient for the court to find that a party has acted unreasonably. Add in three relevant circumstances, however, and it may be.

For example, the *claimant* made the offer. It was *before* she issued the claim. The judgment sum is one-fifth *more* than the offer.

In any event, before making a submission that a party has behaved unreasonably, identify *at least* one circumstance, in addition to the mere fact that there has been a rejection of an offer to settle.

b. Non-attendance

Non-attendance is capable of forming the basis of a submission that the manner in which a party has pursued her case means that she has behaved unreasonably.

The following will often be determinative.

First, whether there was written notice. Secondly, the importance of the likely evidence that the witness is able to give. Thirdly, whether there has been a breach of a CPR, PD, or court order.

i. Party

A party may have behaved unreasonably if she does not attend, and does not give written notice.

If a claimant does *not* attend a final hearing, and does *not* give written notice, the court may *strike out* her claim.

If a defendant does not attend a final hearing, the court may decide the claim on the basis of the claimant's evidence alone. That is, provided that written notice was not given, and the claimant either attended the hearing, or gave written notice.

ii. Witness

In principle, there is *no* requirement to serve a hearsay notice where a witness cannot attend a hearing (CPR 27.2(1)(c)).

In practice, where that witness is *vital,* the other party has *not* been notified, and a good reason has *not* been given for the absence, the court *may* find that a party has behaved unreasonably.

For example, in cases where liability is in dispute following a road traffic collision, the absent witness may determine liability.

The parties are under an obligation to help the court to further the overriding objective (CPR 1.3).

This includes the following (CPR 1.1(2)).

First, saving expense. Secondly, allotting to the case an appropriate share of the court's resources, while taking into account the need to allot resources to other cases. Thirdly, enforcing compliance with court orders.

Standard directions include a time estimate. The notice of allocation will usually include the following direction: 'If a party is aware of a reason why this estimate might be substantially inaccurate, that party must notify the court immediately.'

If so, there is a breach of the CPR, and a court order.

4. Exaggeration

This is important for two reasons.

First, *exaggerated* claims mean *higher* costs and disbursements.

For example, if the claim form is served by the court, the legal representative's fee is £80 where the amount claimed is £5,000; and £100 where the amount claimed is more than £5,000.

A case is not dealt with justly and at proportionate cost by ordering the defendant to pay *exaggerated* costs and disbursements.

It is *irrelevant* whether or not the defence succeeded.

Secondly, *exaggeration* makes it difficult for a defendant to *assess* the true value of a claim, and to *settle* at an earlier stage.

Whilst there is no distinction in the rules between *in*tentional and *un*intentional exaggeration, the former *must* be considered in any assessment of costs (*Painting v University of Oxford* [2005] EWCA Civ 161, [2005] 3 Costs LR 394 at [22]).

5. Unnecessary applications

The parties are under an obligation to help the court to further the overriding objective (CPR 1.3).

This includes the following (CPR 1.1(2)).

First, saving expense. Secondly, ensuring that the matter is dealt with expeditiously and fairly. Thirdly, allotting the case an appropriate share of the court's resources, taking into account the need to allot resources to other cases.

Take a written application to strike out the defence. It may have been necessary to incur the cost of a skeleton argument to counter it. The application, and then the claim, may have been dismissed.

Of itself, this is unlikely to attract a finding that a party has behaved unreasonably. Coupled with *another* circumstance, however, and this *unnecessary application* may tip the balance.

6. Communications

Any communication with the court *must* be disclosed.

If it is in writing, whether paper or electronic, it *must* be copied to the other party (CPRs 27.2(1)(h) and 39.8).

This applies to any matter of *substance,* or *procedure.*

There are three exceptions.

First, for purely routine, uncontentious, and administrative, correspondence. Secondly, where there is a compelling reason for not doing so, and this is clearly stated in the communication.

Thirdly, where authorised by a CPR, or PD.

Correspondence to the court must state three matters.

First, that it is being copied to the other party. Secondly, the identity of the author. Thirdly, her capacity. For example, 'solicitor for the claimant'.

Unless the court otherwise directs, failure to do so *should* result in the court returning the correspondence, with*out* being considered, but with a brief explanation as to *why* it is being returned.

Where there has been a failure to disclose, and to copy to the other party, any communication on a matter of substance or procedure, the court *should* hear from the parties. Having done so, the court may impose sanctions, or exercise its powers of case management.

Corresponding with the court, so as to deprive the other party of an opportunity to respond, amounts to "a serious procedural irregularity" (*National Westminster Bank Plc v Rushmer* [2010] EWHC 554 (Ch), [2010] 2 FLR 362 at [35]).

The overriding objective includes ensuring that the parties are on an *equal footing*. This is *not* achieved if one party corresponds with the court on a matter of substance or procedure, *without notice* to the other party, so that the other party can*not* respond.

7. Opportunism

Opportunistically resisting an application that is bound to succeed requires "heavy costs sanctions" to be imposed (*Denton & Ors v TH White Ltd & Ors* [2014] EWCA Civ 906, [2015] 1 All ER 880 at [43]).

This is *in*compatible with the duty of the parties to help the court to further the overriding objective. It *frustrates* the court's duty to actively case-manage. In particular, to encourage cooperation.

d. Summary assessment

In principle, costs should be summarily assessed at the end of the hearing, unless there is a *good* reason not to do so (PD 44 at [9.2]).

In practice, the exception will be *rare*.

For example, where the party who has behaved unreasonably shows *substantial* grounds for disputing the amount of costs.

e. Statement of costs

Parties and their legal representatives must assist the court to make a summary assessment of costs.

To do so, a written "statement of costs" should be drafted.

In principle, it should follow Form N260 as closely as possible.

In practice, this form is used. In any event, it must be signed, either by the party, or that party's legal representatives (PD 44 at [9.5]).

i. Particulars

The following should be in a separate schedule (PD 44 at [9.5(2)]).

First, number of hours. Secondly, hourly rate. Thirdly, grade of fee earner. Fourthly, amount and nature of any disbursement (other than counsel's fee for appearing at the hearing). Fifthly, amount of legal representative's costs to be claimed for attending, or appearing at, the hearing. Sixthly, counsel's fees. Seventhly, any VAT.

If the party who you are representing is a limited company, confirm whether it is *registered* for VAT, and whether it can *reclaim* the VAT on costs. The court may ask, and, if you are not able to confirm, VAT on costs may not be awarded.

1. Grade & number of hours

Be prepared to justify the number of hours that are claimed.

Reasonableness will likely depend on two factors. First, *extent* and *complexity* of the procedural history. Secondly, *grade* of fee earner.

If there are a number of previous applications, the number of hours invested in the case is likely to be high.

In a straightforward claim for the cost of repairs following a road traffic collision, absent pre-final hearing applications, however, the court will expect a *modest* number of hours.

It is hard to justify a Grade 'A' fee earner.

Where the claim or defence is *abusive,* there is a stronger argument that the issues are more *complex,* requiring a guiding, *experienced* fee-earner.

There is, of course, a *limit.* There is also a *balance.*

A *lower* grade of fee earner means a *larger* number of hours.

2. Rate

Solicitors' guideline hourly rates can be found online at www.gov.uk/guidance/solicitors-guideline-hourly-rates.

See appendix I.

a. London

Band 1 encompasses very heavy *commercial* and *corporate* work by *centrally-based London firms,* and is *not* restricted by postcode.

Band 2 encompasses EC1-EC4, W1, WC1, WC2 and SW1.

Band 3 encompasses all other boroughs, Dartford and Gravesend.

b. National

Band 1 encompasses 12 *counties* and 12 *areas.*

The *counties* are: Berkshire; Buckinghamshire; Dorset; Essex; Hampshire (and the Isle of Wight); Kent; Middlesex; Oxfordshire; Suffolk; Surrey; Sussex; and Wiltshire.

The *areas* are: Birkenhead; (Inner) Birmingham; Bristol; Cambridge City; (Inner) Cardiff; (Inner) Leeds (within 2km of the City Art Gallery); Liverpool; (Central) Manchester; Newcastle City (within two miles of St Nicholas Cathedral); Norwich City; Nottingham City; and Watford.

Band 2 encompasses all places that are not included in London 1-3 and National Band 1.

ii. Notice

The statement of costs *must* be filed at court, and a copy must be *served* on the other party, *as soon as possible.*

In any event, this should be *not less than 24 hours* before the hearing. In practice, this means *one working day* before the hearing.

Without reasonable excuse, failure to do so *will* be taken into account when deciding what order to make (PD 44 at [9.6]).

It is prudent to print off *spare copies* of the statement of costs, with the correspondence *filing,* and *serving,* it, stapled to the front.

In practice, the correspondence is likely to be a single email to the court, copying in any other party.

If there are two cover letters because it has been posted, order the cover letter filing the statement of costs with the court first, then the cover letter serving it, followed by the statement of costs.

Evidencing filing and service usually short circuits any dispute over the same. In practice, such disputes are common.

iii. Absence

For barristers, where there is no statement of costs, practice managers, or professional clients, should be able to confirm fees.

This sum plus any applicable VAT is often awarded. It deals with the issue of costs swiftly, without the need for a further hearing.

25. Appeals

It is part of your implied instructions to make an oral application for permission to appeal where properly arguable.

a. Court

The "appeal court" is the court to which an appeal *must* be made.

The "lower court" is the court from whose decision an appeal is brought (CPR 52.1(3)(b) and (c)).

For a first appeal, the appeal court from a (deputy) district judge is the circuit judge at the same county court (if there is one).

In the rare circumstance that a circuit judge heard the claim, the appeal court is a High Court judge.

It does not depend on whether the decision was interim, or final.

For a second appeal, the appeal court is the Court of Appeal (PD 52A at [3.4]–[3.5], and Table 1).

b. Centre

Appeals *must* be brought in the appropriate "appeal centre".

All other notices, such as the respondent's notice, *must* also be filed at that appeal centre.

The venue for an appeal will be determined by the Designated Civil Judge. This may be different to the appeal centre (PD 52B at [2.2] and Table A).

c. Permission

Permission *must* be given to bring an appeal.

There are two tests. First appeals, and second appeals.

An oral, or a written, application, can be made.

Two other applications can also be made.

First, for a stay of the lower court's order. Secondly, for an extension of time in which to file an appellant's notice.

i. Need

Any party wishing to appeal requires permission (CPR 52.3(1)).

This includes a party wishing to appeal against an order made without a hearing, or in her absence in accordance with her request (PD 27A at [8.2]).

In principle, an application for permission to appeal may be made to the lower court that made the decision being appealed (CPR 52.3(2)(a)). In practice, this is often refused.

Further application *must* be to the *appeal* court (CPR 52.3(3)(a)).

ii. Test

The test is different for first, and second, appeals.

1. First appeal

Permission *may* only be given in two circumstances (CPR 52.6(1)).

First, the court considers that the appeal would have a *real prospect of success*. Secondly, there is some *other compelling reason* for the appeal to be heard.

Permission is *not* granted as of right, even where the test is satisfied. The court has a *discretion*. This is clear from the word "may".

In practice, the first limb of the test is most frequently relied upon.

In *R (A Child)* [2019] EWCA Civ 895, [2019] FLR 1033 at [31], Peter Jackson LJ (with whom Baker LJ agreed) said that "there must be a realistic, as opposed to a fanciful, prospect of success. There is no requirement that success should be probable, or more likely than not."

2. Second appeal

The Court of Appeal *will not* give permission, *unless* it considers that one of the following is *satisfied* (CPR 52.7(2)).

First, the appeal would have a real prospect of success, *and raise an important point of principle or practice*. Secondly, there is some other compelling reason *for the Court of Appeal* to hear it.

From a decision of the county court, which was itself made on appeal, *only the Court of Appeal* can give permission (CPR 52.7(1)).

Permission is *not* granted as of right. Even where the test is met.

In practice, the *first* limb of the test is most frequently relied upon.

The *first* part of the *first* limb of the second appeal test is the same as the *first* limb of the *first* appeal test.

The *second* part of the *first* limb – 'raise an important point of principle or practice' – means one "that has not yet been established".

This was confirmed by McCombe LJ (with whom Richards LJ agreed) in *BS (Congo) & Ors v Secretary of State for the Home Department* [2015] EWCA Civ 639 at [17].

iii. Oral application

After judgment and costs, an oral application may be made.

Reasons for the application should be clear, and concise.

It is part of your implied instructions to make an oral application for permission to appeal where properly arguable. If you do not, an opportunity to gain permission will have been lost.

A written application attracts a fee. An oral application does not.

iv. Appellant's notice

Where permission is sought from the appeal court, it must be in the form of an "appellant's notice".

This is Form N164 (PDs 27A at [8A] and 52B at [4.1]).

Guidance is available in Form N161A.

As a general rule, it *must* be filed at the appeal court within *21* days of the *date of the decision* of the lower court.

This may be longer, or shorter, as directed by the lower court.

CPRs, and PDs, regarding time limits, apply (PD 52D).

Unless the appeal court orders otherwise, it *must* be served on each respondent as soon as practicable. In any event, it *must* be no later than *seven* days after it is filed.

1. Fee

It *must* be accompanied by the *fee* of £142, a fee *remission* application, or *certificate* (PD 52B at [4.1]).

2. Documents

The following *must* be filed with the notice (PD 52B at [4.2]).

First, three copies of the appellant's notice, and one additional copy for each respondent.

Secondly, a copy of the sealed order under appeal.

Thirdly, where an application was made to the lower court for permission to appeal, a copy of any order granting or refusing permission, together with a copy of the reasons, if any, for allowing, or refusing, permission.

Fourthly, grounds of appeal.

3. Grounds

Grounds of appeal *must* be set out on a *separate* sheet, and *attached* to the appellant's notice. They *must* set out why the decision of the lower court was one of the following (CPR 52.21(3)).

First, *wrong*. Secondly, *unjust* because of a serious procedural, or other, irregularity.

Language used must be simple, clear and concise.

4. Transcript

There is no requirement for a transcript of the judgment of the lower court, or other record of reasons (PD 52B at [6.2]).

In practice, it will likely assist the appeal court.

v. Respondent's notice

A respondent *may* file and serve a "respondent's notice".

This is Form N162.

Guidance is available in Form N162A.

It *must* be filed in two circumstances (CPR 52.13(2)).

First, where permission to appeal is sought from the *appeal* court by the *respondent.* Secondly, the respondent wishes to ask the appeal court to uphold the decision of the lower court for reasons *different* from, or *additional* to, those given by the lower court.

1. Permission

Where permission is sought from the appeal court, it *must* be in a respondent's notice.

It *must* be filed within such period as directed by the lower court, or 14 days after the "relevant date".

Where permission to appeal was *granted* by the *lower* court, or permission to appeal is *not* required, the relevant date is when the respondent is *served* with the appellant's notice.

When the *respondent* is served with notification that the *appeal* court has *given* the appellant permission, this is the relevant date.

When the *respondent* is served with notification that the *application* for permission to appeal and the *appeal* itself are to be heard together, this is the relevant date.

2. Service

Unless otherwise ordered by the appeal court, the respondent's notice *must* be served on the appellant, and any other respondent, *as soon as practicable,* and no later than *seven* days after filing.

d. Skeleton arguments

Skeleton arguments should *not* be relied on as a matter of course.

They should *only* be used in two circumstances (PD 52B at [8.3]).

First, where they are *justified* on the basis of the *complexity* of the issues of *fact,* or *law,* in the appeal.

Secondly, they would otherwise assist the court in respects that are *not readily apparent from the documents* in the appeal.

In general, the cost of a skeleton argument is not recoverable.

e. Appeal bundle

As soon as practicable, but in any event, within *35* days of filing the appellant's notice, the appellant *must* file an appeal bundle.

It *must* contain *only* those documents that are "relevant" to the appeal. This is subject to any order made by the court.

It *must* be paginated and indexed (PD 52B at [6.3]).

i. Relevant

There are six "relevant" documents (PD 52B at [6.4(1)]).

First, the appellant's notice. Secondly, any respondent's notice. Thirdly, any skeleton argument. Fourthly, the order under appeal.

Fifthly, the order of the lower court, granting or refusing permission to appeal, with a copy of the judge's reasons (if any). Sixthly, a copy of any order allocating the case to the small claims track.

Relevant documents obtained, or created, after the appeal bundle has been filed, should be added to the appeal bundle as soon as practicable. In any event, this *must* be no less than *seven* days before the hearing of the appeal, or any application (PD 52B at [6.6]).

ii. May be relevant

If *relevant,* include the following (PD 52B at [6.4(2)]).

First, statements of case. Secondly, application notices. Thirdly, other orders made in the case. Fourthly, chronology of events.

Fifthly, witness statements made in support of any application in the appellant's notice. Sixthly, other witness statements. Seventhly, documents that a party considers would assist the court.

iii. Service

The appeal bundle must be served as follows (PD 52B at [6.5]).

Where permission to appeal was *granted* by the *lower* court, at the *same time* as filing the *appeal bundle.*

Where the *appeal* court has *granted* permission to appeal, as soon as practicable after notification, and, in any event, within *14* days of the *grant of permission.*

Where the *appeal* court directs that the *application* for permission to appeal will be heard on the *same* occasion as the *appeal,* as soon as practicable, and, in any event, within *14* days after *notification of the hearing date.*

iv. Respondent's documents

Where a respondent considers that relevant documents have been omitted, she may file and serve on all parties a "respondent's supplemental appeal bundle".

It should contain the omitted documents. It *must* be filed and served as soon as practicable, and, in any event, no less than *seven* days before the hearing (PD 52B at 8.2).

f. Applications

Applications should be made to the *lower* court.

Where the time limit for filing an appellant's notice has expired, they should be made to the *appeal* court.

i. Stay

Application can be made to stay the order of the lower court.

This should be in the appellant's notice. Any application for a transcript at public expense should be in this notice (PD 52B at [4.3]).

ii. Extension

Application can be made for an extension of time to file an appellant's notice.

Where the time limit for filing an appellant's notice has expired, the appellant must include an application within the appellant's notice (PD 52B at [3.2] and [4.3]).

It *must* state the following (PD 52B at [3.2]).

First, the *reason* for delay. Secondly, the *steps taken* before making the application.

The court *may* make an order granting, or refusing, an extension of time. This may be with, or without, a hearing.

Where it is with*out* a hearing, a party seeking to set aside, or vary, the order, may apply for a hearing within *14* days of service of the order (PD 52B at [3.3]).

g. Determination

Applications may be determined with, or without, a hearing. This includes an application for permission to appeal (PD 52B at [7.1]).

Where permission to appeal is refused without a hearing, a party may *request* this to be reconsidered at a hearing.

Where the court determines any other application without a hearing, any party affected by that determination may *apply* to have the order set aside, or varied.

In any event, the following are *mandatory* (PD 52B at [7.4]).

First, the request or application *must* be made within *seven* days of *service of notification of the determination* upon the party making the application.

Secondly, a copy of the request, or application, *must* be served on *all other parties* at the *same* time. Thirdly, the court *will* give directions for the determination of the application.
Where an appeal is allowed, the appeal court will, if possible, dispose of the case at the *same* time. That is, with*out* ordering a further hearing in the lower court. The court may do so without hearing further evidence (PD 27A at [8.3]).

h. Costs

The costs regime under CPR 27.14 applies to appeals.

In *Akhtar v Boland* [2014] EWCA Civ 943, [2014] CP Rep 41 at [7], Sir Stanley Burnton (with whom Floyd and Gloster LJJ agreed) said (with emphasis added) that:

> "If I could, I would order the appellant to pay the respondent's costs of his appeal to this Court. However, the power of this Court to make a costs order is constrained by the CPR. *The wording of CPR 27.14 is clear, and extends to the costs of an appeal,* and I see no basis for construing that as inapplicable to an appeal to this Court. ... Regrettably, therefore, I would make no order for costs on the appeal to this Court, on the ground that any such order is precluded by CPR r.27.14."

In *Dammermann v Lanyon Bowdler LLP* [2017] EWCA Civ 269, [2017] 2 Costs LR 393 at [15], Longmore LJ and McFarlane LJ (as he then was) said (with emphasis added) that:

> "The first point to note about *the provisions in Part 27.14* is that they *apply to an appeal.* Ms Tildesley was therefore right to draw the provision to the judge's attention ... see *Akhtar v Boland* [2014] EWCA Civ 943."

26. Attendance notes

An attendance note ("a note") may be condensed, or contain a complete, word-for-word alternative to a transcript.

In any event, the practice of writing a couple of sentences on a back sheet is dying out for a number of reasons.

There are no set rules for notes, albeit there are pieces of information that any note should strive to contain.

This includes the name of the court, judge, legal representative (if there is one), and the terms of any order.

In a competitive market, professional clients repeatedly instruct counsel where there is evidence (a note) of the following.

First, ability to *foresee* problems, take *prompt* action to flag them up, and *mitigate* against any unavoidable hurdles.

Secondly, gain the *trust and confidence* of a witness in a pre-hearing conference.

Thirdly, ability to deliver sound legal submissions, which, on looking at the reasoning in the judgment, have *had the desired impact.*

a. Utility

Notes are helpful. For counsel, those instructing, and the party who they represent. In different ways, and for different reasons.

i. Counsel

For counsel, it offers an opportunity to make a clear, *contemporaneous,* comprehensive note of what has been said, complete with any relevant context.

For example, the time that a conference started, that the witness had an opportunity to read an unmarked copy of her statement, and that she confirmed the accuracy and truth of it, without any suggested amendments.

During cross-examination, the witness may admit that she was not wearing a seat belt. This may conflict with her written evidence.

The note may provide that the witness did not take the opportunity in conference to correct her written evidence. If this inconsistency is cited in the judgment as a reason that the credibility of this witness was undermined, then, the note may provide counsel with reassurance that they gave the witness an opportunity to re-read the statement, and amend it, ahead of the final hearing.

If there is any dispute as to what was said, perhaps days, months, or even *years*, later, a detailed note provides a persuasive answer.

ii. Professional client

For a professional client, the following are vital.

First, what points were successful, and the reasons why. Secondly, what points were not successful, and the reasons why. Thirdly, the total amount of the judgment sum. Fourthly, a breakdown of the amounts awarded for each head of loss. Fifthly, any payment terms. For example, payment within 21 (as opposed to 14) days.

If your lay client asks your professional client what was discussed in conference, what oral evidence was given, or what were the reasons for judgment against them, your professional client will be able to respond. Promptly, in detail, and with confidence.

This is a reason that your note should promptly be sent to your professional client. They must be able to field questions from their client. This is often shortly after a hearing.

A professional client will not appreciate being kept in the dark.

It may compromise their relationship with their client. *In*ability to answer questions, advise on next steps, or prospects of successfully appealing, is *not* conducive to building trust and confidence.

iii. Lay client

For a party, they may wish to confirm, for example, the reasoning in the judgment. They may have been held to be an unreliable historian of events. If so, what was the factual basis?

A comprehensive note of the judgment will enable a professional client to inform a party of the reasoning in the judgment, and the factual findings in support of it.

After the hearing, it is prudent to *telephone* your professional client to relay the result. They may need to revert to their client *promptly.* Even if you take time to proofread your note before emailing it, your professional client will be able to revert to her client, if the result has promptly been relayed over the telephone.

It will also enable a party to instruct counsel to advise whether or not there are prospects of successfully appealing, without having to wait for, and incur the cost of, a transcript.

Remember that your lay client may reasonably request to see your note. This may inform whether you wish to include, for example, your mobile telephone number.

It may also inform whether you include a candid view of the reasonableness of your lay client, or her credibility.

This is *not* code to conceal.

They are reasons to send a *professional* note.

b. Fundamentals

At the top of the note, it is helpful to set out the following details.

First, the names of the parties as they appear on the statements of case. Secondly, the claim number. Thirdly, the name of the court. Fourthly, the number of the courtroom. Fifthly, the title, and the name, of the judge. Sixthly, the date of the hearing.

Seventhly, the type of hearing (preliminary or final). Eighthly, the title, surname, and status (counsel or solicitor) of any advocate representing the other party. Ninthly, the contact details of your professional client, including her name, firm, and email address.

c. Outcome

The outcome should be on the first page.

Usually, this will be the *terms of the order.*

If the hearing has been adjourned, and the party represented by you has been directed to do something, this should **stand out.**

It should also **stand out** in the email attaching your note.

d. Correspondence

It is prudent to note any material correspondence.

This includes correspondence with your *professional* client, instructions taken in conference from your *lay* client, or issues raised by the *other party.*

This is especially helpful where, for example, an offer to settle is made. It is useful to have a note of the terms of that offer after the hearing, when the issue of costs is decided, and for your professional client to assess quantum in future, similar cases.

i. Professional client

For counsel, it may be helpful to record that a key document, such as an invoice, has been requested from a professional client ahead of the hearing via *email;* and followed up with a *telephone* call.

If the head of loss to which that invoice relates is then dismissed, there is a note to the effect that counsel has discharged her duty to *foresee* problems, and to *promptly* attempt to resolve them.

The terms of any offer to settle (including provision for costs) should be noted, including when it was made, and who made it.

The note should also provide when you relayed that offer to your professional client, your advice as to whether or not it was in your client's interests to accept that offer, and any instructions from your professional client.

If an offer to settle is made, and you advise your professional client that, the *best* alternative to a settlement out of court is judgment for the same, or even *less* than that offer, and your client does not beat that offer after a final hearing, the question *why* that offer was not accepted may reasonably be asked.

If you are able to set out the above, and that you did not have authority to accept the offer, despite receipt of your advice, counsel has discharged her professional duty.

ii. Lay client

Instructions taken in conference should be noted.

What time the conference started, when the witness read an unmarked copy of her statement, whether she confirmed the contents of that statement without any suggested amendment, and whether she confirmed her signature.

If that witness changes a material part of her written evidence under cross-examination, thereby undermining her credibility, so that the case that you are instructed to present is dismissed, counsel cannot be criticised in this respect.

The *exact* words of any suggested amendment should be noted, and the *paragraph* of the statement to which they relate.

It is often helpful for a witness to read the other party's statement(s), and to take a note of what that witness says in *response* to material evidence conflicting with the case of the party who you represent.

First, to understand the case that you are instructed to present.

Especially in cases following a road traffic collision, witness statements can be sparse, lacking the necessary detail as to the exact location of the collision, where the impact was in respect of each vehicle, and the mechanism of collision.

Secondly, when cross-examining, you know what facts are in dispute, and what the witness for the party who you represent has to say about them.

iii. Other party

When you speak to the other party before the hearing, summarise the material points that arose out of that discussion.

As well as offers to settle, the issues that are in dispute, and any procedural issues, are helpful to note.

First, to have at your fingertips during the hearing, especially if you are representing the claimant, and summarising the issues in dispute at the outset.

Secondly, so that you can speak to your professional client, relay the same *accurately*, and take *precise* instructions.

Thirdly, so that your professional client is able to understand the other party's position *ahead* of the hearing, and compare that to the judgment *after* the hearing.

e. Tactical & strategic decisions

Any *tactical* or *strategic* decision before a hearing should be noted.

For example, the defendant is required to make an application for relief from sanctions due to failure to serve a key document, such as an invoice. The claimant wishes to rely on video footage of the collision that has not been served until the day of the final hearing.

On instructions, and on receipt of your advice, the decision is taken not to resist the claimant relying on this video. The reason is that this will assist the defendant's application for relief from sanctions. If instructions were taken over the telephone, the time of that call, and the person giving these instructions, may be noted.

The video may feature heavily in the reasoning of the judgment *against the party who you represent.* Succinctly summarising the circumstances in which this decision was made can be helpful for counsel, those instructing, and the lay client.

This is because, if the question is asked why there was no resistance to the video going into evidence, say, a week after the final hearing – when memories have faded – a persuasive answer is in a contemporaneous note.

f. Additional instructions

Additional instructions to those in the brief to counsel, whether obtained over the telephone, or via email, should be noted.

This is so that, in days, months, or years to come, if there is a question as to why something was, or was not, agreed, admitted, or submitted, there is a contemporaneous note recording the reason.

For example, you may have deleted the email, instructing you not to pursue a counterclaim, in accordance with your privacy policy.

g. During hearing

Some advocates make an accurate, word-for-word note of the hearing. Others summarise. Either way, oral evidence, submissions, judgment, and the terms of the order, are useful to note.

i. Shorthand

In case of appeal, where a transcript of the hearing may be requested, the time that the hearing was called on may be helpful.

Counsel for the claimant, Ms Smith, may be shortened to "S".

Whenever Ms Smith addresses the court, a note can be made using shorthand. For example: 'S: this is a claim for credit hire, where need, period, and rate, are the issues that are in dispute.'

The judge can be shortened to "J".

In the above example, if the defendant agrees that these are the issues in dispute, the court will not then allow the defendant to cross-examine on, for example, enforceability. This is why an accurate note of what was said during proceedings is important.

ii. Evidence

In case of appeal, the time that a witness was called may be helpful, in the event that a transcript of the hearing is requested.

The oral evidence given by a witness should be noted carefully.

Instead of noting question and answer, they can be combined.

Take the question: "You could have used public transport?" And the answer: "I have a disabled mother, who I often take to the hospital." This can be combined: "I could not use public transport as I have a disabled mother, who I often take to the hospital."

If a witness makes a concession in cross-examination, and you wish to refer to it in your closing submissions, you can **embolden** it. There are two reasons to do so.

First, it can be easily found. Secondly, it is more persuasive to quote the *actual words* used, rather than paraphrase.

If your witness says something on which you wish to re-examine, again, you can **embolden** it, so that you can quickly find it.

Sometimes, the judge will comment on a piece of evidence, submission, or the conduct of a party.

If it assists your case, again, it can be **emboldened**, for ease of reference. Then, it can be incorporated into your closing submissions, application for costs on the basis that a party has behaved unreasonably, or both.

For example, the judge may strike out a claim, on the basis that it is abusive. If so, the *reasoning* of the *ruling* may be usefully *relayed* when making submissions that costs should be awarded on the basis that the claimant has behaved unreasonably.

You may submit that, *given the reasoning for strike out,* the only *consistent* ruling is that the claimant has *behaved unreasonably.*

If the judge asked the other party a question, it may be a point that you would like to address in submissions. If so, **emboldening** it will enable you to find it, and answer it at the appropriate time.

iii. Submissions

Note the other party's closing submissions for three reasons.

First, if there is anything that you need to address, this will remind you to do so. Secondly, if a concession is made, you can rely on it in your closing submissions. Thirdly, to demonstrate internal inconsistency, and inherent unlikelihood.

iv. Judgment

A word-for-word note of the judgment is helpful for four reasons.

First, to explain to your lay client why her case was dismissed, she was not awarded the full amount claimed, or the reasons that the judge found that her credibility was compromised.

Secondly, to advise on prospects of successfully appealing, or resisting an appeal.

Where there are prospects of appeal, the relevant sentence, paragraph, or passage, can be **emboldened**, so that it stands out from the rest of the judgment.

Thirdly, so that both you, and your professional client, have a note of what submissions succeeded, failed, and did not feature in the reasoning of the judgment. This is so that, in future cases, you can hone your submissions.

Professional client and counsel are thereby better able to fulfil their professional duty to further their client's best interests, and help the *court* to further the overriding objective.

Fourthly, if the order is incompatible with the judgment, there may be an error. If so, this can be corrected using the slip rule.

Without an *accurate* note of the judgment, you are in a weaker position to *advise* whether there has been an error; and what the order *should* read, so that it accurately reflects the *judgment.*

v. Order

The terms of the order should be set out on the first page.

You may also wish to copy and paste the same into the email to your professional client, attaching the note.

This is for the convenience of your *professional* client.

h. Next steps

If the hearing was preliminary, after which the court made case management directions, this is the place to note them.

Any summary advice on next steps should be included. In practice, this should not be longer than, say, a paragraph.

You may have seen the evidence in support of the claim. If so, you may also have advised that an offer for that sum should be made, together with the relevant fixed costs that have been incurred.

Your professional client is then in a position to act on your advice, make the offer, and attempt to settle the matter out of court.

i. Travel expenses

Some advocates set out their travel expenses for two reasons.

First, your practice manager may have agreed with your professional client that they should be billed, in addition to the brief fee, especially where the court is some distance from your chambers.

Secondly, when working out your expenses for tax purposes, your notes provide a convenient, contemporary record.

This is a failsafe if you are not as fastidious in going through your expenses every month or so. When you do come around to it, you should then be able to see your travel expenses in detail.

j. Contact details

At the bottom of a note, the name of your practice manager, her contact details, and your professional address should be set out, in case your professional client wishes to contact you.

Remember that your lay client may reasonably request your note, so bear this in mind if you provide your mobile telephone number.

k. Telephone

Speak to your professional client after the hearing.

First, to relay the result *promptly*, so that your *professional* client is able to answer questions, should the *lay* client telephone. You may take some time proofreading your note.

Secondly, this is an *opportunity to build rapport* with a professional client, who may be based at the other end of the country.

It is easier to build rapport over the telephone than in writing.

l. Email

Once completed, email your note to your professional client.

Ideally, on the day of the hearing

In any event, this should be within 24 hours. Professional clients choose repeatedly to instruct counsel who promptly send notes.

Copy your practice manager into this email for three reasons.

First, she will know that the case can be billed.

Secondly, if there is a further hearing, but, due to another professional commitment, you are unable to attend, your practice manager is able to forward your note to counsel who will attend.

Thirdly, if your professional client contacts your practice manager to say that they have not received your note, your practice manager can forward on your note, *without* having to revert to you.

27. Tools

A number of tools are useful to a junior advocate.

A smart phone, laptop, and access to online, electronic legal resources are invaluable. They enable you to correspond, type up attendance notes, orders, and look up an authority that has arisen just before, during, or after, a hearing.

The rise in remote working, telephone and audio-visual hearings, have also given increased importance to software.

a. Smart phone

Most carry a mobile telephone.

It is necessary to swiftly send requests for, and to rapidly receive, instructions, from your professional client.

For example: to relay that a witness is late; and to receive instructions that the good reason for this is that she was admitted to an accident and emergency department of a hospital.

It is also necessary to urgently update your practice manager.

For example: to relay that your train has been delayed; or to receive the notification that, in fact, the in-person hearing has been vacated whilst making your way to court.

Offers to settle must *promptly* be relayed to professional clients.

This is so that instructions can swiftly be taken as to whether they should be accepted. The terms of a last-minute counter-offer may need to be relayed before the case is called on.

A *smart phone* is helpful for in-person hearings.

First, to check train times, buy tickets, and plan your route to and from court, using the full range of public transport options. This includes tube, train, and bus.

Secondly, to use online navigation software, and find the court.

Thirdly, so that you can tether your smart phone to your laptop.

This enables access to the internet. Online legal resources may need to be considered. For example, so as to confirm whether an authority has received negative judicial consideration.

b. Laptop

A laptop, and the software to utilise it efficiently, are invaluable.

A laptop charger guards against running out of battery. It is especially important when your case is on an *un*assigned list.

You may be waiting, while getting on with other work, as the prospects increase that your laptop will run out of battery.

i. Hardware

For *remote* hearings, a computer is necessary. It need not be portable. Desktop computers suffice.

Two electronic devices are preferable. One to access the hearing. Another to access electronic copies of the documents.

A preliminary issue may arise as to whether a document has been filed or served. Many professional clients file and serve documents by sending an email, to both the court and the other side, attaching the document to that email. Frequently, the court and the other party are recipients of the same email.

If so, this email can be forwarded to counsel in advance of the hearing. If the issue of filing, or service, arises, that email can be forwarded to the court, copying in any other legal representative.

The date and time of the email, and any attachment, can then swiftly be determined.

Or, an authority may arise just before, or during, a remote hearing. This can be emailed to all court actors when they have a computer, internet, and email.

A laptop is invaluable for *in-person* hearings for three reasons.

First, so that you have an electronic copy of the documents. You may have to hand up your spare, hard copy to the court, or it may be needed as a witness bundle.

Secondly, so that you can take an accurate note of the hearing, swiftly proofread, and then promptly email it to those instructing.

Thirdly, so that you can send and receive emails, access online, electronic legal resources, and view an online diary.

ii. Software

Software enables you to be effective, and efficient.

1. Read Aloud

Read Aloud reads your document.

It is available for Windows, macOS and iOS.

For example, in Microsoft Word on macOS, press 'Review' then 'Read Aloud'. Controls are simple. 'Play'. 'Pause'.

To change paragraphs, press 'Previous' or 'Next'. To exit, press 'x'. Using the icon that looks like a gear on top of a speaker, the reading speed can be altered, and the voice changed.

It is useful for rapid assimilation, and proofreading.

2. Speech

Speech enables PDFs to be selected and read on macOS.

To activate, click the Apple symbol in the top, right-hand corner. Select 'System Settings' then 'Accessibility'. Select the 'VoiceOver' button, so that it moves left-to-right and turns blue.

Reading speed and voice can be changed in 'Speech'.

Speech is for PDFs what Read Aloud is for Word documents.

3. Adobe Acrobat

The main benefit over PDF Expert (without the Premium upgrade) is that a document can be converted into a searchable digital file.

Optical Character Recognition ("OCR") converts images of typed, hand-written, or printed, text, into digital text.

A photocopied bundle will arrive as a photograph. If it is clear enough, text can be converted by OCR into digital text. This enables you to search the document for words, or phrases.

To convert a bundle, open it. Select 'All tools', 'Scan & OCR', 'In This File', 'All Pages', 'English UK', and 'Recognise Text'.

To search that bundle, open it. Click 'Find text or tools', insert the word or phrase, and press 'Enter'.

You can also press and hold 'command' and 'F' to search.

4. PDF Expert

This is *excellent* for constructing bundles.

Documents may be inserted, or removed, from an existing bundle.

Pages may be rearranged.

They can be paginated, indexed, and bookmarked.

Bundles may be annotated with comments, underlining, and highlighting. These may be exported, and printed.

For OCR, use Adobe Acrobat, and open the file in PDF Expert.

To search a converted bundle, open it in PDF Expert. Use the search bar in the top, right-hand corner.

c. Online resources

Access to an electronic version of a professional text will save you from carrying a hard copy to in-person hearings.

Professional texts may be saved electronically, however, online access is preferable.

First, the number of professional texts, and authorities, that you can access online. This has the corresponding impracticality of taking hard copies to an in-person hearing, or of saving electronic copies to your electronic device.

Secondly, when accessed, you can be confident that you are reading a version that is (likely to be more) up to date. A printed copy, or one that has been saved electronically, may be out of date.

You may recall an authority that assists your case. The legal principle that it is authority for has only been raised during submissions. Therefore, you do not have a copy of the authority.

If you have online access to an electronic database, you can find the name, citation, and relevant paragraph. The reason for not providing a copy in advance can be stated.

The best interests of your client can then be served, whilst also assisting the court to further the overriding objective.

This includes dealing with the matter justly, and at proportionate cost, without the need for an adjournment, or an appeal.

d. Notepad

A notepad and a black, ball-point pen are useful.

First, in case your laptop is unworkable. Secondly, to draft consent orders that may be signed when attending an in-person hearing.

A consent order may be scanned, emailed to you, and sent to your professional client, or just stored on your external, encrypted hard drive. In either case, the hard copy can be disposed of confidentially. This assists your practice to become paperless.

It therefore also furthers the objectives of data protection.

Writing should be in black ink. Text should be in capital letters.

When scanned, and photocopied, it will then remain legible.

e. Tablet

A tablet is useful for three reasons.

First, playing a video following a road traffic collision during an in-person hearing, so that all court actors can see it. Secondly, so that it can be used as an electronic witness bundle. Thirdly, during a remote hearing, to navigate around an electronic bundle.

In the likely event that you are required to cross-examine on a video, it is not possible to play the video, whilst simultaneously taking a note of the evidence, on a single electronic device.

All too often, separate witness bundles do not make it to an in-person hearing. If so, the bundle may be accessed using your professional email address and a tablet.

It is preferable to have two electronic devices for remote hearings.

One to access the hearing. Another to access the documents.

g. The Highway Code

Where liability is in dispute, *The Highway Code* is essential for final hearings following a road traffic collision.

It is the starting point for identifying the standard of care that is expected of a reasonable driver.

h. Judicial College Guidelines

Where there is a claim for personal injury, the *Judicial College Guidelines for the Assessment of General Damages in Personal Injury Cases* (17th edn, OUP, 2024) is essential.

i. Props

In cases following a road traffic collision, toy, or model, cars, may be useful for conferences. They may also assist with oral evidence.

Reasons include that a witness can demonstrate the mechanism of collision, point of impact, and corresponding damage.

Other items may also be used. For example, highlighters.

j. External encrypted vault

Electronic devices should promptly be sanitised of confidential material, in accordance with your privacy policy.

Once a case is concluded, there is no good reason to retain confidential material relating to it on a *portable* electronic device.

To comply with data protection and privacy laws, external hard drives containing confidential material *must* be encrypted.

There are two forms of encryption.

Hardware and software.

In general, hardware encryption is preferable. This means that a keypad requires a *numerical code* to be entered before the hard drive will be recognised, and files can be accessed, or transferred.

One encrypted, external hard drive is *vital.* Two are preferable.

The first can be kept under lock and key in chambers.

The second can be kept at another location. For example, your home. This may also be under lock and key.

The first should be periodically updated onto the second.

The second functions as a secure "vault". This shows reasonable steps to mitigate against the worst-case scenario. Fire or theft.

28. Dress

There is guidance on court dress, and emblems of faith.

a. Guidance

'Court dress' (reviewed July 2020) ("the 2020 guidance") recommends appropriate court dress to barristers.

It is 'intended to provide a ready guide as to what clothing will generally be expected and acceptable'.

Unless "court dress" is required, "business attire" is to be worn.

"Court dress" means 'wigs, gowns, wing-collars and bands or collarettes.'

"Business attire" means 'smart dark office wear.' This 'will usually mean a black, dark grey or dark suit with tie for men, and, for women, a similarly coloured jacket and either skirt or trousers'.

Business attire should be worn in the county court for *all* applications, appeals from applications, and final hearings.

The 2020 guidance is not intended to affect any change.

It does not provide guidance on dress for appeals from final hearings, however, 'Court dress: Revised Guidance from the Chairman of the Bar Council' (2 June 2009), suggests court dress.

The 2020 guidance prescribes an exception for *remote* hearings, in which court dress need not be worn.

b. Emblems of faith

The 2020 guidance strikes a balance between 'reflecting the seriousness of the function Counsel perform in Court, the role of Court dress as the uniform of the profession, and the need for such uniform to be inclusive of different religious practice.'

As a general rule, 'clothing that is worn as a requirement or emblem of faith is permitted'. The exception is where 'the clothing in question may affect the just determination of proceedings.'

Four common examples are provided.

First, jewellery bearing crosses or other symbols of religious belief is permitted. Secondly, kippahs may be worn, including under wigs. Thirdly, sober-coloured headscarves may be worn, and Muslims who wear headscarves need not wear wigs. Fourthly, sober-coloured turbans may be worn, and Sikhs who wear turbans need not wear wigs.

29. Ethics

Barristers and solicitors are bound by codes of conduct.

They are taken as read, however, there is some *practical* guidance.

a. Confidants

Prepare in advance of an ethical issue.

It is helpful, and comforting, to store the mobile telephone numbers, and the email addresses of several *appropriately* experienced, reliable, and trustworthy, colleagues.

King's Counsel is *un*likely to be appropriate.

Ideally, they should not be so senior that they are likely to be unfamiliar with claims that are allocated to the small claims track.

You should be confident that, if they can, they will answer your call, or otherwise revert to you, as soon as practicable.

They should have your confidence so that you can confide in them.

Many advocates in claims that are allocated to the small claims track are pupils, or otherwise junior advocates. They will be grateful that their questions are not passed on to colleagues.

Often, a telephone call can be the quickest means of relaying an issue, receiving guidance, and reassurance.

If all of the telephone numbers that you have are engaged, or you cannot otherwise speak to a colleague, send an email.

If time is of the essence, another option is to speak to your practice manager, enquire whether any of your colleagues are available, and request to be put through to the one who is most appropriate.

b. Ethical Enquiries Services

If it is not possible to speak to a colleague, the Bar Council provides an Ethical Enquiries Service.

It provides confidential assistance to *barristers,* and, where appropriate, their *clerks and other members of staff* connected with barristers' professional practices.

It does so by assisting to *identify, interpret, and comply with, professional obligations,* under the BSB Handbook.

Monday to Friday, from 09:15 to 17:15, it is available by calling 020 7611 1307. Emails can be sent to ethics@barcouncil.org.uk.

A response should be within *four* working days.

It is *confidential.* All *information* provided through this service, and any *assistance* given, will be kept *confidential.*

There are two exceptions.

First, where you consent. Secondly, where the law provides.

Assistance is not "guidance" for the the BSB Handbook.

Barristers are *personally* responsible for their own *conduct, ethics,* and *decisions.* The service "assists". It does not "decide".

An important benefit of seeking assistance is that, in the event of a complaint against you, it may be easier to explain your decisions, where you can show that you have sought assistance, and taken into account any response, before making a decision.

To this end, a *note* should be made of any oral assistance, and *confirmed* with the advisor within a *week*. Calls are *not* recorded.

In any event, you must not disclose the identity of the advisor without her prior consent, or that of the Chairman of the Ethics Committee. The exception is when you are responding to a complaint made to the BSB, or the Legal Ombudsman.

30. Etiquette

Etiquette goes hand in hand with professional ethics.

A core duty of counsel is not to behave in a way that is likely to diminish the trust and confidence that the public place in *you,* and generally, in the *profession.*

Failure to show respect and courtesy to court actors, for example, through following the appropriate etiquette, may breach this duty.

a. Outside court

Punctuality, use of an advocates' room, secure disposal of confidential documents, and formal correspondence, are consistent with the customary code of polite, professional behaviour.

i. Punctuality

For an in-person hearing, plan to arrive in the right *place*, at the right *time*, with the right *tools*, and the right *attitude.*

Public transport may be delayed, listings can go awry, and personal circumstances may conspire against you.

The ethical question is often not *whether* you are late, but the reason *why,* and what steps you have taken to *mitigate* the effects.

If you are likely to be late, consider the following guidance.

First, send an email to your professional client. Copy in your practice manager. Relay that you are likely to be late, the reason, and your estimated time of arrival.

Secondly, ask your practice manager to email the court, copying you and your professional client in. The email should relay that you are likely to be late, the reason, and your estimated time of arrival.

Thirdly, ask your professional client to forward the email on to the legal representative for any other party.

If you are late, apologise. *Unreservedly.*

To your professional client, lay client, opponent, and the court.

Briefly explain why you are late.

Let your practice manager, and your instructing solicitor, know that you have arrived. Keep them updated of any complications.

If you need more time to hold a conference before a hearing is called on, inform the usher, and outline the reason why.

Cases are often listed together at 10:00, or 14:00.

The court may be able to accommodate a request for more time by hearing another matter before the one that you are instructed in.

ii. Coats, umbrellas & bags

Advocates should *not* take *un*necessary items into the courtroom.

If they are *un*necessary for the hearing, they are *un*necessary.

One of the reasons for an advocates' room is so that legal representatives do not have to take unnecessary items into court. There is somewhere that they can be left securely.

If there is an advocates' room, and it is *lockable,* it should be used.

Documents and electronic devices containing confidential material, however, should *never* be left unattended.

Even where there is a locked room.

Keep them to hand.

iii. Disposal

His Majesty's Courts and Tribunals Service ("HMCTS") met with the Bar Council to confirm the correct position as to who has responsibility for documents after hearings.

In a joint notice, it was agreed that *only those documents (or bundles) belonging to legal representatives should be removed by the legal representatives.*

If not, and they contain 'special category (formerly sensitive) personal data', HMCTS 'may consider it necessary to report that a personal data breach has occurred'.

Documents filed with the court should *not* be removed by legal representatives. They are *not* "data processors" for the court.

iv. Correspondence

When corresponding with the court, professional clients, or practice managers, follow formalities, revert promptly, and be professional.

1. Judge

Generally, any communication with the court on a matter of substance, or procedure, *must* be served on the other party.

It is etiquette.

It is also prescribed in CPRs (CPRs 27.2(1)(h) and 39.8).

The court may ask a party to draw up a draft minute of order.

If so, the legal representative for the claimant, or applicant, will usually have "carriage".

This means that they are responsible for three actions.

First, drafting. Secondly, ensuring that it is an accurate reflection of the court's order, as prescribed in open court. Thirdly, emailing it to the court. In practice, it is usually to a judicial email address.

If so, the email should start: 'Dear Judge'.

It *must* state that it is being I to the other party, her *identity,* and *capacity.* For example: 'Solicitor for the Claimant'.

If an agreed minute of order is attached, state it.

It should end with the title and surname of the legal representative sending the correspondence, and the party who they represent.

Do not copy in your *lay* client.

Having sent the email, it can be forwarded to your *professional* client, so that they are aware of the date and time that the email was sent, its content, and any attachments.

2. Ushers & other court staff

Be courteous.

First, they deserve it. Secondly, they speak to the judges.

Thirdly, there may be a time when they can assist by calling another case before the one that you are instructed in.

Fourthly, if you would like a photocopy of an order, or you have forgotten to print a document, they may be more inclined to assist.

3. Professional client

Be *courteous.* Revert *promptly.* Meet *deadlines.*

There is nothing that a client hates more than missing a deadline.

Where there is a potential problem, do not put your head in the sand. Speak to your practice manager.

When a professional client instructs counsel, they are putting their neck on the line. They have an enormous stake in the case.

If your professional client is unavailable, it is often possible to take instructions from another member of her team.

4. Practice manager

There should be implicit trust and confidence between counsel and practice manager.

Barristers look after their practice managers; and vice versa.

There is reciprocity.

Emotional intelligence, considered correspondence, and flexibility, are key. They nurture confidence in practice managers when corresponding with you, other members of chambers, and your professional clients.

b. Inside court

The key etiquette *in* court surrounds submissions, and encompasses ethics. In particular, criticism of other professionals.

i. Mobile telephones

During in-person hearings, keep a smart phone on "silent".

First, to tether to your laptop, where the court does not provide a reliable internet connection.

Secondly, to use a calculator function, so as to calculate a money judgment, interest, and costs.

Thirdly, to use a calendar function, so as to work out what the date will be, for example, 21 days from the hearing.

ii. Entering & exiting

For an in-person hearing, wait for the names of the parties to be called by the usher *before* moving to the door of the courtroom.

If you have signed in, the matter will *not* go ahead without you.

Unless you have left the building.

On entering and exiting the courtroom, it is etiquette to bow.

In practice, this is a modest nod of the head, rather than the greeting that one imagines may be used when meeting the King.

When exiting the courtroom, *never* leave the judge sitting in court with another party. Parties should leave together.

That may mean waiting for the other side.

Frequently, after the matter has concluded, the judge will say "good morning / afternoon". It is normal to repeat the greeting.

For an in-person hearing, this is your cue that you may leave the courtroom. For a remote hearing, you may then hang up the telephone, or leave the audio-visual hearing.

After an in-person hearing, you may ask to be excused.

This is very formal. It may take a judge by surprise.

Asking to be excused may originate from the practice that you should not leave court before a judge has risen.

An alternative is to enquire whether the court is rising. Most judges will then understand. You are then likely to be excused.

iii. Seating

For in-person hearings, most courtrooms are of an average, or slightly bigger than average, size.

Judges are not elevated. All court actors are at the same eye-level.

Frequently, there are only three in-built architectural features, so as to convey the authority of the decision-maker.

First, a royal crest above the judge. Secondly, a pronounced gap between where the parties sit, and where the judge sits. Thirdly, a vertical panel in front of the judge's desk, so that the parties cannot see what she is writing.

In other courts, the rooms are larger, and the judge sits higher-up, so that the parties have to look up to catch the judge's eye.

On occasion, in the County Court at Central London, judges sit in courtrooms used by the High Court. Frequently, in the Queen's Building, or the West Green Building. If so, it is preferable to stand, so as to catch the judge's eye, and so not to appear discourteous.

There are conventions surrounding where legal representatives, witnesses, and non-court actors, are located in the courtroom.

The layout will dictate.

When a person is disabled, the courts usually permit that person to fulfil her role in the position in which she is most comfortable.

You can identify whether to make such a request in a conference.

1. Parties

Legal representatives sit at the front tables.

Usually, the claimant sits on the left. The defendant sits on the right. In some courts, however, this is reversed. If so, there will be signs denominating which party is to sit at which table.

A person without a representative also sit at the front table.

2. Witnesses

Witnesses usually sit at a table behind the legal representative for the party who calls them to give evidence.

When giving evidence, witnesses usually move to another table.

Often, it is in between the legal representatives' and the judge's table. Usually, it is off to one side, so that all court actors can comfortably see, and hear, the witness.

A witness bundle usually indicates the witness table.

In absence of a separate table, however, witnesses sit at the table at which the legal representatives (or persons without a representative) sit.

Witnesses should only be able to see an *un*marked witness bundle.

Care should be taken not to appear to give any visual cues, or otherwise project body language, when a witness is giving evidence.

This may require a concerted effort.

3. Non-court actors

Pupils, and mini-pupils, should sit at the back of the courtroom.

It should be clear that they are not a court actor. They have no role in the case. They are not a legal representative, party, or witness.

Introduce non-court actors before the hearing to the other party, and at the start of the hearing for the benefit of the court.

iv. Submissions

There are conventions surrounding the way in which court actors introduce the case, address other court actors, and interruptions.

Do not make a positive submission unless you have instructions to do so, the evidence in support; or, if it is a matter of law, you reasonably believe it to be correct.

Be careful not knowingly to mislead the court by appearing to endorse a proposition of law to which you are not able to agree.

1. Forms of address

In the *un*likely event that you are before a recorder, or a circuit judge, they should be referred to as "Your Honour".

Part-time (deputy district) judges, and full time (district) judges, should be referred to as "Judge".

Alternatively, judges can be referred to as "the court".

The convention is that counsel refer to one another as "my learned friend". Counsel refer to solicitors as "my friend".

The latter can appear old-fashioned, however, so counsel often refer to a solicitor using her title and surname.

There are two ways to refer to a party.

First, "claimant" or "defendant". Secondly, title and surname.

Witnesses are referred to using title and surname.

Ushers are referred to as "madam usher" or "mister usher".

2. Introduction

As a general rule, (the legal representative for) the *claimant* speaks first. It is the *claimant's* case.

Even where there is a counterclaim, if there is an introduction, the claimant usually speaks first.

Where the hearing is listed to dispose of an *application,* the applicant speaks first because it is the *applicant's* application.

It is safer to wait for the judge to invite you to speak before addressing the court. If the judge is writing when you enter the courtroom, she may be finalising the order from the previous case.

Usually, the judge will introduce the case for the recording.

For an in-person hearing, you will have signed in with the usher.

Sometimes, case-management forms have been completed before the hearing. If so, the names of the parties, legal representatives, and witnesses will have been noted.

Accordingly, the judge is likely to state the names of the parties, case number, and the name of any advocate, before the hearing.

If the judge does not state the names of the advocates, it is etiquette to introduce the legal representative for the other side.

Title and surname, followed by the party who they represent.

Introduce yourself, using your first name and surname, followed by the party who you represent. There is no need to include your title. For example: "Mr Adam, Counsel for the Claimant."

In the event that a non-court actor is observing, introduce them. State who they are, and in what capacity they are observing. For example, they might be the claimant's partner.

3. Issues

The judge will usually ask what issues are in dispute.

So as to respond, it is invaluable to speak to the other party before the hearing to confirm the following.

First, the documents that have been filed, served, and the parties wish to rely upon.

Secondly, which heads of loss are still pursued; in respect of each, whether it is admitted, denied, or agreed subject to liability; and the issues relating to each head of loss in dispute.

Thirdly, whether quantum is agreed; and, if so, the sum for each head of loss.

Fourthly, what authority (if any) is relied upon.

This will dictate whether or not there are any preliminary issues.

Having *defined* and *confined* the issues that are in dispute, if you try to raise an issue that has not been flagged up at the outset, you will likely be stopped by the court for three reasons.

First, the court is under a duty to further the overriding objective. This includes ensuring that the parties are on an *equal footing,* and the case is dealt with both *fairly,* and *expeditiously.*

Secondly, the court is under a duty to actively manage cases. This includes *identifying the issues at an early stage,* and fixing timetables, or otherwise controlling the progress of the case.

Thirdly, etiquette. The other party has a legitimate expectation that the issues will not expand throughout the hearing.

4. Interrupting

Do not interrupt another court actor, unless there is a *good* reason.

Judge, legal representative, or witness.

If the judge, or another legal representative interrupts you, yield, and wait. If the interruption is unjustified, you will have the opportunity to explain the reason why. The impact of your explanation will not diminish having demonstrated common courtesy.

An obvious exception is where a witness strays into relaying what was said during a conference. This is privileged.

5. Humility

If you can*not* assist the judge on a particular issue, *say so*.

You should do your best to acquire such knowledge of the facts, and the law, so as to understand the facts that are in dispute, the applicable law, and what you are inviting the court to do.

You must not mislead the court, knowingly, or recklessly.

Better to show *reasonable* humility, and *appropriate* deference, than to invite, or otherwise to encourage, the court to do something against CPRs, PDs, or authority, which is appealable.

6. Gestures

No matter your instinctive reaction to the evidence, submission, order, or judgment, try to retain your composure.

Let a witness be discourteous. It will undermine her evidence.

When a weak submission is made, an effective way to neutralise it may be to demonstrate that it is not persuasive using the evidence, and submissions on the law.

If it is *inherently* weak, the judge is likely to have perceived that it is an unsustainable reason on which to base her judgment. She may not necessarily flag it up, however, it may be unnecessary to give verbose submissions as to why it is inherently weak.

Orders *will* be made, and judgments *will* be given, with which you do not agree. They are the *responsibility* of the *judge.*

Not counsel, solicitor, or litigant.

If it is arguably susceptible to an appeal, an oral application for permission to appeal can be made at the end of the hearing.

You are likely to be instructed in many more cases before *that* judge. You will undermine your professional reputation with that judge, and perhaps also her colleagues, the usher, and court staff, if you visibly show your disapproval.

7. Criticism

Criticism should be *measured*, *reasoned*, and, unless there is a good reason, on *instructions.* The hearing will be recorded.

a. Experts

Criticism of experts, and their reports, should be carefully considered, and without good reason, only with *written* instructions.

There may be an "expert" report on diminution in the value of a vehicle following a road traffic collision, over and above the reasonable cost of repair.

If there is no permission to rely on expert evidence, the following three submissions can be effective, and time-efficient, without criticising the expert personally, or her report.

First, no expert may give evidence at a hearing, whether oral or written, without the permission of the court (CPR 27.5).

Secondly, the court is under a duty to restrict expert evidence (CPRs 27.2(1)(e) and 35.1).

Thirdly, if the party seeking to rely on expert evidence has indicated that they wish to do so in their directions questionnaire, the court has already had notice of the request, and it has been refused.

Alternatively, if that party has failed to indicate that they wish to rely on expert evidence, there has been a failure to complete the directions questionnaire accurately.

In the case of the former, an application should have been made for permission to rely on an expert. In the case of the latter, the overriding objective will be compromised if permission is granted.

The parties will no longer be on an equal footing. The case will not have been dealt with fairly. Compliance with the direction to complete direc tions questionnaires accurately has not been enforced.

Whether or not there is permission to rely on an expert, the author of an expert report is unlikely to attend a hearing. If so, she will not give oral evidence. There is no opportunity to respond to any criticism, as it cannot be put in cross-examination.

In practice, this means that it is often difficult to persuade a judge that an "expert" report is unreliable. To do so, the *reasoning* behind the conclusion should be addressed in cogent submissions.

b. Legal representatives

Attacks on the conduct of a legal representative should also be *carefully* considered, and, unless there is a good reason, only with explicit, *written* instructions.

The conduct of legal representatives is relevant for deciding what order to make as to costs.

For example, in responding to requests for key documents, such as invoices, so as to narrow, and potentially settle, the issues.

When identified ahead of the hearing, a *very* short witness statement from your professional client, setting out any non-compliance, can assist. Relevant correspondence may be exhibited.

If there is legitimate criticism to be made as to the manner in which a legal representative has litigated, it may also be possible expressly to state that no criticism is made of counsel. If so, say so.

Appendix A
CPR 1.1
The Overriding Objective

(1) These Rules are a procedural code with the overriding objective of enabling the court to deal with cases justly and at proportionate cost.

(2) Dealing with a case justly and at proportionate cost includes, so far as is practicable—

(a) ensuring that the parties are on an equal footing and can participate fully in proceedings, and that parties and witnesses can give their best evidence;

(b) saving expense;

(c) dealing with the case in ways which are proportionate—

(i) to the amount of money involved;
(ii) to the importance of the case;
(iii) to the complexity of the issues; and
(iv) to the financial position of each party;

(d) ensuring that it is dealt with expeditiously and fairly;

(e) allotting to it an appropriate share of the court's resources, while taking into account the need to allot resources to other cases; and

(f) promoting or using alternative dispute resolution; and

(g) enforcing compliance with rules, practice directions and orders.

Appendix B
CPR 1.4
Court's Duty To Manage Cases

(1) The court must further the overriding objective by actively managing cases.

(2) Active case management includes—

(a) encouraging the parties to co-operate with each other in the conduct of the proceedings;

(b) identifying the issues at an early stage;

(c) deciding promptly which issues need full investigation and trial and accordingly disposing summarily of the others;

(d) deciding the order in which issues are to be resolved;

(e) ordering or encouraging the parties to use, and facilitating the use of, alternative dispute resolution;

(f) helping the parties to settle the whole or part of the case;

(g) fixing timetables or otherwise controlling the progress of the case;

(h) considering whether the likely benefits of taking a particular step justify the cost of taking it;

(i) dealing with as many aspects of the case as it can on the same occasion;

(j) dealing with the case without the parties needing to attend at court;

(k) making use of technology; and

(l) giving directions to ensure that the trial of a case proceeds quickly and efficiently.

Appendix C
CPR 27
The Small Claims Track

CPR 27.1 — Scope of this Part

(1) This Part—

- (a) sets out the special procedure for dealing with claims which have been allocated to the small claims track under Part 26; and
- (b) limits the amount of costs that can be recovered in respect of a claim which has been allocated to the small claims track.

(Rule 27.14 deals with costs on the small claims track.)

(2) A claim being dealt with under this Part is called a small claim.

(Rule 26.9 provides for the scope of the small claims track. A claim for a remedy for harassment or unlawful eviction relating, in either case, to residential premises or to a dwelling where the claim is under the Renting Homes (Wales) Act 2016 shall not be allocated to the small claims track whatever the financial value of the claim. Otherwise, the small claims track will be the normal track for—

- any claim which has a financial value of not more than £10,000 subject to the special provisions about claims for personal injuries and housing disrepair claims;
- any claim for personal injuries which has a financial value of not more than £10,000 where the claim for damages for personal injuries is not more than the relevant value specified in

rule 26.9(1)(a)(ii)(aa), (bb) or (cc), being £5,000, £1,000 or £1,500, respectively; and

- any claim which includes a claim by a tenant of residential premises against his landlord for repairs or other work to the premises where the estimated cost of the repairs or other work is not more than £1,000 and the financial value of any other claim for damages is not more than £1,000;
- any claim which includes a claim under the Renting Home (Wales) Act 2016 by a contract-holder of a dwelling against their landlord for repairs or other work to the dwelling where the estimated cost of the repairs or other work is not more than £1,000 and the financial value of any other claim for damages is not more than £1,000).

CPR 27.2 — Extent to which other Parts apply

(1) The following Parts of these Rules do not apply to small claims—

(a) Part 25 (interim remedies) except as it relates to interim injunctions;

(b) Part 31 (disclosure and inspection);

(c) Part 32 (evidence) except rule 32.1 (power of court to control evidence);

(d) Part 33 (miscellaneous rules about evidence);

(e) Part 35 (experts and assessors) except rules 35.1 (duty to restrict expert evidence), 35.3 (experts—overriding duty to the court), 35.7 (court's power to direct that evidence is to be given by single joint expert) and 35.8 (instructions to a single joint expert);

(f) Subject to paragraph (3), Part 18 (further information);

(g) Part 36 (offers to settle); and

(h) Part 39 (hearings) except rule 39.2 (general rule—hearing to be in public), rule 39.8 (communications with the court) and rule 39.9 (recording and transcription of proceedings).

(2) The other Parts of these Rules apply to small claims except to the extent that a rule or a practice direction under this Part limits such application.

(2A) A rule or practice direction may, in relation to a specified type of small claim—

(a) require or permit the use of the procedure set out in this Part; and

(b) disapply or modify any of the rules set out in this Part.

(3) The court of its own initiative may order a party to provide further information if it considers it appropriate to do so.

CPR 27.3 — Court's power to grant a final remedy

The court may grant any final remedy in relation to a small claim which it could grant if the proceedings were on the fast track, the intermediate track, or the multi-track.

CPR 27.4 — Preparation for the hearing

(1) After allocation the court will—

(a) give standard directions and fix a date for the final hearing;

(b) give special directions and fix a date for the final hearing;

(c) give special directions and direct that the court will consider what further directions are to be given no later than 28 days after the date the special directions were given;

(d) fix a date for a preliminary hearing under rule 27.6; or

(e) give notice that it proposes to deal with the claim without a hearing under rule 27.10 and invite the parties to notify the court by a specified date if they agree the proposal.

(2) The court will—

(a) give parties at least 21 days' notice of the date fixed for the final hearing, unless the parties agree to accept less notice; and

(b) inform them of the amount of time allowed for the final hearing.

(3) In this rule—

(a) *"standard directions"* means—

(i) a direction that each party shall, at least 14 days before the date fixed for the final hearing, file and serve on every other party copies of all documents (including any expert's report) on which he intends to rely at the hearing; and

(ii) any other standard directions set out in Practice Direction 27A; and

(b) *"special directions"* means directions given in addition to or instead of the standard directions.

CPR 27.5 — Experts

No expert may give evidence, whether written or oral, at a hearing without the permission of the court.

CPR 27.6 — Preliminary hearing

(1) The court may hold a preliminary hearing for the consideration of the claim, but only—

(a) where—

(i) it considers that special directions, as defined in rule 27.4, are needed to ensure a fair hearing; and

(ii) it appears necessary for a party to attend at court to ensure that he understands what he must do to comply with the special directions; or

(b) to enable it to dispose of the claim on the basis that one or other of the parties has no real prospect of success at a final hearing; or

(c) to enable it to strike out a statement of case or part of a statement of case on the basis that the statement of case, or the part to be struck out, discloses no reasonable grounds for bringing or defending the claim.

(2) When considering whether or not to hold a preliminary hearing, the court must have regard to the desirability of limiting the expense to the parties of attending court.

(3) Where the court decides to hold a preliminary hearing, it will give the parties at least 14 days' notice of the date of the hearing.

(4) The court may treat the preliminary hearing as the final hearing of the claim if all the parties agree.

(5) At or after the preliminary hearing the court will—

(a) fix the date of the final hearing (if it has not been fixed already) and give the parties at least 21 days' notice of the date fixed unless the parties agree to accept less notice;

(b) inform them of the amount of time allowed for the final hearing; and

(c) give any appropriate directions.

CPR 27.7 — Power of court to add to, vary or revoke directions

The court may add to, vary or revoke directions.

CPR 27.8 — Conduct of the hearing

(1) The court may adopt any method of proceeding at a hearing that it considers to be fair.

(2) Hearings will be informal.

(3) The strict rules of evidence do not apply.

(4) The court need not take evidence on oath.

(5) The court may limit cross-examination.

(6) The court must give reasons for its decision.

CPR 27.9 — Non-attendance of parties at a final hearing

(1) If a party who does not attend a final hearing—

(a) has given written notice to the court and the other party at least 7 days before the hearing date that he will not attend;

(b) has served on the other party at least 7 days before the hearing date any other documents which he has filed with the court; and

(c) has, in his written notice, requested the court to decide the claim in his absence and has confirmed his compliance with paragraphs (a) and (b) above,

the court will take into account that party's statement of case and any other documents he has filed and served when it decides the claim.

(2) If a claimant does not—

(a) attend the hearing; and

(b) give the notice referred to in paragraph (1),

the court may strike out the claim.

(3) If—

(a) a defendant does not—

(i) attend the hearing; or

(ii) give the notice referred to in paragraph (1); and

(b) the claimant either—

(i) does attend the hearing; or

(ii) gives the notice referred to in paragraph (1),

the court may decide the claim on the basis of the evidence of the claimant alone.

(4) If neither party attends or gives the notice referred to in paragraph (1), the court may strike out the claim and any defence and counterclaim.

CPR 27.10 — Disposal without a hearing

The court may, if all parties agree, deal with the claim without a hearing.

CPR 27.11 — Setting judgment aside and re-hearing

(1) A party—

(a) who was neither present nor represented at the hearing of the claim; and

(b) who has not given written notice to the court under rule 27.9(1),

may apply for an order that a judgment under this Part shall be set aside and the claim re-heard.

(2) A party who applies for an order setting aside a judgment under this rule must make the application not more than 14 days after the day on which notice of the judgment was served on him.

(3) The court may grant an application under paragraph (2) only if the applicant—

(a) had a good reason for not attending or being represented at the hearing or giving written notice to the court under rule 27.9(1); and

(b) has a reasonable prospect of success at the hearing.

(4) If a judgment is set aside—

(a) the court must fix a new hearing for the claim; and

(b) the hearing may take place immediately after the hearing of the application to set the judgment aside and may be dealt with by the judge who set aside the judgment.

(5) A party may not apply to set aside a judgment under this rule if the court dealt with the claim without a hearing under rule 27.10.

(Rules 27.12 and 27.13 are revoked.)

CPR 27.14 — Costs on the small claims track

(1) This rule applies to any case which has been allocated to the small claims track.

(Rule 46.13 makes provision in relation to orders for costs made before a claim has been allocated to the small claims track.)

(2) The court may not order a party to pay a sum to another party in respect of that other party's costs, fees and expenses, including those relating to an appeal, except—

(a) the fixed costs attributable to issuing the claim, calculated in accordance with Table 2 in Practice Direction 45;

(b) in proceedings which included a claim for an injunction or an order for specific performance a sum not exceeding the amount specified in Practice Direction 27A for legal advice and assistance relating to that claim;

(c) any court fees paid by that other party;

(d) expenses which a party or witness has reasonably incurred in travelling to and from a hearing or in staying away from home for the purposes of attending a hearing;

(e) a sum not exceeding the amount specified in Practice Direction 27A for any loss of earnings or loss of leave by a party or witness due to attending a hearing or to staying away from home for the purpose of attending a hearing;

(f) a sum not exceeding the amount specified in Practice Direction 27A for an expert's fees;

(g) such further costs as the court may assess by the summary procedure and order to be paid by a party who has behaved unreasonably;

(h) the applicable Stage 1 and, where relevant, the Stage 2 fixed costs in Table 10 and Table 11 in Practice Direction 45 where—

 (i) the claim was within the scope of the Pre-Action Protocol for Low Value Personal Injury Claims in Road Traffic Accidents ("the RTA Protocol") or the Pre-action Protocol for Low Value Personal Injury (Employers' Liability and Public Liability) Claims ("the EL/PL Protocol");

 (ii) the claimant reasonably believed that the claim was valued at more than the small claims track limit in accordance with paragraph 4.1(4) of the relevant Protocol; and

 (iii) the defendant admitted liability under the process set out in the relevant Protocol; but

 (iv) the defendant did not pay those Stage 1 and, where relevant, Stage 2 fixed costs; and

(i) in an appeal, the cost of any approved transcript reasonably incurred.

(3) A party's rejection of an offer in settlement will not of itself constitute unreasonable behaviour under paragraph (2)(g) but the court may take it into consideration when it is applying the unreasonableness test.

(4) The limits on costs imposed by this rule also apply to any fee or reward for acting on behalf of a party to the proceedings charged by a person exercising a right of audience by virtue of an order under section 11 of the Courts and Legal Services Act 1990 (a lay representative).

CPR 27.15 — Claim re-allocated from the small claims track to another track

(1) Where a claim is allocated to the small claims track and subsequently re-allocated to another track, the costs which may be allowed are those applicable to the track to which the claim is reallocated, as if the claim been allocated to that track at the outset.

(2) Where a claim is reallocated to the small claims track from the multi-track, rule 27.14 shall apply to the period before, as well as after, reallocation, except where a court order or a rule or practice direction provides otherwise.

Appendix D
PD 27A
Small Claims Track

This Practice Direction supplements CPR Part 27

Judges

1 The functions of the court described in Part 27 which are to be carried out by a judge will generally be carried out by a District Judge but may be carried out by a Circuit Judge.

Case Management Directions

2.1 Rule 27.4 explains how directions will be given, and rule 27.6 contains provisions about the holding of a preliminary hearing and the court's powers at such a hearing.

2.2 Appendix A sets out details of the case that the court usually needs in the type of case described. Appendix B sets out the Standard Directions that the court may give. Appendix C sets out Special Directions that the court may give.

2.3 Before allocating the claim to the Small Claims Track and giving directions for a hearing the court may require a party to give further information about that party's case.

2.4 A party may ask the court to give particular directions about the conduct of the case.

2.5 In deciding whether to make an order for exchange of witness statements the court will have regard to the following—

(a) whether either or both the parties are represented;

(b) the amount in dispute in the proceedings;

(c) the nature of the matters in dispute;

(d) whether the need for any party to clarify his case can better be dealt with by an order under paragraph 2.3;

(e) the need for the parties to have access to justice without undue formality, cost or delay.

Representation at a Hearing

3.1 In this paragraph—

(1) a lawyer means a barrister, a solicitor or a legal executive employed by a solicitor or any other person authorised under the Legal Services Act 2007 to act as a litigator or advocate, and

(2) a lay representative means any other person.

3.2

(1) A party may present his own case at a hearing or a lawyer or lay representative may present it for him.

(2) The Lay Representatives (Right of Audience) Order 1999 provides that a lay representative may not exercise any right of audience—

(a) where his client does not attend the hearing;

(b) at any stage after judgment; or

(c) on any appeal brought against any decision made by the District Judge in the proceedings.

(3) However the court, exercising its general discretion to hear anybody, may hear a lay representative even in circumstances excluded by the Order.

(4) Any of its officers or employees may represent a corporate party.

Small Claim Hearing

. . .

4.2 A hearing that takes place at the court will generally be in the judge's room but it may take place in a courtroom.

4.3 Rule 27.8 allows the court to adopt any method of proceeding that it considers to be fair and to limit cross-examination. The judge may in particular—

(1) ask questions of any witness himself before allowing any other person to do so,

(2) ask questions of all or any of the witnesses himself before allowing any other person to ask questions of any witnesses,

(3) refuse to allow cross-examination of any witness until all the witnesses have given evidence in chief,

(4) limit cross-examination of a witness to a fixed time or to a particular subject or issue, or both.

Recording Evidence and the Giving of Reasons

5.1 A hearing that takes place at the court will be tape recorded by the court. A party may obtain a transcript of such a recording on payment of the proper transcriber's charges.

5.2 Attention is drawn to section 9 of the Contempt of Court Act 1981 (which deals with the unauthorised use of tape recorders in court) and to the *Practice Direction ([1981] 1 W.L.R. 1526)* which relates to it.

5.3

(1) The judge may give reasons for his judgment as briefly and simply as the nature of the case allows.

(2) He will normally do so orally at the hearing, but he may give them later at a hearing either orally or in writing.

5.4 Where the judge decides the case without a hearing under rule 27.10 or a party who has given notice under rule 27.9(1) does not attend the hearing, the judge will prepare a note of his reasons and the court will send a copy to each party.

5.5 Nothing in this practice direction affects the duty of a judge at the request of a party to make a note of the matters referred to in section 80 of the County Courts Act 1984.

Non-attendance of a Party at a Hearing

6.1 Attention is drawn to rule 27.9 (which enables a party to give notice that he will not attend a final hearing and sets out the effect of his giving such notice and of not doing so), and to paragraph 3 above.

6.2 Nothing in those provisions affects the general power of the court to adjourn a hearing, for example where a party who wishes to attend a hearing on the date fixed cannot do so for a good reason.

Costs

7.1 Attention is drawn to rule 27.14 which contains provisions about the costs which may be ordered to be paid by one party to another.

7.2 The amount which a party may be ordered to pay under rule 27.14(2)(b) (for legal advice and assistance in claims including an injunction or specific performance) is a sum not exceeding £260.

7.3 The amounts which a party may be ordered to pay under rule 27.14(3)(e) (loss of earnings) and (f) (experts' fees) are—

(1) for the loss of earnings or loss of leave of each party or witness due to attending a hearing or staying away from home for the purpose of attending a hearing, a sum not exceeding £95 per day for each person, and

(2) for experts' fees, a sum not exceeding £750 for each expert.

(As to recovery of pre-allocation costs in a case in which an admission by the defendant has reduced the amount in dispute to a figure below £10,000, reference should be made to paragraph 7.4 of Practice Direction 26 and to paragraph 7.1(3) of Practice Direction 46.)

Appeals

8.1 Part 52 deals with appeals and attention is drawn to that Part and Practice Direction 52.

8A An appellant's notice in small claims must be filed and served in Form N164.

8.2 Where the court dealt with the claim to which the appellant is a party—

(1) under rule 27.10 without a hearing; or

(2) in his absence because he gave notice under rule 27.9 requesting the court to decide the claim in his absence,

an application for permission to appeal must be made to the appeal court.

8.3 Where an appeal is allowed the appeal court will, if possible, dispose of the case at the same time without referring the claim to the lower court or ordering a new hearing. It may do so without hearing further evidence.

Appendix A — Information and Documentation the Court Usually Needs in Particular Types of Case

ROAD ACCIDENT CASES (where the information or documentation is available)

- witness statements (including statements from the parties themselves);
- invoices and estimates for repairs;
- agreements and invoices for any car hire costs;
- the Police accident report;
- sketch plan which should wherever possible be agreed;
- photographs of the scene of the accident and of the damage.

BUILDING DISPUTES, REPAIRS, GOODS SOLD AND SIMILAR CONTRACTUAL CLAIMS (where the information or documentation is available)

- any written contract;
- photographs;
- any plans;
- a list of works complained of;
- a list of any outstanding works;
- any relevant estimate, invoice or receipt including any relating to repairs to each of the defects;
- invoices for work done or goods supplied;

- estimates for work to be completed;
- a valuation of work done to date.

LANDLORD AND TENANT CLAIMS, AND LANDLORD AND CONTRACT-HOLDER CLAIMS UNDER THE RENTING HOMES (WALES) ACT 2016 (where the information or documentation is available)

- a calculation of the amount of any rent alleged to be owing, showing amounts received;
- details of breaches of an agreement which are said to justify withholding any deposit itemised showing how the total is made up and with invoices and estimates to support them.

BREACH OF DUTY CASES (negligence, deficient professional services and the like)

Details of the following:

- what it is said by the claimant was done negligently by the defendant;
- why it is said that the negligence is the fault of the defendant;
- what damage is said to have been caused;
- what injury or losses have been suffered and how any (and each) sum claimed has been calculated;
- the response of the defendant to each of the above.

Appendix B — Standard Directions

(For use where the district judge specifies no other directions)

The Court Directs:

1. Each party must deliver to every other party and to the court office copies of all documents on which he intends to rely at the hearing no later than […] [14 days before the hearing]. (These should include the letter making the claim and the reply.)

2. The original documents must be brought to the hearing.

3. [Notice of hearing date and time allowed.]

4. The parties are encouraged to contact each other with a view to trying to settle the case or narrow the issues. However the court must be informed immediately if the case is settled by agreement before the hearing date.

5. No party may rely at the hearing on any report from an expert unless express permission has been granted by the court beforehand. Anyone wishing to rely on an expert must write to the court immediately on receipt of this Order and seek permission, giving an explanation why the assistance of an expert is necessary.

NOTE: Failure to comply with the directions may result in the case being adjourned and in the party at fault having to pay costs. The parties are encouraged always to try to settle the case by negotiating with each other. The court must be informed immediately if the case is settled before the hearing.

Appendix C — Special Directions

The … must clarify his case.

He must do this by delivering to the court office and to the … no later than … [a list of …] [details of …]

The … must allow the … to inspect by appointment within … days of receiving a request to do so.

The hearing will not take place at the court but at …

The … must bring to court at the hearing the …

Signed statements setting out the evidence of all witnesses on whom each party intends to rely must be prepared and copies included in the documents mentioned in paragraph 1. This includes the evidence of the parties themselves and of any other witness, whether or not he is going to come to court to give evidence.

The court may decide not to take into account a document [or video] or the evidence of a witness if these directions have not been complied with.

If he does not [do so] […] his [Claim] [Defence] [and Counterclaim] will be struck out and (specify consequence).

It appears to the court that expert evidence is necessary on the issue of … and that that evidence should be given by a single expert to be instructed by the parties jointly. If the parties cannot agree about who to choose and what arrangements to make about paying his fee, either party MUST apply to the court for further directions. The evidence is to be given in the form of a written report. Either party may ask the expert questions and must then send copies of the questions and replies to the other party and to the court. Oral expert evidence may be allowed in exceptional circumstances but only after a further order of the court. Attention is drawn to the limit of £750 on expert's fees that may be recovered.

If either party intends to show a video as evidence he must –

(a) contact the court at once to make arrangements for him to do so, because the court may not have the necessary equipment, and

(b) provide the other party with a copy of the video or the opportunity to see it at least … days before the hearing.

Appendix E PD — Pre-Action Conduct & Protocols

Introduction

1 Pre-action protocols explain the conduct and set out the steps the court would normally expect parties to take before commencing proceedings for particular types of civil claims. They are approved by the Master of the Rolls and are annexed to the Civil Procedure Rules (CPR). (The current pre-action protocols are listed in paragraph 18.)

2 This Practice Direction applies to disputes where no pre-action protocol approved by the Master of the Rolls applies. A person who knowingly makes a false statement in a pre-action protocol letter or other document prepared in anticipation of legal proceedings may be subject to proceedings for contempt of court.

Objectives of pre-action conduct and Protocols

3 Before commencing proceedings, the court will expect the parties to have exchanged sufficient information to—

(a) understand each other's position;

(b) make decisions about how to proceed;

(c) try to settle the issues without proceedings;

(d) consider a form of Alternative Dispute Resolution (ADR) to assist with settlement;

(e) support the efficient management of those proceedings; and

(f) reduce the costs of resolving the dispute.

Proportionality

4 A pre-action protocol or this Practice Direction must not be used by a party as a tactical device to secure an unfair advantage over another party. Only reasonable and proportionate steps should be taken by the parties to identify, narrow and resolve the legal, factual or expert issues.

5 The costs incurred in complying with a pre-action protocol or this Practice Direction should be proportionate (CPR 44.3(5)). Where parties incur disproportionate costs in complying with any pre-action protocol or this Practice Direction, those costs will not be recoverable as part of the costs of the proceedings.

Steps before issuing a claim at court

6 Where there is a relevant pre–action protocol, the parties should comply with that protocol before commencing proceedings. Where there is no relevant pre-action protocol, the parties should exchange correspondence and information to comply with the objectives in paragraph 3, bearing in mind that compliance should be proportionate. The steps will usually include—

(a) the claimant writing to the defendant with concise details of the claim. The letter should include the basis on which the claim is made, a summary of the facts, what the claimant wants from the defendant, and if money, how the amount is calculated;

(b) the defendant responding within a reasonable time—14 days in a straight forward case and no more than 3 months in a very complex one. The reply should include confirmation as to whether the claim is accepted and, if it is not accepted, the reasons why, together with an explanation as to which facts and parts of the claim are disputed and whether the defendant is making a counterclaim as well as providing details of any counterclaim; and

(c) the parties disclosing key documents relevant to the issues in dispute.

Experts

7 Parties should be aware that the court must give permission before expert evidence can be relied upon (see CPR 35.4(1)) and that the court may limit the fees recoverable. Many disputes can be resolved without expert advice or evidence. If it is necessary to obtain expert evidence, particularly in low value claims, the parties should consider using a single expert, jointly instructed by the parties, with the costs shared equally.

Settlement and ADR

8 Litigation should be a last resort. As part of a relevant pre-action protocol or this Practice Direction, the parties should consider whether negotiation or some other form of ADR might enable them to settle their dispute without commencing proceedings.

9 Parties should continue to consider the possibility of reaching a settlement at all times, including after proceedings have been started. … offers may be made before proceedings are issued.

10 Parties may negotiate to settle a dispute or may use a form of ADR including—

(a) mediation, a third party facilitating a resolution;

(b) arbitration, a third party deciding the dispute;

(c) early neutral evaluation, a third party giving an informed opinion on the dispute; and

(d) Ombudsmen schemes.

Information on mediation and other forms of ADR is available in the Jackson ADR Handbook (available from Oxford University Press) or at—http://www.gov.uk/guidance/a-guide-to-civil-mediation

11 If proceedings are issued, the parties may be required by the court to provide evidence that ADR has been considered. A party's silence in response to an invitation to participate or a refusal to participate in ADR might be considered unreasonable by the court and could lead to the court ordering that party to pay additional court costs.

Stocktake and list of issues

12 Where a dispute has not been resolved after the parties have followed a pre-action protocol or this Practice Direction, they should review their respective positions. They should consider the papers and the evidence to see if proceedings can be avoided and at least seek to narrow the issues in dispute before the claimant issues proceedings.

Compliance with this Practice Direction and the Protocols

13 If a dispute proceeds to litigation, the court will expect the parties to have complied with a relevant pre-action protocol or this Practice Direction. The court will take into account non-compliance when giving directions for the management of proceedings (see CPR 3.1(4) to (6)) and when making orders for costs (see CPR

44.3(5)(a)). The court will consider whether all parties have complied in substance with the terms of the relevant pre-action protocol or this Practice Direction and is not likely to be concerned with minor or technical infringements, especially when the matter is urgent (for example an application for an injunction).

14 The court may decide that there has been a failure of compliance when a party has—

(a) not provided sufficient information to enable the objectives in paragraph 3 to be met;

(b) not acted within a time limit set out in a relevant protocol, or within a reasonable period; or

(c) unreasonably refused to use a form of ADR, or failed to respond at all to an invitation to do so.

15 Where there has been non-compliance with a pre-action protocol or this Practice Direction, the court may order that:

(a) the parties are relieved of the obligation to comply or further comply with the pre-action protocol or this Practice Direction;

(b) the proceedings are stayed while particular steps are taken to comply with the pre-action protocol or this Practice Direction;

(c) sanctions are to be applied.

16 The court will consider the effect of any non-compliance when deciding whether to impose any sanctions which may include—

(a) an order that the party at fault pays the costs of the proceedings, or part of the costs of the other party or parties;

(b) an order that the party at fault pay those costs on an indemnity basis;

(c) if the party at fault is a claimant who has been awarded a sum of money, an order depriving that party of interest on that sum for a specified period, and / or awarding interest at a lower rate than would otherwise have been awarded;

(d) if the party at fault is a defendant, and the claimant has been awarded a sum of money, an order awarding interest on that sum for a specified period at a higher rate, (not exceeding 10% above base rate), than the rate which would otherwise have been awarded.

Limitation

17 This Practice Direction and the pre-action protocols do not alter the statutory time limits for starting court proceedings. If a claim is issued after the relevant limitation period has expired, the defendant will be entitled to use that as a defence to the claim. If proceedings are started to comply with the statutory time limit before the parties have followed the procedures in this Practice Direction or the relevant pre-action protocol, the parties should apply to the court for a stay of the proceedings while they so comply.

Protocols in force

18 The table sets out the protocols currently in force and from which date.

Protocol	Came into force
Personal Injury	6 April 2015
Resolution of Clinical Disputes	6 April 2015
Construction & Engineering	9 November 2016
Defamation	2 October 2000
Professional Negligence	16 July 2000
Judicial Review	6 April 2015
Disease & Illness	8 December 2003
Housing Disrepair	6 April 2015
Possession Claims by Social Landlords	6 April 2015
Possession Claims for Mortgage Arrears	6 April 2015
Dilapidation of Commercial Property	1 January 2012
Low Value Personal Injury Road Traffic Accident Claims	30 April 2010 extended from 31 July 2013
Low Value Personal Injury Employers' & Public Liability Claims	31 July 2013
Debt Claims	1 October 2017
Personal Injury Claims Below the Small Claims Limit in Road Traffic Accidents	31 May 2021

Appendix F
Issue Fees

Amount claimed	Fee
Not more than £300	£35
£300.01 to £500	£50
£500.01 to £1,000	£70
£1,000.01 to £1,500	£80
£1,500.01 to £3,000	£115
£3,000.01 to £5,000	£205
£5,000.01 to £10,000	£455
£10,000.01 to £100,000	5% of the amount claimed

To calculate five percent of the amount claimed, multiply it by 0.05, and round the sum to the nearest penny.

Appendix G
Hearing Fees

Amount claimed	Hearing fee
Not more than £300	£27
£300.01 to £500	£59
£500.01 to £1,000	£85
£1,000.01 to £1,500	£123
£1,500.01 to £3,000	£181
More than £3,000	£346

Appendix H
Legal Representative's Costs

Amount claimed	A	B	C
£25 to £500	£50	£60	£15
£500.01 to £1,000	£70	£80	£15
£1,000.01 to £5,000*	£80	£90	£15
More than £5,000	£100	£110	£15

A: Where the claim form is served by the court, or by any other method, other than personal service by the claimant.

B: Where the claim form is served personally by the claimant, and there is only one defendant.

C: Where there are multiple defendants, for each additional defendant personally served at a separate address by the claimant.

* This is the relevant row where the only claim is for delivery of goods, and no value is specified on the claim form.

Appendix I
Guideline Hourly Rates

Grade	Fee earner	Band				
		London			National	
		1	2	3	1	2
A	Solicitors & legal executives over eight years' experience	£546	£398	£301	£278	£272
B	Solicitors & legal executives over four years' experience	£371	£308	£247	£233	£233
C	Other solicitors or legal executives & fee earners of equivalent experience	£288	£260	£197	£190	£189
D	Trainee solicitors, paralegals & other fee earners	£198	£148	£138	£134	£134

MORE BOOKS BY LAW BRIEF PUBLISHING

A selection of our other titles available now:-

'A Practical Guide to Probation Breaches and Other Applications' by Mark Thomas
'A Practical Guide to Remarriage and Divorce' by Cordelia Williams & Claire Howard
'A Practical Guide to Privacy, Transparency, Reporting Restrictions and Closed Proceedings in the Court of Protection' by Laura Mannering
'Beaumont on Barristers – A Guide to Defending Disciplinary Proceedings (Second Edition)' by Marc Beaumont
'A Practical Guide to Payments for Environmental Services' by Ben Sharples
'A Practical Guide to the Law of Pregnancy and Maternity at Work' by Rebecca Thomas
'A Practical Guide to Redundancy – Second Edition' by Philip Hyland & Collette Moore
'A Practical Guide to International Issues for Scottish Family Lawyers' by Susie Mountain, Donna McKay, Ken MacDonald
'A Practical Guide to the Law on Deprivation of Liberty' by Ben Troke
'A Practical Guide to Rights over Airspace and Subsoil – Second Edition' by Daniel Gatty
'A Practical Guide to the Law in Relation to Inquests' by Ramya Nagesh
'A Practical Guide to the Construction and Rectification of Wills and Trust Instruments (Second Edition)' by Edward Hewitt
'A Practical Guide to Data Protection in Social Housing' by Clare Paterson
'A Practical Guide to Spousal Maintenance – Second Edition' by Liz Cowell
'A Practical Guide to International Parental Child Abduction Law (England and Wales)' by Dr Onyója Momoh
'A Practical Guide to Deprivation of British Citizenship' by Sean Ell
'A Practical Guide to Commercial Property Service Charges' by Rachel Garton
'A Practical Guide to Clinical Negligence – Third Edition' by Geoffrey Simpson-Scott (Geoff)
'A Practical Guide to the Rights of Grandparents in Children Proceedings – Second Edition' by Stuart Barlow

'The Electronic Communications Code: A Practical Guide – Second Edition' by Kerry Bretherton KC, James Castle, Mark Loveday
'A Practical Guide to the Independent School Standards – September 2023 Edition' by Sarah McKimm
'A Practical Guide to Estate Administration and Crypto Assets' by Richard Marshall
'A Practical Guide to Parental Alienation in Private and Public Law Children Cases' by Sam King QC & Frankie Shama
'Contested Heritage – Removing Art from Land and Historic Buildings' by Richard Harwood QC, Catherine Dobson, David Sawtell
'The Limits of Separate Legal Personality: When Those Running a Company Can Be Held Personally Liable for Losses Caused to Third Parties Outside of the Company' by Dr Mike Wilkinson
'A Practical Guide to Transgender Law' by Robin Moira White & Nicola Newbegin
'A Practical Guide to 'Stranded Spouses' in Family Law' by Mani Singh Basi
'A Practical Guide to Residential Freehold Conveyancing' by Lorraine Richardson
'A Practical Guide to Pensions on Divorce for Lawyers' by Bryan Scant
'A Practical Guide to Challenging Sham Marriage Allegations in Immigration Law' by Priya Solanki
'A Practical Guide to Digital Communications Evidence in Criminal Law' by Sam Willis
'A Practical Guide to Legal Rights in Scotland' by Sarah-Jane Macdonald
'A Practical Guide to New Build Conveyancing' by Paul Sams & Rebecca East
'A Practical Guide to Inherited Wealth on Divorce' by Hayley Trim
'A Practical Guide to Practice Direction 12J and Domestic Abuse in Private Law Children Proceedings' by Rebecca Cross & Malvika Jaganmohan
'A Practical Guide to Confiscation and Restraint' by Narita Bahra QC, John Carl Townsend, David Winch
'A Practical Guide to the Law of Forests in Scotland' by Philip Buchan
'A Practical Guide to Health and Medical Cases in Immigration Law' by Rebecca Chapman & Miranda Butler
'A Practical Guide to Bad Character Evidence for Criminal Practitioners by Aparna Rao
'A Practical Guide to Extradition Law post-Brexit' by Myles Grandison et al
'A Practical Guide to Hoarding and Mental Health for Housing Lawyers' by Rachel Coyle

'Stephens on Contractual Indemnities' by Richard Stephens
'A Practical Guide to the EU Succession Regulation' by Richard Frimston
'A Practical Guide to Solicitor and Client Costs – Second Edition' by Robin Dunne
'Constructive Dismissal – Practice Pointers and Principles' by Benjimin Burgher
'A Practical Guide to Religion and Belief Discrimination Claims in the Workplace' by Kashif Ali
'A Practical Guide to the Law of Medical Treatment Decisions' by Ben Troke
'Fundamental Dishonesty and QOCS in Personal Injury Proceedings: Law and Practice' by Jake Rowley
'A Practical Guide to the Law in Relation to School Exclusions' by Charlotte Hadfield & Alice de Coverley
'A Practical Guide to Divorce for the Silver Separators' by Karin Walker
'The Right to be Forgotten – The Law and Practical Issues' by Melissa Stock
'A Practical Guide to Planning Law and Rights of Way in National Parks, the Broads and AONBs' by James Maurici QC, James Neill et al
'A Practical Guide to Election Law' by Tom Tabori
'A Practical Guide to the Law in Relation to Surrogacy' by Andrew Powell
'A Practical Guide to Claims Arising from Fatal Accidents – Second Edition' by James Patience
'A Practical Guide to Asbestos Claims' by Jonathan Owen & Gareth McAloon
'A Practical Guide to Stamp Duty Land Tax in England and Northern Ireland' by Suzanne O'Hara
'A Practical Guide to the Law of Farming Partnerships' by Philip Whitcomb
'A Practical Guide to the Law of Unlawful Eviction and Harassment – Second Edition' by Stephanie Lovegrove
'A Practical Guide to Costs in Personal Injury Claims – Second Edition' by Matthew Hoe
'A Practical Guide to the General Data Protection Regulation (GDPR) – Second Edition' by Keith Markham
'A Practical Guide to Working with Litigants in Person and McKenzie Friends in Family Cases' by Stuart Barlow
'Protecting Unregistered Brands: A Practical Guide to the Law of Passing Off' by Lorna Brazell
'A Practical Guide to Secondary Liability and Joint Enterprise Post-Jogee' by Joanne Cecil & James Mehigan

'A Practical Guide to the Pre-Action RTA Claims Protocol for Personal Injury Lawyers' by Antonia Ford

'A Practical Guide to Neighbour Disputes and the Law' by Alexander Walsh

'A Practical Guide to Coercive Control for Legal Practitioners and Victims' by Rachel Horman

'A Practical Guide to the Law of Driverless Cars – Second Edition'

by Alex Glassbrook, Emma Northey & Scarlett Milligan

'A Practical Guide to TOLATA Claims' by Greg Williams

'A Practical Guide to Elderly Law – Second Edition' by Justin Patten

'A Practical Guide to Responding to Housing Disrepair and Unfitness Claims' by Iain Wightwick

'A Practical Guide to the Law of Bullying and Harassment in the Workplace' by Philip Hyland

'How to Be a Freelance Solicitor: A Practical Guide to the SRA-Regulated Freelance Solicitor Model' by Paul Bennett

'A Practical Guide to Prison Injury Claims' by Malcolm Johnson

'A Practical Guide to Advising Clients at the Police Station' by Colin Stephen McKeown-Beaumont

'A Practical Guide to Antisocial Behaviour Injunctions – Second Edition' by Iain Wightwick

'Practical Mediation: A Guide for Mediators, Advocates, Advisers, Lawyers, and Students in Civil, Commercial, Business, Property, Workplace, and Employment Cases' by Jonathan Dingle with John Sephton

'The Mini-Pupillage Workbook' by David Boyle

'A Practical Guide to Crofting Law' by Brian Inkster

'A Practical Guide to the Law of Domain Names and Cybersquatting' by Andrew Clemson

'A Practical Guide to the Law of Gender Pay Gap Reporting' by Harini Iyengar

'NHS Whistleblowing and the Law' by Joseph England

'Employment Law and the Gig Economy' by Nigel Mackay & Annie Powell

'A Practical Guide to Noise Induced Hearing Loss (NIHL) Claims' by Andrew Mckie, Ian Skeate, Gareth McAloon

'An Introduction to Beauty Negligence Claims – A Practical Guide for the Personal Injury Practitioner' by Greg Almond

'Intercompany Agreements for Transfer Pricing Compliance' by Paul Sutton

'Zen and the Art of Mediation' by Martin Plowman

'A Practical Guide to Adoption for Family Lawyers' by Graham Pegg

'A Practical Guide to Industrial Disease Claims' by Andrew Mckie & Ian Skeate
'A Practical Guide to Conducting a Sheriff Court Proof' by Andrew Stevenson
'A Practical Guide to Vicarious Liability' by Mariel Irvine
'A Practical Guide to Applications for Landlord's Consent and Variation of Leases' by Mark Shelton
'A Practical Guide to Relief from Sanctions Post-Mitchell and Denton' by Peter Causton
'A Practical Guide to Equity Release for Advisors' by Paul Sams
'A Practical Guide to Financial Services Claims' by Chris Hegarty
'A Practical Guide to Financial Ombudsman Service Claims' by Adam Temple & Robert Scrivenor
'A Practical Guide to Running Housing Disrepair and Cavity Wall Claims – Second Edition' by Andrew Mckie & Ian Skeate
'A Practical Guide to Holiday Sickness Claims – Second Edition' by Andrew Mckie & Ian Skeate
'Arguments and Tactics for Personal Injury and Clinical Negligence Claims' by Dorian Williams
'A Practical Guide to Drone Law' by Rufus Ballaster, Andrew Firman, Eleanor Clot
'On Experts: CPR35 for Lawyers and Experts' by David Boyle
'An Introduction to Personal Injury Law' by David Boyle

These books and more are available to order online direct from the publisher at www.lawbriefpublishing.com, where you can also read free sample chapters. For any queries, call us on 0844 587 2383 or email us at mail@lawbriefpublishing.com.

Our books are all generally in stock at www.amazon.co.uk with free next day delivery for Prime members, and at good legal bookshops such as Wildy & Sons.

We are regularly launching new books in our series of practical day-to-day practitioners' guides. Visit our website and join our free newsletter to be kept informed and to receive special offers, free chapters, etc.

You can also follow us on Twitter at www.twitter.com/lawbriefpub.